The Quran With Tafsir Ibn Kathir Part 7 of 30: Al Ma'idah 082 To Al An'am 110

The Quran With Tafsir Ibn Kathir
Part 7 of 30:
Al Ma'idah 082 To
Al An'am 110

With
Arabic Script, Transliteration of Arabic, Meaning in English
and Ibn Kathir's Abridged Tafsir (Explanation)

Muhammad Saed Abdul-Rahman
BSc, DipHE

© Muhammad Saed Abdul-Rahman,2012
ISBN 978-1-86179-846-6

All Rights reserved

British Library Cataloguing in Publication Data. A Catalogue record for this book is available from the British Library

Designed, Typeset and produced by:
MSA Publication Limited, 4 Bello Close, Herne Hill,
London SE24 9BW
United Kingdom

Cover design: Houriyah Abdul-Rahman

TABLE OF CONTENTS

- TABLE OF CONTENTS V
- PRELUDE XI
  - OPENING SERMAN XI
  - OUR MISSION XII
  - BIOGRAPHY OF HAFIZ IBN KATHIR (701 H - 774 H) XII
    - Ibn Kathir's Teachers xii
    - Ibn Kathir's Students xiii
    - Ibn Kathir's Books xiii
    - Ibn Kathir's Death xiv
- PREFACE XV
  - ABOUT THIS BOOK XV
  - PERFORMING PROSTRATION WHILE READING THE QUR'AN XV
- PART 7 FULL ARABIC TEXT 1
- INTRODUCTION TO CHAPTER (SURAH) 5: AL-MAIDAH (THE TABLE, THE TABLE SPREAD) 13
  - IBN KATHIR'S INTRODUCTION 13
    - The Virtues of Surat Al-Ma'idah; When It was Revealed 13
- CHAPTER (SURAH) 5: AL-MAIDAH (THE TABLE, THE TABLE SPREAD), VERSES 082-120 13
  - *Surah: 5 Ayah: 82 Ayah: 83, Ayah: 84, Ayah: 85 & Ayah: 86* 13
    - Ibn Kathir Tafsir: 14
      - The Reason Behind Revealing these Ayat 14
  - *Surah 5: Ayah: 87 & Ayah: 88* 16
    - Tafsir Ibn Kathir 17
      - There is No Monasticism in Islam 17
  - *Surah 5: Ayah: 89* 18
    - Tafsir Ibn Kathir 18
      - Unintentional Oaths 18
      - Expiation for Breaking the Oaths 18
  - *Surah 5: Ayah: 90, Ayah: 91, Ayah: 92 & Ayah: 93* 20
    - Tafsir Ibn Kathir 21
      - Prohibiting Khamr (Intoxicants) and Maysir (Gambling) 21
      - Meaning of Ansab and Azlam 21
      - Hadiths that Prohibit Khamr (Intoxicants) 22
      - Another Hadith 23
      - Another Hadith 24
      - Another Hadith 24
      - Another Hadith 24
      - Another Hadith 25

- Surah 5: Ayah: 94 & Ayah: 95 26
  - Tafsir Ibn Kathir 27
    - Prohibiting Hunting Game in the Sacred Area and During the State of Ihram 27
    - The Penalty of Killing Game in the Sacred Area or in the State of Ihram 28
- Surah 5: Ayah: 96, Ayah: 97, Ayah: 98 & Ayah: 99 30
  - Tafsir Ibn Kathir 31
    - Water Game is Allowed for the Muhrim 31
    - Hunting Land Game is Prohibited During Ihram 32
- Surah 5: Ayah: 100, Ayah: 101 & Ayah: 102 34
  - Tafsir Ibn Kathir 35
    - Unnecessary Questioning is Disapproved of 36
- Surah 5: Ayah: 103 & Ayah: 104 38
  - Tafsir Ibn Kathir 39
    - The Meaning of Bahirah, Sa'ibah, Wasilah and Ham 39
- Surah 5: Ayah: 105 42
  - Tafsir Ibn Kathir 43
    - One is Required to Reform Himself First 43
- Surah 5: Ayah: 106, Ayah: 107 & Ayah: 108 43
  - Tafsir Ibn Kathir 44
    - Testimony of Two Just Witnesses for the Final Will and Testament 44
- Surah 5: Ayah: 109 46
  - Tafsir Ibn Kathir 46
    - The Messengers Will be Asked About Their Nations 46
- Surah 5: Ayah: 110 & Ayah: 111 47
  - Tafsir Ibn Kathir 48
    - Reminding `Isa of the Favors that Allah Granted him 48
- Surah 5: Ayah: 112, Ayah: 113, Ayah: 114 & Ayah: 115 50
  - Tafsir Ibn Kathir 51
    - Sending Down the Ma'idah 51
- Surah 5: Ayah: 116, Ayah: 117 & Ayah: 118 52
  - Tafsir Ibn Kathir 53
    - `Isa Rejects Shirk and Affirms Tawhid 53
- Surah 5: Ayah: 119 & Ayah: 120 55
  - Tafsir Ibn Kathir 55
    - Only Truth will be of Benefit on the Day of Resurrection 55

INTRODUCTION TO CHAPTER (SURAH) 6: AL-AN'AM (CATTLE, LIVESTOCK) 56

- IBN KATHIR'S INTRODUCTION 56
  - The Virtue of Surat Al-An`am and When it Was Revealed 56

CHAPTER (SURAH) 6: AL-AN'AM (CATTLE, LIVESTOCK), VERSES 001-110 56

- Surah: 6 Ayah: 1, Ayah: 2 & Ayah: 3 56
  - Tafsir Ibn Kathir 57
    - All Praise is Due to Allah for His Glorious Ability and Great Power 57

Table of Contents

Surah: 6 Ayah: 4, Ayah: 5 & Ayah: 6 59
   Tafsir Ibn Kathir 59
      Threatening the Idolators for their Stubbornness 59
Surah: 6 Ayah: 7, Ayah: 8, Ayah: 9, Ayah: 10 & Ayah: 11 60
   Tafsir Ibn Kathir 61
      Censuring the Rebellious and their Refusal to Accept Human Messengers 61
Surah: 6 Ayah: 12, Ayah: 13, Ayah: 14, Ayah: 15 & Ayah: 16 63
   Tafsir Ibn Kathir 64
      Allah is the Creator and the Sustainer 64
Surah: 6 Ayah: 17, Ayah: 18, Ayah: 19, Ayah: 20 & Ayah: 21 66
   Tafsir Ibn Kathir 67
      Allah is the Irresistible, Able to Bring Benefit and Protect from Harm 67
      People of the Book Recognize the Prophet Just as They Recognize Their Own Children .. 68
Surah: 6 Ayah: 22, Ayah: 23, Ayah: 24, Ayah: 25 & Ayah: 26 68
   Tafsir Ibn Kathir 70
      The Polythiests Shall be Questioned About the Shirk They Committed 70
      The Miserable Do Not Benefit from the Qur'an 70
Surah: 6 Ayah: 27, Ayah: 28, Ayah: 29 & Ayah: 30 71
   Tafsir Ibn Kathir 72
      Wishes and Hopes Do Not Help One When He Sees the Torment 72
Surah: 6 Ayah: 31 & Ayah: 32 73
   Tafsir Ibn Kathir 74
      Allah describes the regret of the disbelievers when facing Him, and their disappointment at the commencement, along with their sorrow for not performing good deeds and for their evil deeds. 74
Surah: 6 Ayah: 33, Ayah: 34, Ayah: 35 & Ayah: 36 75
   Tafsir Ibn Kathir 76
      Comforting the Prophet 76
Surah: 6 Ayah: 37, Ayah: 38 & Ayah: 39 78
   Tafsir Ibn Kathir 79
      The Idolators Ask for a Miracle 79
      The Meaning of Umam 79
      The Disbelievers will be Deaf and Mute in Darkness 80
Surah: 6 Ayah: 40, Ayah: 41, Ayah: 42, Ayah: 43, Ayah: 44 & Ayah: 45 80
   Tafsir Ibn Kathir 82
      The Idolators Call On Allah Alone During Torment and Distress 82
Surah: 6 Ayah: 46, Ayah: 47, Ayah: 48 & Ayah: 49 83
   Tafsir Ibn Kathir 84
Surah: 6 Ayah: 50, Ayah: 51, Ayah: 52, Ayah: 53 & Ayah: 54 85
      The Messenger Neither has the Key to Allah's Treasures, Nor Knows the Unseen 87
      Prohibiting the Messenger from Turning the Weak Away and the Order to Honor Them 88
Surah: 6 Ayah: 55, Ayah: 56, Ayah: 57, Ayah: 58 & Ayah: 59 90
      The Prophet Understands What He Conveys; Torment is in Allah's Hands Not the Prophet's 91

    Only Allah Knows the Unseen 93
Surah: 6 Ayah: 60, Ayah: 61 & Ayah: 62... 94
    The Servants are in Allah's Hands Before and After Death 94
Surah: 6 Ayah: 63, Ayah: 64 & Ayah: 65... 97
    Allah's Compassion and Generosity, and His Power and Torment.................... 98
    Another Hadith.. 100
    Another Hadith.. 100
Surah: 6 Ayah: 66, Ayah: 67, Ayah: 68 & Ayah: 69... 101
    The Invitation to the Truth is Guidance Without Coercion 102
    The Prohibition of Sitting with Those Who Deny and Mock Allah's Ayat 102
Surah: 6 Ayah: 70 103
Surah: 6 Ayah: 71, Ayah: 72 & Ayah: 73... 105
    The Parable of Those Who Revert to Disbelief After Faith and Good Deeds 106
    As-Sur; The Trumpet... 107
Surah: 6 Ayah: 74, Ayah: 75, Ayah: 76, Ayah: 77, Ayah: 78 & Ayah: 79.............. 107
    Ibrahim Advises his Father 109
    Tawhid Becomes Apparent to Ibrahim.. 109
    Prophet Ibrahim Debates with his People 110
Surah: 6 Ayah: 80, Ayah: 81, Ayah: 82 & Ayah: 83... 111
    Shirk is the Greatest Zulm (Wrong) 113
Surah: 6 Ayah: 84, Ayah: 85, Ayah: 86, Ayah: 87, Ayah: 88, Ayah: 89 & Ayah: 90 115
    Ibrahim Receives the News of Ishaq and Ya`qub During His Old Age.............. 116
    Qualities of Nuh and Ibrahim 117
    Shirk Eradicates the Deeds, Even the Deeds of the Messengers...................... 118
Surah: 6 Ayah: 91 & Ayah: 92.. 120
    The Messenger is but a Human to Whom the Book was Revealed by Inspiration 121
Surah: 6 Ayah: 93 & Ayah: 94.. 123
    None is Worse Than One who Invents a Lie Against Allah and Claims that Revelation Came to Him.. 124
    The Condition of These Unjust People Upon Death and on the Day of Resurrection 124
Surah: 6 Ayah: 95, Ayah: 96 & Ayah: 97... 126
    Recognizing Allah Through Some of His Ayat 127
Surah: 6 Ayah: 98 & Ayah: 99.. 129
Surah: 6 Ayah: 100 132
Surah: 6 Ayah: 101 133
    Meaning of Badi' 133
Surah: 6 Ayah: 102 & Ayah: 103.. 134
    Allah is Your Lord.. 134
Surah: 6 Ayah: 104 & Ayah: 105.. 136
    The Meaning of Basa'ir 136
Surah: 6 Ayah: 106 & Ayah: 107.. 138
    The Command to Follow the Revelation 138
Surah: 6 Ayah: 108 139

The Prohibition of Insulting the False gods of the Disbelievers, So that they Do not Insult Allah..139
Surah: 6 Ayah: 109 & Ayah: 110... *140*
　Tafsir Ibn Kathir 140
　　Asking for Miracles and Swearing to Believe if They Come 140

PRELUDE

Opening Serman

Indeed, all praise is due to Allah. We praise Him and seek His help and forgiveness. We seek refuge with Allah from our soul's evil and our wrong doings. He whom Allah guides, no one can misguide; and he whom He misguides, no one can guide

I bear witness that there is no (true) god except Allah – alone without a partner, and I bear witness that Muhammad (peace and blessings of Allah be upon him) is His 'abd (servant) and messenger.

يَٰٓأَيُّهَا ٱلَّذِينَ ءَامَنُوا۟ ٱتَّقُوا۟ ٱللَّهَ حَقَّ تُقَاتِهِۦ وَلَا تَمُوتُنَّ إِلَّا وَأَنتُم مُّسْلِمُونَ

O you who believe! Fear Allâh (by doing all that He has ordered and by abstaining from all that He has forbidden) as He should be feared. (Obey Him, be thankful to Him, and remember Him always), and die not except in a state of Islâm (as Muslims (with complete submission to Allâh)).

يَٰٓأَيُّهَا ٱلنَّاسُ ٱتَّقُوا۟ رَبَّكُمُ ٱلَّذِى خَلَقَكُم مِّن نَّفْسٍ وَٰحِدَةٍ وَخَلَقَ مِنْهَا زَوْجَهَا وَبَثَّ مِنْهُمَا رِجَالًا كَثِيرًا وَنِسَآءً وَٱتَّقُوا۟ ٱللَّهَ ٱلَّذِى تَسَآءَلُونَ بِهِۦ وَٱلْأَرْحَامَ إِنَّ ٱللَّهَ كَانَ عَلَيْكُمْ رَقِيبًا

O mankind! Be dutiful to your Lord, Who created you from a single person (Adam), and from him (Adam) He created his wife (Hawwâ (Eve)) and from them both He created many men and women; and fear Allâh through Whom you demand (your mutual rights), and (do not cut the relations of) the wombs (kinship). Surely, Allâh is Ever an All-Watcher over you.

يُصْلِحْ لَكُمْ أَعْمَٰلَكُمْ وَيَغْفِرْ لَكُمْ ذُنُوبَكُمْ وَمَن يُطِعِ ٱللَّهَ وَرَسُولَهُۥ فَقَدْ فَازَ فَوْزًا عَظِيمًا

He will direct you to do righteous good deeds and will forgive you your sins. And whosoever obeys Allâh and His Messenger (peace be upon him), he has indeed achieved a great achievement (i.e. he will be saved from the Hell-fire and will be admitted to Paradise).

Indeed, the best speech is Allah's Book and the best guidance is Muhammad's () guidance. The worst affairs (of religion) are those innovated (by people), for every such innovation is an act of misguidance leading to the Fire

Our Mission

Our mission is to gather in one place, for the English-speaking public, all relevant information needed to make the Qur'an more understandable and easier to study. This book tries to do this by providing the following:

1. The Arabic Text for those who are able to read Arabic
2. Transliteration of the Arabic text for those who are unable to read the Arabic script. This will give them a sample of the sound of the Qur'an, which they could not otherwise comprehend from reading the English meaning.
3. The meaning of the qur'an (translated by Dr. Muhammad Taqi-ud-Din Al-Hilali, Ph.D. and Dr. Muhammad Muhsin Khan)
4. Explanation (abridged Tafsir) by Ibn Kathir (translated by Safi-ur-Rahman al-Mubarakpuri)

We hope that by doing this an ordinary English-speaker will be able to pick up a copy of this book and study and comprehend The Glorious Qur'an in a way that is acceptable to the understanding of the Rightly-guided Muslim Ummah (Community).

Biography of Hafiz Ibn Kathir (701 H - 774 H)

By the Honored Shaykh `Abdul-Qadir Al-Arna'ut, may Allah protect him.

He is the respected Imam, Abu Al-Fida', `Imad Ad-Din Isma il bin 'Umar bin Kathir Al-Qurashi Al-Busrawi - Busraian in origin; Dimashqi in training, learning and residence.

Ibn Kathir was born in the city of Busra in 701 H. His father was the Friday speaker of the village, but he died while Ibn Kathir was only four years old. Ibn Kathir's brother, Shaykh Abdul-Wahhab, reared him and taught him until he moved to Damascus in 706 H., when he was five years old.

Ibn Kathir's Teachers

Ibn Kathir studied Fiqh - Islamic jurisprudence - with Burhan Ad-Din, Ibrahim bin `Abdur-Rahman Al-Fizari, known as Ibn Al-Firkah (who died in 729 H). Ibn Kathir heard Hadiths from `Isa bin Al-Mutim, Ahmad bin Abi Talib, (Ibn Ash-Shahnah) (who died in 730 H), Ibn Al-Hajjar, (who died in 730 H), and the Hadith narrator of Ash-Sham (modern day Syria and surrounding areas); Baha Ad-Din Al-Qasim bin Muzaffar bin `Asakir (who died in 723 H), and Ibn Ash-Shirdzi, Ishaq bin Yahya Al-Ammuddi, also known as `Afif Ad-Din, the Zahiriyyah Shaykh who died in 725 H, and Muhammad bin Zarrad. He remained with Jamal Ad-Din, Yusuf bin Az-Zaki AlMizzi who died in 724 H, he benefited from his knowledge and also married his daughter. He also read with Shaykh Al-Islam, Taqi Ad-Din Ahmad bin `Abdul-Halim bin `Abdus-Salam bin Taymiyyah who died in 728 H. He also read with the Imam Hafiz and historian Shams Ad-Din, Muhammad bin Ahmad bin Uthman bin Qaymaz Adh-Dhahabi, who died in 748 H. Also, Abu Musa Al-Qarafai, Abu Al-Fath Ad-Dabbusi and

'Ali bin 'Umar As-Suwani and others who gave him permission to transmit the knowledge he learned with them in Egypt.

In his book, Al-Mu jam Al-Mukhtas, Al-Hafiz Adh-Dhaliabi wrote that Ibn Kathir was, "The Imam, scholar of jurisprudence, skillful scholar of Hadith, renowned Faqih and scholar of Tafsir who wrote several beneficial books."

Further, in Ad-Durar Al-Kdminah, Al-Hafiz Ibn Hajar AlAsqalani said, "Ibn Kathir worked on the subject of the Hadith in the areas of texts and chains of narrators. He had a good memory, his books became popular during his lifetime, and people benefited from them after his death."

Also, the renowned historian Abu Al-Mahasin, Jamal Ad-Din Yusuf bin Sayf Ad-Din (Ibn Taghri Bardi), said in his book, AlManhal As-Safi, "He is the Shaykh, the Imam, the great scholar 'Imad Ad-Din Abu Al-Fida'. He learned extensively and was very active in collecting knowledge and writing. He was excellent in the areas of Fiqh, Tafsir and Hadith. He collected knowledge, authored (books), taught, narrated Hadith and wrote. He had immense knowledge in the fields of Hadith, Tafsir, Fiqh, the Arabic language, and so forth. He gave Fatawa (religious verdicts) and taught until he died, may Allah grant him mercy. He was known for his precision and vast knowledge, and as a scholar of history, Hadith and Tafsir."

Ibn Kathir's Students

Ibn Hajji was one of Ibn Kathir's students, and he described Ibn Kathir: "He had the best memory of the Hadith texts. He also had the most knowledge concerning the narrators and authenticity, his contemporaries and teachers admitted to these qualities. Every time I met him I gained some benefit from him."

Also, Ibn Al-'Imad Al-Hanbali said in his book, Shadhardt Adh-Dhahab, "He is the renowned Hafiz 'Imad Ad-Din, whose memory was excellent, whose forgetfulness was miniscule, whose understanding was adequate, and who had good knowledge in the Arabic language." Also, Ibn Habib said about Ibn Kathir, "He heard knowledge and collected it and wrote various books. He brought comfort to the ears with his Fatwas and narrated Hadith and brought benefit to other people. The papers that contained his Fatwas were transmitted to the various (Islamic) provinces. Further, he was known for his precision and encompassing knowledge."

Ibn Kathir's Books

1 - One of the greatest books that Ibn Kathir wrote was his Tafsir of the Noble Qur'an, which is one of the best Tafsir that rely on narrations [of Ahadith, the Tafsir of the Companions, etc.]. The Tafsir by Ibn Kathir was printed many times and several scholars have summarized it.

2- The History Collection known as Al-Biddyah, which was printed in 14 volumes under the name Al-Bidayah wanNihdyah, and contained the stories of the Prophets and previous nations, the Prophet's Seerah (life story) and Islamic history until his time. He also added a book Al-Fitan, about the Signs of the Last Hour.

3- At-Takmil ft Ma`rifat Ath-Thiqat wa Ad-Du'afa wal Majdhil which Ibn Kathir collected from the books of his two Shaykhs Al-Mizzi and Adh-Dhahabi; Al-Kdmal and Mizan Al-Ftiddl. He added several benefits regarding the subject of Al-Jarh and AtT'adil.

4- Al-Hadi was-Sunan ft Ahadith Al-Masdnfd was-Sunan which is also known by, Jami` Al-Masdnfd. In this book, Ibn Kathir collected the narrations of Imams Ahmad bin Hanbal, Al-Bazzar, Abu Ya`la Al-Mawsili, Ibn Abi Shaybah and from the six collections of Hadith: the Two Sahihs [Al-Bukhari and Muslim] and the Four Sunan [Abu Dawud, At-Tirmidhi, AnNasa and Ibn Majah]. Ibn Kathir divided this book according to areas of Fiqh.

5-Tabaqat Ash-Shaf iyah which also contains the virtues of Imam Ash-Shafi.

6- Ibn Kathir wrote references for the Ahadith of Adillat AtTanbfh, from the Shafi school of Fiqh.

7- Ibn Kathir began an explanation of Sahih Al-Bukhari, but he did not finish it.

8- He started writing a large volume on the Ahkam (Laws), but finished only up to the Hajj rituals.

9- He summarized Al-Bayhaqi's 'Al-Madkhal. Many of these books were not printed.

10- He summarized `Ulum Al-Hadith, by Abu `Amr bin AsSalah and called it Mukhtasar `Ulum Al-Hadith. Shaykh Ahmad Shakir, the Egyptian Muhaddith, printed this book along with his commentary on it and called it Al-Ba'th Al-Hathfth fi Sharh Mukhtasar `Ulum Al-Hadith.

11- As-Sfrah An-Nabawiyyah, which is contained in his book Al-Biddyah, and both of these books are in print.

12- A research on Jihad called Al-Ijtihad ft Talabi Al-Jihad, which was printed several times.

Ibn Kathir's Death

Al-Hafiz Ibn Hajar Al-Asgalani said, "Ibn Kathir lost his sight just before his life ended. He died in Damascus in 774 H." May Allah grant mercy upon Ibn Kathir and make him among the residents of His Paradise.

PREFACE

In the name of Allah, Most Gracious, Most Merciful.

About this book

The previous publication of this book included some background information to the chapters of the Qur'an by an Islamic scholar known as Abul Ala Maududi. This information was used to shed more light on the chapters by giving a summery of why each chapter was given its name, It's period of revelation and the circumstances surrounding its revelatiom. However, some Muslims objected to the inclusion of the contributions of Maududi.

In this new publication of Tafsir Ibn Kathir, we have removed all traces of the contribution of Abul Ala Maududi. Personally, I do not know the reasons for the objections to Maududi, but this work concerns only the tafsir of Ibn Kathir, so we have not included anything from Maududi in it. We have also corrected all the typing and formatting errors found in the previous publication. We have not alter the structure of the book. The reader is still able to read the full Arabic Text of the thirty Parts of the Qur'an and follow its meanings in the English language. The transliteration of the Arabic text should also give the reader a taste of the sound of the original Arabic.

May Almighty Allah accept this effort from us, and make it a source of blessings for us in this world and in the next. I bear witness that there is none worthy of worship but Allah and I bear witness that Muhammad (may the peace and blessings of Allah be upon him) is the slave and messenger of Allah.

Performing Prostration While Reading the Qur'an

Question:

Could you please give a list of the Qur'anic verses when a prostration is recommended? What happens if we read these verses and not perform a prostration?

A. Jalil

Answer:

There are 15 verses in the Qur'an that mention prostration before God Almighty as a good action by God-fearing believers. Therefore, it is strongly recommended to perform such a prostration when we read or listen to any of these verses, whether during prayer or in any situation.

Some scholars are of the view that even if one has not performed ablution, one should prostrate oneself. These verses are given here, starting with the Arabic title of the surah which is followed by two numbers, the first indicating the surah, and the second indicating the verse,: Al-Araf 7: 206; Al-Raad 13: 15; Al-Nahl 16: 50; Al-Isra 17: 109; Maryam 19: 58; Al-Hajj 22: 18 & 22: 77; Al-Furqan 25: 60; Al-Naml 27: 26;

Al-Sajdah 32: 15; Saad 38: 25; Fussilat 41: 38; Al-Najm 53: 62; Al-Inshiqaq 84: 21 and Al-Alaq 96: 19.

If you do not perform a prostration when you read or listen to any of these verses, you have done badly because you miss out on the reward of performing a prostration for God. You incur no sin and violate no divine order.

Reference:
http://archive.arabnews.com/?page=5&section=0&article=97811&d=1&m=7&y=2007

The Glorious Qur'an Juz' 7 (Part 7): Chapter (Surah) 5: Al Ma'idah (The Table, The Table Spread) 082 To Chapter (Surah) 6: Al An'am (Cattle) 110

PART 7 FULL ARABIC TEXT

Chapter (Surah) 5: Al-Ma'idah 082-120

۞ لَتَجِدَنَّ أَشَدَّ ٱلنَّاسِ عَدَٰوَةً لِّلَّذِينَ ءَامَنُواْ ٱلْيَهُودَ وَٱلَّذِينَ أَشْرَكُواْ ۖ وَلَتَجِدَنَّ أَقْرَبَهُم مَّوَدَّةً لِّلَّذِينَ ءَامَنُواْ ٱلَّذِينَ قَالُوٓاْ إِنَّا نَصَٰرَىٰ ۚ ذَٰلِكَ بِأَنَّ مِنْهُمْ قِسِّيسِينَ وَرُهْبَانًا وَأَنَّهُمْ لَا يَسْتَكْبِرُونَ ۝ وَإِذَا سَمِعُواْ مَآ أُنزِلَ إِلَى ٱلرَّسُولِ تَرَىٰٓ أَعْيُنَهُمْ تَفِيضُ مِنَ ٱلدَّمْعِ مِمَّا عَرَفُواْ مِنَ ٱلْحَقِّ ۖ يَقُولُونَ رَبَّنَآ ءَامَنَّا فَٱكْتُبْنَا مَعَ ٱلشَّٰهِدِينَ ۝ وَمَا لَنَا لَا نُؤْمِنُ بِٱللَّهِ وَمَا جَآءَنَا مِنَ ٱلْحَقِّ وَنَطْمَعُ أَن يُدْخِلَنَا رَبُّنَا مَعَ ٱلْقَوْمِ ٱلصَّٰلِحِينَ ۝ فَأَثَٰبَهُمُ ٱللَّهُ بِمَا قَالُواْ جَنَّٰتٍ تَجْرِى مِن تَحْتِهَا ٱلْأَنْهَٰرُ خَٰلِدِينَ فِيهَا ۚ وَذَٰلِكَ جَزَآءُ ٱلْمُحْسِنِينَ ۝ وَٱلَّذِينَ كَفَرُواْ وَكَذَّبُواْ بِـَٔايَٰتِنَآ أُوْلَٰٓئِكَ أَصْحَٰبُ ٱلْجَحِيمِ ۝ يَٰٓأَيُّهَا ٱلَّذِينَ ءَامَنُواْ لَا تُحَرِّمُواْ طَيِّبَٰتِ مَآ أَحَلَّ ٱللَّهُ لَكُمْ وَلَا تَعْتَدُوٓاْ ۚ إِنَّ ٱللَّهَ لَا يُحِبُّ ٱلْمُعْتَدِينَ ۝ وَكُلُواْ مِمَّا رَزَقَكُمُ ٱللَّهُ حَلَٰلًا طَيِّبًا ۚ وَٱتَّقُواْ ٱللَّهَ ٱلَّذِىٓ أَنتُم بِهِۦ مُؤْمِنُونَ ۝ لَا يُؤَاخِذُكُمُ ٱللَّهُ بِٱللَّغْوِ فِىٓ أَيْمَٰنِكُمْ وَلَٰكِن يُؤَاخِذُكُم بِمَا عَقَّدتُّمُ ٱلْأَيْمَٰنَ ۖ فَكَفَّٰرَتُهُۥٓ إِطْعَامُ عَشَرَةِ مَسَٰكِينَ مِنْ أَوْسَطِ مَا تُطْعِمُونَ أَهْلِيكُمْ أَوْ كِسْوَتُهُمْ أَوْ تَحْرِيرُ رَقَبَةٍ ۖ فَمَن لَّمْ يَجِدْ فَصِيَامُ ثَلَٰثَةِ أَيَّامٍ ۚ ذَٰلِكَ كَفَّٰرَةُ أَيْمَٰنِكُمْ إِذَا حَلَفْتُمْ ۚ وَٱحْفَظُوٓاْ أَيْمَٰنَكُمْ ۚ كَذَٰلِكَ يُبَيِّنُ ٱللَّهُ لَكُمْ ءَايَٰتِهِۦ لَعَلَّكُمْ تَشْكُرُونَ ۝ يَٰٓأَيُّهَا ٱلَّذِينَ ءَامَنُوٓاْ إِنَّمَا

ٱلْخَمْرُ وَٱلْمَيْسِرُ وَٱلْأَنصَابُ وَٱلْأَزْلَـٰمُ رِجْسٌ مِّنْ عَمَلِ ٱلشَّيْطَـٰنِ فَٱجْتَنِبُوهُ لَعَلَّكُمْ تُفْلِحُونَ ۝ إِنَّمَا يُرِيدُ ٱلشَّيْطَـٰنُ أَن يُوقِعَ بَيْنَكُمُ ٱلْعَدَاوَةَ وَٱلْبَغْضَآءَ فِى ٱلْخَمْرِ وَٱلْمَيْسِرِ وَيَصُدَّكُمْ عَن ذِكْرِ ٱللَّهِ وَعَنِ ٱلصَّلَوٰةِ ۖ فَهَلْ أَنتُم مُّنتَهُونَ ۝ وَأَطِيعُوا۟ ٱللَّهَ وَأَطِيعُوا۟ ٱلرَّسُولَ وَٱحْذَرُوا۟ ۚ فَإِن تَوَلَّيْتُمْ فَٱعْلَمُوٓا۟ أَنَّمَا عَلَىٰ رَسُولِنَا ٱلْبَلَـٰغُ ٱلْمُبِينُ ۝ لَيْسَ عَلَى ٱلَّذِينَ ءَامَنُوا۟ وَعَمِلُوا۟ ٱلصَّـٰلِحَـٰتِ جُنَاحٌ فِيمَا طَعِمُوٓا۟ إِذَا مَا ٱتَّقَوا۟ وَّءَامَنُوا۟ وَعَمِلُوا۟ ٱلصَّـٰلِحَـٰتِ ثُمَّ ٱتَّقَوا۟ وَّءَامَنُوا۟ ثُمَّ ٱتَّقَوا۟ وَّأَحْسَنُوا۟ ۗ وَٱللَّهُ يُحِبُّ ٱلْمُحْسِنِينَ ۝ يَـٰٓأَيُّهَا ٱلَّذِينَ ءَامَنُوا۟ لَيَبْلُوَنَّكُمُ ٱللَّهُ بِشَىْءٍ مِّنَ ٱلصَّيْدِ تَنَالُهُۥٓ أَيْدِيكُمْ وَرِمَاحُكُمْ لِيَعْلَمَ ٱللَّهُ مَن يَخَافُهُۥ بِٱلْغَيْبِ ۚ فَمَنِ ٱعْتَدَىٰ بَعْدَ ذَٰلِكَ فَلَهُۥ عَذَابٌ أَلِيمٌ ۝ يَـٰٓأَيُّهَا ٱلَّذِينَ ءَامَنُوا۟ لَا تَقْتُلُوا۟ ٱلصَّيْدَ وَأَنتُمْ حُرُمٌ ۚ وَمَن قَتَلَهُۥ مِنكُم مُّتَعَمِّدًا فَجَزَآءٌ مِّثْلُ مَا قَتَلَ مِنَ ٱلنَّعَمِ يَحْكُمُ بِهِۦ ذَوَا عَدْلٍ مِّنكُمْ هَدْيًۢا بَـٰلِغَ ٱلْكَعْبَةِ أَوْ كَفَّـٰرَةٌ طَعَامُ مَسَـٰكِينَ أَوْ عَدْلُ ذَٰلِكَ صِيَامًا لِّيَذُوقَ وَبَالَ أَمْرِهِۦ ۗ عَفَا ٱللَّهُ عَمَّا سَلَفَ ۚ وَمَنْ عَادَ فَيَنتَقِمُ ٱللَّهُ مِنْهُ ۗ وَٱللَّهُ عَزِيزٌ ذُو ٱنتِقَامٍ ۝ أُحِلَّ لَكُمْ صَيْدُ ٱلْبَحْرِ وَطَعَامُهُۥ مَتَـٰعًا لَّكُمْ وَلِلسَّيَّارَةِ ۖ وَحُرِّمَ عَلَيْكُمْ صَيْدُ ٱلْبَرِّ مَا دُمْتُمْ حُرُمًا ۗ وَٱتَّقُوا۟ ٱللَّهَ ٱلَّذِىٓ إِلَيْهِ تُحْشَرُونَ ۝ ۞ جَعَلَ ٱللَّهُ ٱلْكَعْبَةَ ٱلْبَيْتَ ٱلْحَرَامَ قِيَـٰمًا لِّلنَّاسِ وَٱلشَّهْرَ ٱلْحَرَامَ وَٱلْهَدْىَ وَٱلْقَلَـٰٓئِدَ ۚ ذَٰلِكَ لِتَعْلَمُوٓا۟ أَنَّ ٱللَّهَ يَعْلَمُ مَا فِى ٱلسَّمَـٰوَٰتِ وَمَا فِى ٱلْأَرْضِ وَأَنَّ ٱللَّهَ بِكُلِّ شَىْءٍ عَلِيمٌ ۝ ٱعْلَمُوٓا۟ أَنَّ ٱللَّهَ شَدِيدُ ٱلْعِقَابِ وَأَنَّ ٱللَّهَ غَفُورٌ رَّحِيمٌ ۝ مَّا عَلَى ٱلرَّسُولِ إِلَّا ٱلْبَلَـٰغُ ۗ وَٱللَّهُ يَعْلَمُ مَا تُبْدُونَ وَمَا تَكْتُمُونَ ۝ قُل لَّا يَسْتَوِى ٱلْخَبِيثُ وَٱلطَّيِّبُ وَلَوْ أَعْجَبَكَ كَثْرَةُ ٱلْخَبِيثِ ۚ فَٱتَّقُوا۟ ٱللَّهَ يَـٰٓأُو۟لِى ٱلْأَلْبَـٰبِ لَعَلَّكُمْ تُفْلِحُونَ ۝ يَـٰٓأَيُّهَا ٱلَّذِينَ ءَامَنُوا۟ لَا تَسْـَٔلُوا۟ عَنْ أَشْيَآءَ إِن تُبْدَ لَكُمْ

تَسُؤْكُمْ وَإِن تَسْـَٔلُوا۟ عَنْهَا حِينَ يُنَزَّلُ ٱلْقُرْءَانُ تُبْدَ لَكُمْ عَفَا ٱللَّهُ عَنْهَا ۗ وَٱللَّهُ غَفُورٌ حَلِيمٌ ۝ قَدْ سَأَلَهَا قَوْمٌ مِّن قَبْلِكُمْ ثُمَّ أَصْبَحُوا۟ بِهَا كَٰفِرِينَ ۝ مَا جَعَلَ ٱللَّهُ مِنۢ بَحِيرَةٍ وَلَا سَآئِبَةٍ وَلَا وَصِيلَةٍ وَلَا حَامٍ ۙ وَلَٰكِنَّ ٱلَّذِينَ كَفَرُوا۟ يَفْتَرُونَ عَلَى ٱللَّهِ ٱلْكَذِبَ ۖ وَأَكْثَرُهُمْ لَا يَعْقِلُونَ ۝ وَإِذَا قِيلَ لَهُمْ تَعَالَوْا۟ إِلَىٰ مَآ أَنزَلَ ٱللَّهُ وَإِلَى ٱلرَّسُولِ قَالُوا۟ حَسْبُنَا مَا وَجَدْنَا عَلَيْهِ ءَابَآءَنَآ ۚ أَوَلَوْ كَانَ ءَابَآؤُهُمْ لَا يَعْلَمُونَ شَيْـًٔا وَلَا يَهْتَدُونَ ۝ يَٰٓأَيُّهَا ٱلَّذِينَ ءَامَنُوا۟ عَلَيْكُمْ أَنفُسَكُمْ ۖ لَا يَضُرُّكُم مَّن ضَلَّ إِذَا ٱهْتَدَيْتُمْ ۚ إِلَى ٱللَّهِ مَرْجِعُكُمْ جَمِيعًا فَيُنَبِّئُكُم بِمَا كُنتُمْ تَعْمَلُونَ ۝ يَٰٓأَيُّهَا ٱلَّذِينَ ءَامَنُوا۟ شَهَٰدَةُ بَيْنِكُمْ إِذَا حَضَرَ أَحَدَكُمُ ٱلْمَوْتُ حِينَ ٱلْوَصِيَّةِ ٱثْنَانِ ذَوَا عَدْلٍ مِّنكُمْ أَوْ ءَاخَرَانِ مِنْ غَيْرِكُمْ إِنْ أَنتُمْ ضَرَبْتُمْ فِى ٱلْأَرْضِ فَأَصَٰبَتْكُم مُّصِيبَةُ ٱلْمَوْتِ ۚ تَحْبِسُونَهُمَا مِنۢ بَعْدِ ٱلصَّلَوٰةِ فَيُقْسِمَانِ بِٱللَّهِ إِنِ ٱرْتَبْتُمْ لَا نَشْتَرِى بِهِۦ ثَمَنًا وَلَوْ كَانَ ذَا قُرْبَىٰ ۙ وَلَا نَكْتُمُ شَهَٰدَةَ ٱللَّهِ إِنَّآ إِذًا لَّمِنَ ٱلْءَاثِمِينَ ۝ فَإِنْ عُثِرَ عَلَىٰٓ أَنَّهُمَا ٱسْتَحَقَّآ إِثْمًا فَـَٔاخَرَانِ يَقُومَانِ مَقَامَهُمَا مِنَ ٱلَّذِينَ ٱسْتَحَقَّ عَلَيْهِمُ ٱلْأَوْلَيَٰنِ فَيُقْسِمَانِ بِٱللَّهِ لَشَهَٰدَتُنَآ أَحَقُّ مِن شَهَٰدَتِهِمَا وَمَا ٱعْتَدَيْنَآ إِنَّآ إِذًا لَّمِنَ ٱلظَّٰلِمِينَ ۝ ذَٰلِكَ أَدْنَىٰٓ أَن يَأْتُوا۟ بِٱلشَّهَٰدَةِ عَلَىٰ وَجْهِهَآ أَوْ يَخَافُوٓا۟ أَن تُرَدَّ أَيْمَٰنٌۢ بَعْدَ أَيْمَٰنِهِمْ ۗ وَٱتَّقُوا۟ ٱللَّهَ وَٱسْمَعُوا۟ ۗ وَٱللَّهُ لَا يَهْدِى ٱلْقَوْمَ ٱلْفَٰسِقِينَ ۝ ۞ يَوْمَ يَجْمَعُ ٱللَّهُ ٱلرُّسُلَ فَيَقُولُ مَاذَآ أُجِبْتُمْ ۖ قَالُوا۟ لَا عِلْمَ لَنَآ ۖ إِنَّكَ أَنتَ عَلَّٰمُ ٱلْغُيُوبِ ۝ إِذْ قَالَ ٱللَّهُ يَٰعِيسَى ٱبْنَ مَرْيَمَ ٱذْكُرْ نِعْمَتِى عَلَيْكَ وَعَلَىٰ وَٰلِدَتِكَ إِذْ أَيَّدتُّكَ بِرُوحِ ٱلْقُدُسِ تُكَلِّمُ ٱلنَّاسَ فِى ٱلْمَهْدِ وَكَهْلًا ۖ وَإِذْ عَلَّمْتُكَ ٱلْكِتَٰبَ وَٱلْحِكْمَةَ وَٱلتَّوْرَىٰةَ وَٱلْإِنجِيلَ ۖ وَإِذْ تَخْلُقُ مِنَ ٱلطِّينِ كَهَيْـَٔةِ ٱلطَّيْرِ بِإِذْنِى فَتَنفُخُ فِيهَا فَتَكُونُ طَيْرًۢا بِإِذْنِى ۖ وَتُبْرِئُ ٱلْأَكْمَهَ

وَٱلْأَبْرَصَ بِإِذْنِى ۖ وَإِذْ تُخْرِجُ ٱلْمَوْتَىٰ بِإِذْنِى ۖ وَإِذْ كَفَفْتُ بَنِىٓ إِسْرَٰٓءِيلَ عَنكَ إِذْ جِئْتَهُم بِٱلْبَيِّنَٰتِ فَقَالَ ٱلَّذِينَ كَفَرُوا۟ مِنْهُمْ إِنْ هَٰذَآ إِلَّا سِحْرٌ مُّبِينٌ ۝ وَإِذْ أَوْحَيْتُ إِلَى ٱلْحَوَارِيِّـۧنَ أَنْ ءَامِنُوا۟ بِى وَبِرَسُولِى قَالُوٓا۟ ءَامَنَّا وَٱشْهَدْ بِأَنَّنَا مُسْلِمُونَ ۝ إِذْ قَالَ ٱلْحَوَارِيُّونَ يَٰعِيسَى ٱبْنَ مَرْيَمَ هَلْ يَسْتَطِيعُ رَبُّكَ أَن يُنَزِّلَ عَلَيْنَا مَآئِدَةً مِّنَ ٱلسَّمَآءِ ۖ قَالَ ٱتَّقُوا۟ ٱللَّهَ إِن كُنتُم مُّؤْمِنِينَ ۝ قَالُوا۟ نُرِيدُ أَن نَّأْكُلَ مِنْهَا وَتَطْمَئِنَّ قُلُوبُنَا وَنَعْلَمَ أَن قَدْ صَدَقْتَنَا وَنَكُونَ عَلَيْهَا مِنَ ٱلشَّٰهِدِينَ ۝ قَالَ عِيسَى ٱبْنُ مَرْيَمَ ٱللَّهُمَّ رَبَّنَآ أَنزِلْ عَلَيْنَا مَآئِدَةً مِّنَ ٱلسَّمَآءِ تَكُونُ لَنَا عِيدًا لِّأَوَّلِنَا وَءَاخِرِنَا وَءَايَةً مِّنكَ ۖ وَٱرْزُقْنَا وَأَنتَ خَيْرُ ٱلرَّٰزِقِينَ ۝ قَالَ ٱللَّهُ إِنِّى مُنَزِّلُهَا عَلَيْكُمْ ۖ فَمَن يَكْفُرْ بَعْدُ مِنكُمْ فَإِنِّىٓ أُعَذِّبُهُۥ عَذَابًا لَّآ أُعَذِّبُهُۥٓ أَحَدًا مِّنَ ٱلْعَٰلَمِينَ ۝ وَإِذْ قَالَ ٱللَّهُ يَٰعِيسَى ٱبْنَ مَرْيَمَ ءَأَنتَ قُلْتَ لِلنَّاسِ ٱتَّخِذُونِى وَأُمِّىَ إِلَٰهَيْنِ مِن دُونِ ٱللَّهِ ۖ قَالَ سُبْحَٰنَكَ مَا يَكُونُ لِىٓ أَنْ أَقُولَ مَا لَيْسَ لِى بِحَقٍّ ۚ إِن كُنتُ قُلْتُهُۥ فَقَدْ عَلِمْتَهُۥ ۚ تَعْلَمُ مَا فِى نَفْسِى وَلَآ أَعْلَمُ مَا فِى نَفْسِكَ ۚ إِنَّكَ أَنتَ عَلَّٰمُ ٱلْغُيُوبِ ۝ مَا قُلْتُ لَهُمْ إِلَّا مَآ أَمَرْتَنِى بِهِۦٓ أَنِ ٱعْبُدُوا۟ ٱللَّهَ رَبِّى وَرَبَّكُمْ ۚ وَكُنتُ عَلَيْهِمْ شَهِيدًا مَّا دُمْتُ فِيهِمْ ۖ فَلَمَّا تَوَفَّيْتَنِى كُنتَ أَنتَ ٱلرَّقِيبَ عَلَيْهِمْ ۚ وَأَنتَ عَلَىٰ كُلِّ شَىْءٍ شَهِيدٌ ۝ إِن تُعَذِّبْهُمْ فَإِنَّهُمْ عِبَادُكَ ۖ وَإِن تَغْفِرْ لَهُمْ فَإِنَّكَ أَنتَ ٱلْعَزِيزُ ٱلْحَكِيمُ ۝ قَالَ ٱللَّهُ هَٰذَا يَوْمُ يَنفَعُ ٱلصَّٰدِقِينَ صِدْقُهُمْ ۚ لَهُمْ جَنَّٰتٌ تَجْرِى مِن تَحْتِهَا ٱلْأَنْهَٰرُ خَٰلِدِينَ فِيهَآ أَبَدًا ۚ رَّضِىَ ٱللَّهُ عَنْهُمْ وَرَضُوا۟ عَنْهُ ۚ ذَٰلِكَ ٱلْفَوْزُ ٱلْعَظِيمُ ۝ لِلَّهِ مُلْكُ ٱلسَّمَٰوَٰتِ وَٱلْأَرْضِ وَمَا فِيهِنَّ ۚ وَهُوَ عَلَىٰ كُلِّ شَىْءٍ قَدِيرٌ ۝

(Al-Maidah 082-120)

Chapter (Surah) 6: Al-An'am 001-110

بِسْمِ اللَّهِ الرَّحْمَٰنِ الرَّحِيمِ

﴿ ٱلْحَمْدُ لِلَّهِ ٱلَّذِى خَلَقَ ٱلسَّمَٰوَٰتِ وَٱلْأَرْضَ وَجَعَلَ ٱلظُّلُمَٰتِ وَٱلنُّورَ ۖ ثُمَّ ٱلَّذِينَ كَفَرُوا۟ بِرَبِّهِمْ يَعْدِلُونَ ۝ هُوَ ٱلَّذِى خَلَقَكُم مِّن طِينٍ ثُمَّ قَضَىٰٓ أَجَلًا ۖ وَأَجَلٌ مُّسَمًّى عِندَهُۥ ۖ ثُمَّ أَنتُمْ تَمْتَرُونَ ۝ وَهُوَ ٱللَّهُ فِى ٱلسَّمَٰوَٰتِ وَفِى ٱلْأَرْضِ ۖ يَعْلَمُ سِرَّكُمْ وَجَهْرَكُمْ وَيَعْلَمُ مَا تَكْسِبُونَ ۝ وَمَا تَأْتِيهِم مِّنْ ءَايَةٍ مِّنْ ءَايَٰتِ رَبِّهِمْ إِلَّا كَانُوا۟ عَنْهَا مُعْرِضِينَ ۝ فَقَدْ كَذَّبُوا۟ بِٱلْحَقِّ لَمَّا جَآءَهُمْ ۖ فَسَوْفَ يَأْتِيهِمْ أَنۢبَٰٓؤُا۟ مَا كَانُوا۟ بِهِۦ يَسْتَهْزِءُونَ ۝ أَلَمْ يَرَوْا۟ كَمْ أَهْلَكْنَا مِن قَبْلِهِم مِّن قَرْنٍ مَّكَّنَّٰهُمْ فِى ٱلْأَرْضِ مَا لَمْ نُمَكِّن لَّكُمْ وَأَرْسَلْنَا ٱلسَّمَآءَ عَلَيْهِم مِّدْرَارًا وَجَعَلْنَا ٱلْأَنْهَٰرَ تَجْرِى مِن تَحْتِهِمْ فَأَهْلَكْنَٰهُم بِذُنُوبِهِمْ وَأَنشَأْنَا مِنۢ بَعْدِهِمْ قَرْنًا ءَاخَرِينَ ۝ وَلَوْ نَزَّلْنَا عَلَيْكَ كِتَٰبًا فِى قِرْطَاسٍ فَلَمَسُوهُ بِأَيْدِيهِمْ لَقَالَ ٱلَّذِينَ كَفَرُوٓا۟ إِنْ هَٰذَآ إِلَّا سِحْرٌ مُّبِينٌ ۝ وَقَالُوا۟ لَوْلَآ أُنزِلَ عَلَيْهِ مَلَكٌ ۖ وَلَوْ أَنزَلْنَا مَلَكًا لَّقُضِىَ ٱلْأَمْرُ ثُمَّ لَا يُنظَرُونَ ۝ وَلَوْ جَعَلْنَٰهُ مَلَكًا لَّجَعَلْنَٰهُ رَجُلًا وَلَلَبَسْنَا عَلَيْهِم مَّا يَلْبِسُونَ ۝ وَلَقَدِ ٱسْتُهْزِئَ بِرُسُلٍ مِّن قَبْلِكَ فَحَاقَ بِٱلَّذِينَ سَخِرُوا۟ مِنْهُم مَّا كَانُوا۟ بِهِۦ يَسْتَهْزِءُونَ ۝ قُلْ سِيرُوا۟ فِى ٱلْأَرْضِ ثُمَّ ٱنظُرُوا۟ كَيْفَ كَانَ عَٰقِبَةُ ٱلْمُكَذِّبِينَ ۝ قُل لِّمَن مَّا فِى ٱلسَّمَٰوَٰتِ وَٱلْأَرْضِ ۖ قُل لِّلَّهِ ۚ كَتَبَ عَلَىٰ نَفْسِهِ ٱلرَّحْمَةَ ۚ لَيَجْمَعَنَّكُمْ إِلَىٰ يَوْمِ ٱلْقِيَٰمَةِ لَا رَيْبَ فِيهِ ۚ ٱلَّذِينَ خَسِرُوٓا۟ أَنفُسَهُمْ فَهُمْ لَا يُؤْمِنُونَ ۝ ۞ وَلَهُۥ مَا سَكَنَ فِى ٱلَّيْلِ وَٱلنَّهَارِ ۚ وَهُوَ ٱلسَّمِيعُ ٱلْعَلِيمُ ۝ قُلْ أَغَيْرَ ٱللَّهِ أَتَّخِذُ وَلِيًّا فَاطِرِ ٱلسَّمَٰوَٰتِ وَٱلْأَرْضِ وَهُوَ يُطْعِمُ وَلَا يُطْعَمُ ۗ قُلْ إِنِّىٓ أُمِرْتُ أَنْ أَكُونَ أَوَّلَ مَنْ أَسْلَمَ ۖ وَلَا تَكُونَنَّ مِنَ ٱلْمُشْرِكِينَ ۝ قُلْ إِنِّىٓ أَخَافُ إِنْ عَصَيْتُ رَبِّى عَذَابَ يَوْمٍ عَظِيمٍ ۝ مَّن

يُصۡرَفۡ عَنۡهُ يَوۡمَئِذࣲ فَقَدۡ رَحِمَهُۥۚ وَذَٰلِكَ ٱلۡفَوۡزُ ٱلۡمُبِينُ ۝ وَإِن يَمۡسَسۡكَ ٱللَّهُ بِضُرࣲّ فَلَا كَاشِفَ لَهُۥۤ إِلَّا هُوَۖ وَإِن يَمۡسَسۡكَ بِخَيۡرࣲ فَهُوَ عَلَىٰ كُلِّ شَيۡءࣲ قَدِيرࣱ ۝ وَهُوَ ٱلۡقَاهِرُ فَوۡقَ عِبَادِهِۦۚ وَهُوَ ٱلۡحَكِيمُ ٱلۡخَبِيرُ ۝ قُلۡ أَيُّ شَيۡءٍ أَكۡبَرُ شَهَٰدَةࣰۖ قُلِ ٱللَّهُۖ شَهِيدُۢ بَيۡنِي وَبَيۡنَكُمۡۚ وَأُوحِيَ إِلَيَّ هَٰذَا ٱلۡقُرۡءَانُ لِأُنذِرَكُم بِهِۦ وَمَنۢ بَلَغَۚ أَئِنَّكُمۡ لَتَشۡهَدُونَ أَنَّ مَعَ ٱللَّهِ ءَالِهَةً أُخۡرَىٰۚ قُل لَّاۤ أَشۡهَدُۚ قُلۡ إِنَّمَا هُوَ إِلَٰهࣱ وَٰحِدࣱ وَإِنَّنِي بَرِيٓءࣱ مِّمَّا تُشۡرِكُونَ ۝ ٱلَّذِينَ ءَاتَيۡنَٰهُمُ ٱلۡكِتَٰبَ يَعۡرِفُونَهُۥ كَمَا يَعۡرِفُونَ أَبۡنَاۤءَهُمُۘ ٱلَّذِينَ خَسِرُوۤاْ أَنفُسَهُمۡ فَهُمۡ لَا يُؤۡمِنُونَ ۝ وَمَنۡ أَظۡلَمُ مِمَّنِ ٱفۡتَرَىٰ عَلَى ٱللَّهِ كَذِبًا أَوۡ كَذَّبَ بِـَٔايَٰتِهِۦۤۚ إِنَّهُۥ لَا يُفۡلِحُ ٱلظَّٰلِمُونَ ۝ وَيَوۡمَ نَحۡشُرُهُمۡ جَمِيعࣰا ثُمَّ نَقُولُ لِلَّذِينَ أَشۡرَكُوۤاْ أَيۡنَ شُرَكَاۤؤُكُمُ ٱلَّذِينَ كُنتُمۡ تَزۡعُمُونَ ۝ ثُمَّ لَمۡ تَكُن فِتۡنَتُهُمۡ إِلَّاۤ أَن قَالُواْ وَٱللَّهِ رَبِّنَا مَا كُنَّا مُشۡرِكِينَ ۝ ٱنظُرۡ كَيۡفَ كَذَبُواْ عَلَىٰۤ أَنفُسِهِمۡۚ وَضَلَّ عَنۡهُم مَّا كَانُواْ يَفۡتَرُونَ ۝ وَمِنۡهُم مَّن يَسۡتَمِعُ إِلَيۡكَۖ وَجَعَلۡنَا عَلَىٰ قُلُوبِهِمۡ أَكِنَّةً أَن يَفۡقَهُوهُ وَفِيۤ ءَاذَانِهِمۡ وَقۡرࣰاۚ وَإِن يَرَوۡاْ كُلَّ ءَايَةࣲ لَّا يُؤۡمِنُواْ بِهَاۚ حَتَّىٰۤ إِذَا جَاۤءُوكَ يُجَٰدِلُونَكَ يَقُولُ ٱلَّذِينَ كَفَرُوۤاْ إِنۡ هَٰذَاۤ إِلَّاۤ أَسَٰطِيرُ ٱلۡأَوَّلِينَ ۝ وَهُمۡ يَنۡهَوۡنَ عَنۡهُ وَيَنۡـَٔوۡنَ عَنۡهُۖ وَإِن يُهۡلِكُونَ إِلَّاۤ أَنفُسَهُمۡ وَمَا يَشۡعُرُونَ ۝ وَلَوۡ تَرَىٰۤ إِذۡ وُقِفُواْ عَلَى ٱلنَّارِ فَقَالُواْ يَٰلَيۡتَنَا نُرَدُّ وَلَا نُكَذِّبَ بِـَٔايَٰتِ رَبِّنَا وَنَكُونَ مِنَ ٱلۡمُؤۡمِنِينَ ۝ بَلۡ بَدَا لَهُم مَّا كَانُواْ يُخۡفُونَ مِن قَبۡلُۖ وَلَوۡ رُدُّواْ لَعَادُواْ لِمَا نُهُواْ عَنۡهُ وَإِنَّهُمۡ لَكَٰذِبُونَ ۝ وَقَالُوۤاْ إِنۡ هِيَ إِلَّا حَيَاتُنَا ٱلدُّنۡيَا وَمَا نَحۡنُ بِمَبۡعُوثِينَ ۝ وَلَوۡ تَرَىٰۤ إِذۡ وُقِفُواْ عَلَىٰ رَبِّهِمۡۚ قَالَ أَلَيۡسَ هَٰذَا بِٱلۡحَقِّۚ قَالُواْ بَلَىٰ وَرَبِّنَاۚ قَالَ فَذُوقُواْ ٱلۡعَذَابَ بِمَا كُنتُمۡ تَكۡفُرُونَ ۝ قَدۡ خَسِرَ ٱلَّذِينَ كَذَّبُواْ بِلِقَاۤءِ ٱللَّهِۖ حَتَّىٰۤ إِذَا جَاۤءَتۡهُمُ ٱلسَّاعَةُ بَغۡتَةࣰ قَالُواْ يَٰحَسۡرَتَنَا عَلَىٰ مَا فَرَّطۡنَا فِيهَا وَهُمۡ يَحۡمِلُونَ أَوۡزَارَهُمۡ عَلَىٰ ظُهُورِهِمۡۚ أَلَا سَاۤءَ مَا يَزِرُونَ

وَمَا ٱلْحَيَوٰةُ ٱلدُّنْيَآ إِلَّا لَعِبٌ وَلَهْوٌ ۖ وَلَلدَّارُ ٱلْءَاخِرَةُ خَيْرٌ لِّلَّذِينَ يَتَّقُونَ ۗ أَفَلَا تَعْقِلُونَ ۝ قَدْ نَعْلَمُ إِنَّهُۥ لَيَحْزُنُكَ ٱلَّذِى يَقُولُونَ ۖ فَإِنَّهُمْ لَا يُكَذِّبُونَكَ وَلَٰكِنَّ ٱلظَّٰلِمِينَ بِـَٔايَٰتِ ٱللَّهِ يَجْحَدُونَ ۝ وَلَقَدْ كُذِّبَتْ رُسُلٌ مِّن قَبْلِكَ فَصَبَرُوا۟ عَلَىٰ مَا كُذِّبُوا۟ وَأُوذُوا۟ حَتَّىٰٓ أَتَىٰهُمْ نَصْرُنَا ۚ وَلَا مُبَدِّلَ لِكَلِمَٰتِ ٱللَّهِ ۚ وَلَقَدْ جَآءَكَ مِن نَّبَإِى۟ ٱلْمُرْسَلِينَ ۝ وَإِن كَانَ كَبُرَ عَلَيْكَ إِعْرَاضُهُمْ فَإِنِ ٱسْتَطَعْتَ أَن تَبْتَغِىَ نَفَقًا فِى ٱلْأَرْضِ أَوْ سُلَّمًا فِى ٱلسَّمَآءِ فَتَأْتِيَهُم بِـَٔايَةٍ ۚ وَلَوْ شَآءَ ٱللَّهُ لَجَمَعَهُمْ عَلَى ٱلْهُدَىٰ ۚ فَلَا تَكُونَنَّ مِنَ ٱلْجَٰهِلِينَ ۝ ۞ إِنَّمَا يَسْتَجِيبُ ٱلَّذِينَ يَسْمَعُونَ ۘ وَٱلْمَوْتَىٰ يَبْعَثُهُمُ ٱللَّهُ ثُمَّ إِلَيْهِ يُرْجَعُونَ ۝ وَقَالُوا۟ لَوْلَا نُزِّلَ عَلَيْهِ ءَايَةٌ مِّن رَّبِّهِۦ ۚ قُلْ إِنَّ ٱللَّهَ قَادِرٌ عَلَىٰٓ أَن يُنَزِّلَ ءَايَةً وَلَٰكِنَّ أَكْثَرَهُمْ لَا يَعْلَمُونَ ۝ وَمَا مِن دَآبَّةٍ فِى ٱلْأَرْضِ وَلَا طَٰٓئِرٍ يَطِيرُ بِجَنَاحَيْهِ إِلَّآ أُمَمٌ أَمْثَالُكُم ۚ مَّا فَرَّطْنَا فِى ٱلْكِتَٰبِ مِن شَىْءٍ ۚ ثُمَّ إِلَىٰ رَبِّهِمْ يُحْشَرُونَ ۝ وَٱلَّذِينَ كَذَّبُوا۟ بِـَٔايَٰتِنَا صُمٌّ وَبُكْمٌ فِى ٱلظُّلُمَٰتِ ۗ مَن يَشَإِ ٱللَّهُ يُضْلِلْهُ وَمَن يَشَأْ يَجْعَلْهُ عَلَىٰ صِرَٰطٍ مُّسْتَقِيمٍ ۝ قُلْ أَرَءَيْتَكُمْ إِنْ أَتَىٰكُمْ عَذَابُ ٱللَّهِ أَوْ أَتَتْكُمُ ٱلسَّاعَةُ أَغَيْرَ ٱللَّهِ تَدْعُونَ إِن كُنتُمْ صَٰدِقِينَ ۝ بَلْ إِيَّاهُ تَدْعُونَ فَيَكْشِفُ مَا تَدْعُونَ إِلَيْهِ إِن شَآءَ وَتَنسَوْنَ مَا تُشْرِكُونَ ۝ وَلَقَدْ أَرْسَلْنَآ إِلَىٰٓ أُمَمٍ مِّن قَبْلِكَ فَأَخَذْنَٰهُم بِٱلْبَأْسَآءِ وَٱلضَّرَّآءِ لَعَلَّهُمْ يَتَضَرَّعُونَ ۝ فَلَوْلَآ إِذْ جَآءَهُم بَأْسُنَا تَضَرَّعُوا۟ وَلَٰكِن قَسَتْ قُلُوبُهُمْ وَزَيَّنَ لَهُمُ ٱلشَّيْطَٰنُ مَا كَانُوا۟ يَعْمَلُونَ ۝ فَلَمَّا نَسُوا۟ مَا ذُكِّرُوا۟ بِهِۦ فَتَحْنَا عَلَيْهِمْ أَبْوَٰبَ كُلِّ شَىْءٍ حَتَّىٰٓ إِذَا فَرِحُوا۟ بِمَآ أُوتُوٓا۟ أَخَذْنَٰهُم بَغْتَةً فَإِذَا هُم مُّبْلِسُونَ ۝ فَقُطِعَ دَابِرُ ٱلْقَوْمِ ٱلَّذِينَ ظَلَمُوا۟ ۚ وَٱلْحَمْدُ لِلَّهِ رَبِّ ٱلْعَٰلَمِينَ ۝ قُلْ أَرَءَيْتُمْ إِنْ أَخَذَ ٱللَّهُ سَمْعَكُمْ وَأَبْصَٰرَكُمْ وَخَتَمَ عَلَىٰ قُلُوبِكُم مَّنْ إِلَٰهٌ غَيْرُ ٱللَّهِ يَأْتِيكُم بِهِ ۗ ٱنظُرْ كَيْفَ نُصَرِّفُ

ٱلْءَايَٰتِ ثُمَّ هُمْ يَصْدِفُونَ ۝ قُلْ أَرَءَيْتَكُمْ إِنْ أَتَىٰكُمْ عَذَابُ ٱللَّهِ بَغْتَةً أَوْ جَهْرَةً هَلْ يُهْلَكُ إِلَّا ٱلْقَوْمُ ٱلظَّٰلِمُونَ ۝ وَمَا نُرْسِلُ ٱلْمُرْسَلِينَ إِلَّا مُبَشِّرِينَ وَمُنذِرِينَ ۖ فَمَنْ ءَامَنَ وَأَصْلَحَ فَلَا خَوْفٌ عَلَيْهِمْ وَلَا هُمْ يَحْزَنُونَ ۝ وَٱلَّذِينَ كَذَّبُوا۟ بِـَٔايَٰتِنَا يَمَسُّهُمُ ٱلْعَذَابُ بِمَا كَانُوا۟ يَفْسُقُونَ ۝ قُل لَّا أَقُولُ لَكُمْ عِندِى خَزَآئِنُ ٱللَّهِ وَلَآ أَعْلَمُ ٱلْغَيْبَ وَلَآ أَقُولُ لَكُمْ إِنِّى مَلَكٌ ۖ إِنْ أَتَّبِعُ إِلَّا مَا يُوحَىٰٓ إِلَىَّ ۚ قُلْ هَلْ يَسْتَوِى ٱلْأَعْمَىٰ وَٱلْبَصِيرُ ۚ أَفَلَا تَتَفَكَّرُونَ ۝ وَأَنذِرْ بِهِ ٱلَّذِينَ يَخَافُونَ أَن يُحْشَرُوٓا۟ إِلَىٰ رَبِّهِمْ ۙ لَيْسَ لَهُم مِّن دُونِهِۦ وَلِىٌّ وَلَا شَفِيعٌ لَّعَلَّهُمْ يَتَّقُونَ ۝ وَلَا تَطْرُدِ ٱلَّذِينَ يَدْعُونَ رَبَّهُم بِٱلْغَدَوٰةِ وَٱلْعَشِىِّ يُرِيدُونَ وَجْهَهُۥ ۖ مَا عَلَيْكَ مِنْ حِسَابِهِم مِّن شَىْءٍ وَمَا مِنْ حِسَابِكَ عَلَيْهِم مِّن شَىْءٍ فَتَطْرُدَهُمْ فَتَكُونَ مِنَ ٱلظَّٰلِمِينَ ۝ وَكَذَٰلِكَ فَتَنَّا بَعْضَهُم بِبَعْضٍ لِّيَقُولُوٓا۟ أَهَٰٓؤُلَآءِ مَنَّ ٱللَّهُ عَلَيْهِم مِّنۢ بَيْنِنَآ ۗ أَلَيْسَ ٱللَّهُ بِأَعْلَمَ بِٱلشَّٰكِرِينَ ۝ وَإِذَا جَآءَكَ ٱلَّذِينَ يُؤْمِنُونَ بِـَٔايَٰتِنَا فَقُلْ سَلَٰمٌ عَلَيْكُمْ ۖ كَتَبَ رَبُّكُمْ عَلَىٰ نَفْسِهِ ٱلرَّحْمَةَ ۖ أَنَّهُۥ مَنْ عَمِلَ مِنكُمْ سُوٓءًۢا بِجَهَٰلَةٍ ثُمَّ تَابَ مِنۢ بَعْدِهِۦ وَأَصْلَحَ فَأَنَّهُۥ غَفُورٌ رَّحِيمٌ ۝ وَكَذَٰلِكَ نُفَصِّلُ ٱلْءَايَٰتِ وَلِتَسْتَبِينَ سَبِيلُ ٱلْمُجْرِمِينَ ۝ قُلْ إِنِّى نُهِيتُ أَنْ أَعْبُدَ ٱلَّذِينَ تَدْعُونَ مِن دُونِ ٱللَّهِ ۚ قُل لَّآ أَتَّبِعُ أَهْوَآءَكُمْ ۙ قَدْ ضَلَلْتُ إِذًا وَمَآ أَنَا۠ مِنَ ٱلْمُهْتَدِينَ ۝ قُلْ إِنِّى عَلَىٰ بَيِّنَةٍ مِّن رَّبِّى وَكَذَّبْتُم بِهِۦ ۚ مَا عِندِى مَا تَسْتَعْجِلُونَ بِهِۦٓ ۚ إِنِ ٱلْحُكْمُ إِلَّا لِلَّهِ ۖ يَقُصُّ ٱلْحَقَّ ۖ وَهُوَ خَيْرُ ٱلْفَٰصِلِينَ ۝ قُل لَّوْ أَنَّ عِندِى مَا تَسْتَعْجِلُونَ بِهِۦ لَقُضِىَ ٱلْأَمْرُ بَيْنِى وَبَيْنَكُمْ ۗ وَٱللَّهُ أَعْلَمُ بِٱلظَّٰلِمِينَ ۝ ۞ وَعِندَهُۥ مَفَاتِحُ ٱلْغَيْبِ لَا يَعْلَمُهَآ إِلَّا هُوَ ۚ وَيَعْلَمُ مَا فِى ٱلْبَرِّ وَٱلْبَحْرِ ۚ وَمَا تَسْقُطُ مِن وَرَقَةٍ إِلَّا يَعْلَمُهَا وَلَا حَبَّةٍ فِى ظُلُمَٰتِ ٱلْأَرْضِ وَلَا رَطْبٍ وَلَا يَابِسٍ إِلَّا فِى كِتَٰبٍ مُّبِينٍ ۝ وَهُوَ ٱلَّذِى

يَتَوَفَّىٰكُم بِٱلَّيْلِ وَيَعْلَمُ مَا جَرَحْتُم بِٱلنَّهَارِ ثُمَّ يَبْعَثُكُمْ فِيهِ لِيُقْضَىٰٓ أَجَلٌ مُّسَمًّى ۖ ثُمَّ إِلَيْهِ مَرْجِعُكُمْ ثُمَّ يُنَبِّئُكُم بِمَا كُنتُمْ تَعْمَلُونَ ۞ وَهُوَ ٱلْقَاهِرُ فَوْقَ عِبَادِهِۦ ۖ وَيُرْسِلُ عَلَيْكُمْ حَفَظَةً حَتَّىٰٓ إِذَا جَآءَ أَحَدَكُمُ ٱلْمَوْتُ تَوَفَّتْهُ رُسُلُنَا وَهُمْ لَا يُفَرِّطُونَ ۞ ثُمَّ رُدُّوٓا۟ إِلَى ٱللَّهِ مَوْلَىٰهُمُ ٱلْحَقِّ ۚ أَلَا لَهُ ٱلْحُكْمُ وَهُوَ أَسْرَعُ ٱلْحَٰسِبِينَ ۞ قُلْ مَن يُنَجِّيكُم مِّن ظُلُمَٰتِ ٱلْبَرِّ وَٱلْبَحْرِ تَدْعُونَهُۥ تَضَرُّعًا وَخُفْيَةً لَّئِنْ أَنجَىٰنَا مِنْ هَٰذِهِۦ لَنَكُونَنَّ مِنَ ٱلشَّٰكِرِينَ ۞ قُلِ ٱللَّهُ يُنَجِّيكُم مِّنْهَا وَمِن كُلِّ كَرْبٍ ثُمَّ أَنتُمْ تُشْرِكُونَ ۞ قُلْ هُوَ ٱلْقَادِرُ عَلَىٰٓ أَن يَبْعَثَ عَلَيْكُمْ عَذَابًا مِّن فَوْقِكُمْ أَوْ مِن تَحْتِ أَرْجُلِكُمْ أَوْ يَلْبِسَكُمْ شِيَعًا وَيُذِيقَ بَعْضَكُم بَأْسَ بَعْضٍ ۗ ٱنظُرْ كَيْفَ نُصَرِّفُ ٱلْءَايَٰتِ لَعَلَّهُمْ يَفْقَهُونَ ۞ وَكَذَّبَ بِهِۦ قَوْمُكَ وَهُوَ ٱلْحَقُّ ۚ قُل لَّسْتُ عَلَيْكُم بِوَكِيلٍ ۞ لِّكُلِّ نَبَإٍ مُّسْتَقَرٌّ ۚ وَسَوْفَ تَعْلَمُونَ ۞ وَإِذَا رَأَيْتَ ٱلَّذِينَ يَخُوضُونَ فِىٓ ءَايَٰتِنَا فَأَعْرِضْ عَنْهُمْ حَتَّىٰ يَخُوضُوا۟ فِى حَدِيثٍ غَيْرِهِۦ ۚ وَإِمَّا يُنسِيَنَّكَ ٱلشَّيْطَٰنُ فَلَا تَقْعُدْ بَعْدَ ٱلذِّكْرَىٰ مَعَ ٱلْقَوْمِ ٱلظَّٰلِمِينَ ۞ وَمَا عَلَى ٱلَّذِينَ يَتَّقُونَ مِنْ حِسَابِهِم مِّن شَىْءٍ وَلَٰكِن ذِكْرَىٰ لَعَلَّهُمْ يَتَّقُونَ ۞ وَذَرِ ٱلَّذِينَ ٱتَّخَذُوا۟ دِينَهُمْ لَعِبًا وَلَهْوًا وَغَرَّتْهُمُ ٱلْحَيَوٰةُ ٱلدُّنْيَا ۚ وَذَكِّرْ بِهِۦٓ أَن تُبْسَلَ نَفْسٌۢ بِمَا كَسَبَتْ لَيْسَ لَهَا مِن دُونِ ٱللَّهِ وَلِىٌّ وَلَا شَفِيعٌ وَإِن تَعْدِلْ كُلَّ عَدْلٍ لَّا يُؤْخَذْ مِنْهَآ ۗ أُو۟لَٰٓئِكَ ٱلَّذِينَ أُبْسِلُوا۟ بِمَا كَسَبُوا۟ ۖ لَهُمْ شَرَابٌ مِّنْ حَمِيمٍ وَعَذَابٌ أَلِيمٌۢ بِمَا كَانُوا۟ يَكْفُرُونَ ۞ قُلْ أَنَدْعُوا۟ مِن دُونِ ٱللَّهِ مَا لَا يَنفَعُنَا وَلَا يَضُرُّنَا وَنُرَدُّ عَلَىٰٓ أَعْقَابِنَا بَعْدَ إِذْ هَدَىٰنَا ٱللَّهُ كَٱلَّذِى ٱسْتَهْوَتْهُ ٱلشَّيَٰطِينُ فِى ٱلْأَرْضِ حَيْرَانَ لَهُۥٓ أَصْحَٰبٌ يَدْعُونَهُۥٓ إِلَى ٱلْهُدَى ٱئْتِنَا ۗ قُلْ إِنَّ هُدَى ٱللَّهِ هُوَ ٱلْهُدَىٰ ۖ وَأُمِرْنَا لِنُسْلِمَ لِرَبِّ ٱلْعَٰلَمِينَ ۞ وَأَنْ أَقِيمُوا۟ ٱلصَّلَوٰةَ وَٱتَّقُوهُ ۚ وَهُوَ ٱلَّذِىٓ إِلَيْهِ

تُحْشَرُونَ ۞ وَهُوَ ٱلَّذِى خَلَقَ ٱلسَّمَٰوَٰتِ وَٱلْأَرْضَ بِٱلْحَقِّ ۖ وَيَوْمَ يَقُولُ كُن فَيَكُونُ ۚ قَوْلُهُ ٱلْحَقُّ ۚ وَلَهُ ٱلْمُلْكُ يَوْمَ يُنفَخُ فِى ٱلصُّورِ ۚ عَٰلِمُ ٱلْغَيْبِ وَٱلشَّهَٰدَةِ ۚ وَهُوَ ٱلْحَكِيمُ ٱلْخَبِيرُ ۞ وَإِذْ قَالَ إِبْرَٰهِيمُ لِأَبِيهِ ءَازَرَ أَتَتَّخِذُ أَصْنَامًا ءَالِهَةً ۖ إِنِّى أَرَىٰكَ وَقَوْمَكَ فِى ضَلَٰلٍ مُّبِينٍ ۞ وَكَذَٰلِكَ نُرِىٓ إِبْرَٰهِيمَ مَلَكُوتَ ٱلسَّمَٰوَٰتِ وَٱلْأَرْضِ وَلِيَكُونَ مِنَ ٱلْمُوقِنِينَ ۞ فَلَمَّا جَنَّ عَلَيْهِ ٱلَّيْلُ رَءَا كَوْكَبًا ۖ قَالَ هَٰذَا رَبِّى ۖ فَلَمَّآ أَفَلَ قَالَ لَآ أُحِبُّ ٱلْءَافِلِينَ ۞ فَلَمَّا رَءَا ٱلْقَمَرَ بَازِغًا قَالَ هَٰذَا رَبِّى ۖ فَلَمَّآ أَفَلَ قَالَ لَئِن لَّمْ يَهْدِنِى رَبِّى لَأَكُونَنَّ مِنَ ٱلْقَوْمِ ٱلضَّآلِّينَ ۞ فَلَمَّا رَءَا ٱلشَّمْسَ بَازِغَةً قَالَ هَٰذَا رَبِّى هَٰذَآ أَكْبَرُ ۖ فَلَمَّآ أَفَلَتْ قَالَ يَٰقَوْمِ إِنِّى بَرِىٓءٌ مِّمَّا تُشْرِكُونَ ۞ إِنِّى وَجَّهْتُ وَجْهِىَ لِلَّذِى فَطَرَ ٱلسَّمَٰوَٰتِ وَٱلْأَرْضَ حَنِيفًا ۖ وَمَآ أَنَا۠ مِنَ ٱلْمُشْرِكِينَ ۞ وَحَآجَّهُۥ قَوْمُهُۥ ۚ قَالَ أَتُحَٰٓجُّوٓنِّى فِى ٱللَّهِ وَقَدْ هَدَىٰنِ ۚ وَلَآ أَخَافُ مَا تُشْرِكُونَ بِهِۦٓ إِلَّآ أَن يَشَآءَ رَبِّى شَيْـًٔا ۗ وَسِعَ رَبِّى كُلَّ شَىْءٍ عِلْمًا ۗ أَفَلَا تَتَذَكَّرُونَ ۞ وَكَيْفَ أَخَافُ مَآ أَشْرَكْتُمْ وَلَا تَخَافُونَ أَنَّكُمْ أَشْرَكْتُم بِٱللَّهِ مَا لَمْ يُنَزِّلْ بِهِۦ عَلَيْكُمْ سُلْطَٰنًا ۚ فَأَىُّ ٱلْفَرِيقَيْنِ أَحَقُّ بِٱلْأَمْنِ ۖ إِن كُنتُمْ تَعْلَمُونَ ۞ ٱلَّذِينَ ءَامَنُوا۟ وَلَمْ يَلْبِسُوٓا۟ إِيمَٰنَهُم بِظُلْمٍ أُو۟لَٰٓئِكَ لَهُمُ ٱلْأَمْنُ وَهُم مُّهْتَدُونَ ۞ وَتِلْكَ حُجَّتُنَآ ءَاتَيْنَٰهَآ إِبْرَٰهِيمَ عَلَىٰ قَوْمِهِۦ ۚ نَرْفَعُ دَرَجَٰتٍ مَّن نَّشَآءُ ۗ إِنَّ رَبَّكَ حَكِيمٌ عَلِيمٌ ۞ وَوَهَبْنَا لَهُۥٓ إِسْحَٰقَ وَيَعْقُوبَ ۚ كُلًّا هَدَيْنَا ۚ وَنُوحًا هَدَيْنَا مِن قَبْلُ ۖ وَمِن ذُرِّيَّتِهِۦ دَاوُۥدَ وَسُلَيْمَٰنَ وَأَيُّوبَ وَيُوسُفَ وَمُوسَىٰ وَهَٰرُونَ ۚ وَكَذَٰلِكَ نَجْزِى ٱلْمُحْسِنِينَ ۞ وَزَكَرِيَّا وَيَحْيَىٰ وَعِيسَىٰ وَإِلْيَاسَ ۖ كُلٌّ مِّنَ ٱلصَّٰلِحِينَ ۞ وَإِسْمَٰعِيلَ وَٱلْيَسَعَ وَيُونُسَ وَلُوطًا ۚ وَكُلًّا فَضَّلْنَا عَلَى ٱلْعَٰلَمِينَ ۞ وَمِنْ ءَابَآئِهِمْ وَذُرِّيَّٰتِهِمْ وَإِخْوَٰنِهِمْ ۖ وَٱجْتَبَيْنَٰهُمْ وَهَدَيْنَٰهُمْ إِلَىٰ

صِرَٰطٍ مُّسْتَقِيمٍ ۝ ذَٰلِكَ هُدَى ٱللَّهِ يَهْدِى بِهِۦ مَن يَشَآءُ مِنْ عِبَادِهِۦ ۚ وَلَوْ أَشْرَكُوا۟ لَحَبِطَ عَنْهُم مَّا كَانُوا۟ يَعْمَلُونَ ۝ أُو۟لَٰٓئِكَ ٱلَّذِينَ ءَاتَيْنَٰهُمُ ٱلْكِتَٰبَ وَٱلْحُكْمَ وَٱلنُّبُوَّةَ ۚ فَإِن يَكْفُرْ بِهَا هَٰٓؤُلَآءِ فَقَدْ وَكَّلْنَا بِهَا قَوْمًا لَّيْسُوا۟ بِهَا بِكَٰفِرِينَ ۝ أُو۟لَٰٓئِكَ ٱلَّذِينَ هَدَى ٱللَّهُ ۖ فَبِهُدَىٰهُمُ ٱقْتَدِهْ ۗ قُل لَّآ أَسْـَٔلُكُمْ عَلَيْهِ أَجْرًا ۖ إِنْ هُوَ إِلَّا ذِكْرَىٰ لِلْعَٰلَمِينَ ۝ وَمَا قَدَرُوا۟ ٱللَّهَ حَقَّ قَدْرِهِۦٓ إِذْ قَالُوا۟ مَآ أَنزَلَ ٱللَّهُ عَلَىٰ بَشَرٍ مِّن شَىْءٍ ۗ قُلْ مَنْ أَنزَلَ ٱلْكِتَٰبَ ٱلَّذِى جَآءَ بِهِۦ مُوسَىٰ نُورًا وَهُدًى لِّلنَّاسِ ۖ تَجْعَلُونَهُۥ قَرَاطِيسَ تُبْدُونَهَا وَتُخْفُونَ كَثِيرًا ۖ وَعُلِّمْتُم مَّا لَمْ تَعْلَمُوٓا۟ أَنتُمْ وَلَآ ءَابَآؤُكُمْ ۖ قُلِ ٱللَّهُ ۖ ثُمَّ ذَرْهُمْ فِى خَوْضِهِمْ يَلْعَبُونَ ۝ وَهَٰذَا كِتَٰبٌ أَنزَلْنَٰهُ مُبَارَكٌ مُّصَدِّقُ ٱلَّذِى بَيْنَ يَدَيْهِ وَلِتُنذِرَ أُمَّ ٱلْقُرَىٰ وَمَنْ حَوْلَهَا ۚ وَٱلَّذِينَ يُؤْمِنُونَ بِٱلْءَاخِرَةِ يُؤْمِنُونَ بِهِۦ ۖ وَهُمْ عَلَىٰ صَلَاتِهِمْ يُحَافِظُونَ ۝ وَمَنْ أَظْلَمُ مِمَّنِ ٱفْتَرَىٰ عَلَى ٱللَّهِ كَذِبًا أَوْ قَالَ أُوحِىَ إِلَىَّ وَلَمْ يُوحَ إِلَيْهِ شَىْءٌ وَمَن قَالَ سَأُنزِلُ مِثْلَ مَآ أَنزَلَ ٱللَّهُ ۗ وَلَوْ تَرَىٰٓ إِذِ ٱلظَّٰلِمُونَ فِى غَمَرَٰتِ ٱلْمَوْتِ وَٱلْمَلَٰٓئِكَةُ بَاسِطُوٓا۟ أَيْدِيهِمْ أَخْرِجُوٓا۟ أَنفُسَكُمُ ۖ ٱلْيَوْمَ تُجْزَوْنَ عَذَابَ ٱلْهُونِ بِمَا كُنتُمْ تَقُولُونَ عَلَى ٱللَّهِ غَيْرَ ٱلْحَقِّ وَكُنتُمْ عَنْ ءَايَٰتِهِۦ تَسْتَكْبِرُونَ ۝ وَلَقَدْ جِئْتُمُونَا فُرَٰدَىٰ كَمَا خَلَقْنَٰكُمْ أَوَّلَ مَرَّةٍ وَتَرَكْتُم مَّا خَوَّلْنَٰكُمْ وَرَآءَ ظُهُورِكُمْ ۖ وَمَا نَرَىٰ مَعَكُمْ شُفَعَآءَكُمُ ٱلَّذِينَ زَعَمْتُمْ أَنَّهُمْ فِيكُمْ شُرَكَٰٓؤُا۟ ۚ لَقَد تَّقَطَّعَ بَيْنَكُمْ وَضَلَّ عَنكُم مَّا كُنتُمْ تَزْعُمُونَ ۝ ۞ إِنَّ ٱللَّهَ فَالِقُ ٱلْحَبِّ وَٱلنَّوَىٰ ۖ يُخْرِجُ ٱلْحَىَّ مِنَ ٱلْمَيِّتِ وَمُخْرِجُ ٱلْمَيِّتِ مِنَ ٱلْحَىِّ ۚ ذَٰلِكُمُ ٱللَّهُ ۖ فَأَنَّىٰ تُؤْفَكُونَ ۝ فَالِقُ ٱلْإِصْبَاحِ وَجَعَلَ ٱلَّيْلَ سَكَنًا وَٱلشَّمْسَ وَٱلْقَمَرَ حُسْبَانًا ۚ ذَٰلِكَ تَقْدِيرُ ٱلْعَزِيزِ ٱلْعَلِيمِ ۝ وَهُوَ ٱلَّذِى جَعَلَ لَكُمُ ٱلنُّجُومَ لِتَهْتَدُوا۟ بِهَا فِى ظُلُمَٰتِ ٱلْبَرِّ وَٱلْبَحْرِ ۗ قَدْ فَصَّلْنَا ٱلْءَايَٰتِ لِقَوْمٍ يَعْلَمُونَ ۝ وَهُوَ ٱلَّذِىٓ أَنشَأَكُم مِّن نَّفْسٍ وَٰحِدَةٍ فَمُسْتَقَرٌّ

وَمُسْتَوْدَعٌ قَدْ فَصَّلْنَا ٱلْءَايَـٰتِ لِقَوْمٍ يَفْقَهُونَ ۝ وَهُوَ ٱلَّذِىٓ أَنزَلَ مِنَ ٱلسَّمَآءِ مَآءً فَأَخْرَجْنَا بِهِۦ نَبَاتَ كُلِّ شَىْءٍ فَأَخْرَجْنَا مِنْهُ خَضِرًا نُّخْرِجُ مِنْهُ حَبًّا مُّتَرَاكِبًا وَمِنَ ٱلنَّخْلِ مِن طَلْعِهَا قِنْوَانٌ دَانِيَةٌ وَجَنَّـٰتٍ مِّنْ أَعْنَابٍ وَٱلزَّيْتُونَ وَٱلرُّمَّانَ مُشْتَبِهًا وَغَيْرَ مُتَشَـٰبِهٍ ٱنظُرُوٓا۟ إِلَىٰ ثَمَرِهِۦٓ إِذَآ أَثْمَرَ وَيَنْعِهِۦٓ إِنَّ فِى ذَٰلِكُمْ لَءَايَـٰتٍ لِّقَوْمٍ يُؤْمِنُونَ ۝ وَجَعَلُوا۟ لِلَّهِ شُرَكَآءَ ٱلْجِنَّ وَخَلَقَهُمْ وَخَرَقُوا۟ لَهُۥ بَنِينَ وَبَنَـٰتٍۭ بِغَيْرِ عِلْمٍ سُبْحَـٰنَهُۥ وَتَعَـٰلَىٰ عَمَّا يَصِفُونَ ۝ بَدِيعُ ٱلسَّمَـٰوَٰتِ وَٱلْأَرْضِ أَنَّىٰ يَكُونُ لَهُۥ وَلَدٌ وَلَمْ تَكُن لَّهُۥ صَـٰحِبَةٌ وَخَلَقَ كُلَّ شَىْءٍ وَهُوَ بِكُلِّ شَىْءٍ عَلِيمٌ ۝ ذَٰلِكُمُ ٱللَّهُ رَبُّكُمْ لَآ إِلَـٰهَ إِلَّا هُوَ خَـٰلِقُ كُلِّ شَىْءٍ فَٱعْبُدُوهُ وَهُوَ عَلَىٰ كُلِّ شَىْءٍ وَكِيلٌ ۝ لَّا تُدْرِكُهُ ٱلْأَبْصَـٰرُ وَهُوَ يُدْرِكُ ٱلْأَبْصَـٰرَ وَهُوَ ٱللَّطِيفُ ٱلْخَبِيرُ ۝ قَدْ جَآءَكُم بَصَآئِرُ مِن رَّبِّكُمْ فَمَنْ أَبْصَرَ فَلِنَفْسِهِۦ وَمَنْ عَمِىَ فَعَلَيْهَا وَمَآ أَنَا۠ عَلَيْكُم بِحَفِيظٍ ۝ وَكَذَٰلِكَ نُصَرِّفُ ٱلْءَايَـٰتِ وَلِيَقُولُوا۟ دَرَسْتَ وَلِنُبَيِّنَهُۥ لِقَوْمٍ يَعْلَمُونَ ۝ ٱتَّبِعْ مَآ أُوحِىَ إِلَيْكَ مِن رَّبِّكَ لَآ إِلَـٰهَ إِلَّا هُوَ وَأَعْرِضْ عَنِ ٱلْمُشْرِكِينَ ۝ وَلَوْ شَآءَ ٱللَّهُ مَآ أَشْرَكُوا۟ وَمَا جَعَلْنَـٰكَ عَلَيْهِمْ حَفِيظًا وَمَآ أَنتَ عَلَيْهِم بِوَكِيلٍ ۝ وَلَا تَسُبُّوا۟ ٱلَّذِينَ يَدْعُونَ مِن دُونِ ٱللَّهِ فَيَسُبُّوا۟ ٱللَّهَ عَدْوًۢا بِغَيْرِ عِلْمٍ كَذَٰلِكَ زَيَّنَّا لِكُلِّ أُمَّةٍ عَمَلَهُمْ ثُمَّ إِلَىٰ رَبِّهِم مَّرْجِعُهُمْ فَيُنَبِّئُهُم بِمَا كَانُوا۟ يَعْمَلُونَ ۝ وَأَقْسَمُوا۟ بِٱللَّهِ جَهْدَ أَيْمَـٰنِهِمْ لَئِن جَآءَتْهُمْ ءَايَةٌ لَّيُؤْمِنُنَّ بِهَا قُلْ إِنَّمَا ٱلْءَايَـٰتُ عِندَ ٱللَّهِ وَمَا يُشْعِرُكُمْ أَنَّهَآ إِذَا جَآءَتْ لَا يُؤْمِنُونَ ۝ وَنُقَلِّبُ أَفْـِٔدَتَهُمْ وَأَبْصَـٰرَهُمْ كَمَا لَمْ يُؤْمِنُوا۟ بِهِۦٓ أَوَّلَ مَرَّةٍ وَنَذَرُهُمْ فِى طُغْيَـٰنِهِمْ يَعْمَهُونَ ۝

(Al-An'am 001-110)

INTRODUCTION TO CHAPTER (SURAH) 5: AL-MAIDAH (THE TABLE, THE TABLE SPREAD)

Ibn kathir's Introduction

The Virtues of Surat Al-Ma'idah; When It was Revealed

At-Tirmidhi recorded that `Abdullah bin `Amr said, "The last Surahs to be revealed were Surat Al-Ma'idah and Surat Al-Fath (chapter 48)." At-Tirmidhi commented, "This Hadith is Hasan, Gharib." and it was also reported that Ibn `Abbas said that the last Surah to be revealed was,

(When there comes the help of Allah and the Conquest,) Al-Hakim collected a narration similar to that of At-Tirmidhi in his Mustadrak, and he said, "It is Sahih according to the criteria of the Two Shaykhs and they did not record it." Al-Hakim narrated that Jubayr bin Nufayr said, "I performed Hajj once and visited `A'ishah and she said to me, `O Jubayr! Do you read (or memorize) Al-Ma'idah ' I answered `Yes.' She said, `It was the last Surah to be revealed. Therefore, whatever permissible matters you find in it, then consider (treat) them permissible. And whatever impermissible matters you find in it, then consider (treat) them impermissible.'" Al-Hakim said, "It is Sahih according to the criteria of the Two Shaykhs and they did not record it. " Imam Ahmad recorded that `Abdur-Rahman bin Mahdi related that Mu`awiyah bin Salih added this statement in the last Hadith, "I (Jubayr) also asked `A'ishah about the Messenger of Allah's conduct and she answered by saying, `The Qur'an.'" An-Nasa'i also recorded it.

CHAPTER (SURAH) 5: AL-MAIDAH (THE TABLE, THE TABLE SPREAD), VERSES 082-120

Surah: 5 Ayah: 82 Ayah: 83, Ayah: 84, Ayah: 85 & Ayah: 86

﴿ ۞ لَتَجِدَنَّ أَشَدَّ ٱلنَّاسِ عَدَٰوَةً لِّلَّذِينَ ءَامَنُواْ ٱلْيَهُودَ وَٱلَّذِينَ أَشْرَكُواْ ۖ وَلَتَجِدَنَّ أَقْرَبَهُم مَّوَدَّةً لِّلَّذِينَ ءَامَنُواْ ٱلَّذِينَ قَالُوٓاْ إِنَّا نَصَٰرَىٰ ۚ ذَٰلِكَ بِأَنَّ مِنْهُمْ قِسِّيسِينَ وَرُهْبَانًا وَأَنَّهُمْ لَا يَسْتَكْبِرُونَ ﴾

82. Verily, you will find the strongest among men in enmity to the believers (Muslims) the Jews and those who are Al-Mushrikûn, and you will find the nearest in love to the believers (Muslims) those who say: "We are Christians." That is because amongst them are priests and monks, and they are not proud.

﴿ وَإِذَا سَمِعُواْ مَآ أُنزِلَ إِلَى ٱلرَّسُولِ تَرَىٰٓ أَعْيُنَهُمْ تَفِيضُ مِنَ ٱلدَّمْعِ مِمَّا عَرَفُواْ مِنَ ٱلْحَقِّ ۖ يَقُولُونَ رَبَّنَآ ءَامَنَّا فَٱكْتُبْنَا مَعَ ٱلشَّٰهِدِينَ ﴾

83. And when they (who call themselves Christians) listen to what has been sent down to the Messenger (Muhammad (peace be upon him)) you see their eyes overflowing with tears because of the truth they have recognized. They say: "Our Lord! We believe; so write us down among the witnesses.

﴿ وَمَا لَنَا لَا نُؤْمِنُ بِٱللَّهِ وَمَا جَآءَنَا مِنَ ٱلْحَقِّ وَنَطْمَعُ أَن يُدْخِلَنَا رَبُّنَا مَعَ ٱلْقَوْمِ ٱلصَّٰلِحِينَ ﴾

84. "And why should we not believe in Allâh and in that which has come to us of the truth (Islâmic Monotheism)? And we wish that our Lord will admit us (in Paradise on the Day of Resurrection) along with the righteous people (Prophet Muhammad (peace be upon him) and his Companions (may Allah be pleased with them))"

﴿ فَأَثَٰبَهُمُ ٱللَّهُ بِمَا قَالُوا۟ جَنَّٰتٍ تَجْرِى مِن تَحْتِهَا ٱلْأَنْهَٰرُ خَٰلِدِينَ فِيهَا وَذَٰلِكَ جَزَآءُ ٱلْمُحْسِنِينَ ﴾

85. So because of what they said, Allâh rewarded them Gardens under which rivers flow (in Paradise), they will abide therein forever. Such is the reward of Al-Muhsinûn (the good-doers).

﴿ وَٱلَّذِينَ كَفَرُوا۟ وَكَذَّبُوا۟ بِـَٔايَٰتِنَآ أُو۟لَٰٓئِكَ أَصْحَٰبُ ٱلْجَحِيمِ ﴾

86. But those who disbelieved and belied Our Ayât (proofs, evidences, verses, lessons, signs, revelations, etc.), they shall be the dwellers of the (Hell) Fire.

Transliteration

82. Latajidanna ashadda alnnasi AAadawatan lillatheena amanoo alyahooda waallatheena ashrakoo walatajidanna aqrabahum mawaddatan lillatheena amanoo allatheena qaloo inna nasara thalika bi-anna minhum qisseeseena waruhbanan waannahum la yastakbiroona 83. Wa-itha samiAAoo ma onzila ila alrrasooli tara aAAyunahum tafeedu mina alddamAAi mimma AAarafoo mina alhaqqi yaqooloona rabbana amanna faoktubna maAAa alshshahideena 84. Wama lana la nu/minu biAllahi wama jaana mina alhaqqi wanatmaAAu an yudkhilana rabbuna maAAa alqawmi alssaliheena 85. Faathabahumu Allahu bima qaloo jannatin tajree min tahtiha al-anharu khalideena feeha wathalika jazao almuhsineena 86. Waallatheena kafaroo wakaththaboo bi-ayatina ola-ika as-habu aljaheemi

Ibn Kathir Tafsir:

The Reason Behind Revealing these Ayat

Sa`id bin Jubayr, As-Suddi and others said that these Ayat were revealed concerning a delegation that An-Najashi (King of Ethiopia) sent to the Prophet in order to hear his words and observe his qualities. When the delegation met with the Prophet and he recited the Qur'an to them, they embraced Islam, cried and were humbled. Then they returned to An-Najashi and told him what happened. `Ata' bin Abi Rabah commented,

"They were Ethiopians who embraced Islam when the Muslims who migrated to Ethiopia resided among them." Qatadah said, "They were some followers of the religion of `Isa, son of Maryam, who when they saw Muslims and heard the Qur'an, they became Muslims without hesitation." Ibn Jarir said that these Ayat were revealed concerning some people who fit this description, whether they were from Ethiopia or otherwise. Allah said,

(Verily, you will find the strongest among men in enmity to the believers the Jews and those who commit Shirk,) This describes the Jews, since their disbelief is that of rebellion, defiance, opposing the truth, belittling other, people and degrading the scholars. This is why the Jews - may Allah's continued curses descend on them until the Day of Resurrection - killed many of their Prophets and tried to kill the Messenger of Allah several times, as well as, performing magic spells against him and poisoning him. They also incited their likes among the polytheists against the Prophet . Allah's statement,

(and you will find the nearest in love to the believers those who say: "We are Christians.") refers to those who call themselves Christians, who follow the religion of the Messiah and the teachings of his Injil. These people are generally more tolerant of Islam and its people, because of the mercy and kindness that their hearts acquired through part of the Messiah's religion. In another Ayah, Allah said;

(And We ordained in the hearts of those who followed him, compassion, mercy, and monasticism...) (57:27). In their book is the saying; "He who strikes you on the right cheek, then turn the left cheek for him." And fighting was prohibited in their creed, and this is why Allah said,

(That is because among them are Qissisin (priests) and Ruhban (monks), and they are not proud.) This means that among them are Qissisin (priests). The word Ruhban refers to one dedicated to worship. Allah said,

(That is because among them are priests and monks, and they are not proud.) This describes them with knowledge, worship and humbleness, along with following the truth and fairness.

(And when they listen to what has been sent down to the Messenger, you see their eyes overflowing with tears because of the truth they have recognized.) This refers to the good news that they have about the advent of Muhammad ,

(They say: "Our Lord! We believe; so write us down among the witnesses.") who testify to the truth and believe in it.

("And why should we not believe in Allah and in that which has come to us of the truth And We wish that our Lord will admit us (in Paradise) along with the righteous people.") Such sect of Christians are those mentioned in Allah's statement,

(And there are, certainly, among the People of the Scripture, those who believe in Allah and in that which has been revealed to you, and in that which has been revealed to them, humbling themselves before Allah.)(3:199) and,

(Those to whom We gave the Scripture before it, they believe in it (the Qur'an). And when it is recited to them, they say, "We believe in it. Verily, it is the truth from our Lord. Indeed even before it we were Muslims")(28:52-53), until,

("We seek not the ignorant.")(28:55) This is why Allah said here,

(So because of what they said, Allah awarded them...) rewarding them for embracing the faith and recognizing and believing in the truth,

(Gardens under which rivers flow (in Paradise), they will abide therein forever.) and they will never be removed from it, for they will dwell and remain in it forever and ever,

(Such is the reward of good-doers) who follow the truth and obey it wherever, whenever and with whomever they find it. Allah then describes the condition of the miserable.

(But those who disbelieved and belied Our Ayat,) defied and opposed them,

(they shall be the dwellers of the (Hell) Fire.) For they are the people of the Fire who will enter and reside in it (eternally).

Surah 5: Ayah: 87 & Ayah: 88

﴿ يَـٰٓأَيُّهَا ٱلَّذِينَ ءَامَنُوا۟ لَا تُحَرِّمُوا۟ طَيِّبَـٰتِ مَآ أَحَلَّ ٱللَّهُ لَكُمْ وَلَا تَعْتَدُوٓا۟ إِنَّ ٱللَّهَ لَا يُحِبُّ ٱلْمُعْتَدِينَ ۝ ﴾

87. O you who believe! Make not unlawful the Taiyibât (all that is good as regards foods, things, deeds, beliefs, persons) which Allâh has made lawful to you, and transgress not. Verily, Allâh does not like the transgressors.

﴿ وَكُلُوا۟ مِمَّا رَزَقَكُمُ ٱللَّهُ حَلَـٰلًا طَيِّبًا ۚ وَٱتَّقُوا۟ ٱللَّهَ ٱلَّذِىٓ أَنتُم بِهِۦ مُؤْمِنُونَ ۝ ﴾

88. And eat of the things which Allâh has provided for you, lawful and good, and fear Allâh in Whom you believe.

Transliteration

87. Ya ayyuha allatheena amanoo la tuharrimoo tayyibati ma ahalla Allahu lakum wala taAAtadoo inna Allaha la yuhibbu almuAAtadeena   88. Wakuloo mimma razaqakumu Allahu halalan tayyiban waittaqoo Allaha allathee antum bihi mu/minoona

Tafsir Ibn Kathir

There is No Monasticism in Islam

`Ali bin Abi Talhah said that Ibn `Abbas said, "This Ayah (5:87) was revealed about some of the Companions of the Prophet who said, `We should cut off our male organs, abandon the desires of this life and travel in the land, just as the Ruhban (monks) do.' When the Prophet heard of this statement, he summoned them and asked them if they made this statement and they answered `Yes.' The Prophet said,

«لكِنِّي أَصُومُ وَأُفْطِرُ، وَأُصَلِّي، وَأَنَامُ، وَأَنْكِحُ النِّسَاءَ، فَمَنْ أَخَذَ بِسُنَّتِي فَهُوَ مِنِّي، وَمَنْ لَمْ يَأْخُذْ بِسُنَّتِي فَلَيْسَ مِنِّي»

(I fast and break my fast, pray and sleep, and marry women. Whoever follows my Sunnah is of me, and whoever abandons my Sunnah is not of me.)" Ibn Abi Hatim also collected this Hadith. Ibn Marduwyah recorded that Al-`Awfi said that Ibn `Abbas narrated a similar Hadith. It is recorded in the Two Sahihs that `A'ishah said that some of the Companions asked the wives of the Prophet about the acts of worship that he performed in private. One of them said, "I will not eat meat," another said, "I will not marry women," while the third said, "I will not sleep on the bed." When the Prophet heard this statement, he said,

«مَا بَالُ أَقْوَامٍ يَقُولُ أَحَدُهُمْ كَذَا وَكَذَا، لكِنِّي أَصُومُ وَأُفْطِرُ، وَأَنَامُ وَأَقُومُ، وَآكُلُ اللَّحْمَ، وَأَتَزَوَّجُ النِّسَاءَ، فَمَنْ رَغِبَ عَنْ سُنَّتِي فَلَيْسَ مِنِّي»

(What is the matter with some people who said such and such I fast and break the fast, sleep and wake to stand to pray, eat meat, and marry women. He who is not pleased with my Sunnah is not of me.) Allah's statement,

(and transgress not.) means, do not exaggerate and make it hard for yourselves by prohibiting the permissible things. Do not transgress the limits by excessively indulging in the permissible matters; only use of it what satisfies your need; and do not fall into extravagance. Allah said in other Ayat,

(And eat and drink but waste not by extravagance.)(7:31), and,

(And those, who, when they spend, are neither extravagant nor miserly, but hold a medium (way) between those (extremes).)(25:67) So Allah legislated a medium way between those who are extreme and those who fall into shortcomings, and it does not allow excessive application, nor lack of application. This is why Allah said here,

(Make not unlawful the good things which Allah has made lawful to you, and transgress not. Verily, Allah does not like the transgressors.) then He said,

(And eat of the things which Allah has provided for you, lawful and good,)(5:88), eat of those items that are pure and lawful for you,

(and have Taqwa of Allah,) in all your affairs, obey Him and seek His pleasure, all the while staying away from defiance and disobedience of Allah,

(and have Taqwa of Allah in Whom you believe.)

Surah 5: Ayah: 89

﴿لَا يُؤَاخِذُكُمُ ٱللَّهُ بِٱللَّغْوِ فِىٓ أَيْمَـٰنِكُمْ وَلَـٰكِن يُؤَاخِذُكُم بِمَا عَقَّدتُّمُ ٱلْأَيْمَـٰنَ فَكَفَّـٰرَتُهُۥٓ إِطْعَامُ عَشَرَةِ مَسَـٰكِينَ مِنْ أَوْسَطِ مَا تُطْعِمُونَ أَهْلِيكُمْ أَوْ كِسْوَتُهُمْ أَوْ تَحْرِيرُ رَقَبَةٍ فَمَن لَّمْ يَجِدْ فَصِيَامُ ثَلَـٰثَةِ أَيَّامٍ ذَٰلِكَ كَفَّـٰرَةُ أَيْمَـٰنِكُمْ إِذَا حَلَفْتُمْ وَٱحْفَظُوٓا۟ أَيْمَـٰنَكُمْ كَذَٰلِكَ يُبَيِّنُ ٱللَّهُ لَكُمْ ءَايَـٰتِهِۦ لَعَلَّكُمْ تَشْكُرُونَ ۝﴾

89. Allâh will not punish you for what is unintentional in your oaths, but He will punish you for your deliberate oaths; for its expiation feed ten Masâkin (poor persons), on a scale of the average of that with which you feed your own families, or clothe them or manumit a slave. But whosoever cannot afford (that), then he should fast for three days. That is the expiation for the oaths when you have sworn. And protect your oaths (i.e. do not swear much). Thus Allâh make clear to you His Ayât (proofs, evidences, verses, lessons, signs, revelations, etc.) that you may be grateful.

Transliteration

89. La yu-akhithukumu Allahu biallaghwi fee aymanikum walakin yu-akhithukum bima AAaqqadtumu al-aymana fakaffaratuhu itAAamu AAasharati masakeena min awsati ma tutAAimoona ahleekum aw kiswatuhum aw tahreeru raqabatin faman lam yajid fasiyamu thalathati ayyamin thalika kaffaratu aymanikum itha halaftum waihfathoo aymanakum kathalika yubayyinu Allahu lakum ayatihi laAAallakum tashkuroona

Tafsir Ibn Kathir

Unintentional Oaths

We mentioned the subject of unintentional oaths in Surat Al-Baqarah, all praise and thanks are due to Allah, and so we do not need to repeat it here. We also mentioned that the Laghw in oaths refers to one's saying, "No by Allah," or, "Yes, by Allah," unintentionally.

Expiation for Breaking the Oaths

Allah said,

(but He will punish you for your deliberate oaths.) in reference to the oaths that you intend in your hearts, (for its expiation (a deliberate oath) feed ten poor,), who are needy, not able to find necessities of the life. Allah's statement,

(on a scale of the Awsat of that with which you feed your own families;) means, "On the average scale of what you feed your families," according to Ibn `Abbas, Sa`id bin Jubayr and `Ikrimah. `Ata' Al-Khurasani commented on the Ayah, "From the best of what you feed your families". Allah's statement,

(or clothe them,) refers to clothing each of the ten persons with what is suitable to pray in, whether the poor person was male or female. Allah knows best. Al-`Awfi said that Ibn `Abbas said that the Ayah means a robe or garment for each poor person (of the ten). Mujahid also said that the least of clothing, referred to in the Ayah, is a garment, and the most is whatever you wish. Al-Hasan, Abu Ja`far Al-Baqir, `Ata', Tawus, Ibrahim An-Nakha`i, Hammad bin Abi Sulayman and Abu Malik said that it means (giving each of the ten poor persons) a garment each. Allah's statement,

(or free a slave) refers to freeing a believing slave. In the Muwatta' of Malik, the Musnad of Ash-Shafi`i and the Sahih of Muslim, a lengthy Hadith was recorded that `Umar bin Al-Hakam As-Sulami said that he once had to free a slave (as atonement) and he brought a black slave girl before the Messenger of Allah , who asked her;

(Where is Allah?) «أَيْنَ اللهُ؟»

She said, "Above the heavens." He said,

(Who am I?) «مَنْ أَنَا؟»

She said, "The Messenger of Allah." He said,

«أَعْتِقْهَا فَإِنَّهَا مُؤْمِنَة»

(Free her, for she is a believer.) There are three types of expiation for breaking deliberate oaths, and whichever one chooses, it will suffice, according to the consensus (of the scholars). Allah mentioned the easiest, then the more difficult options, since feeding is easier than giving away clothes, and giving away clothes is easier than freeing a slave. If one is unable to fulfill any of these options, then he fasts for three days for expiation, just as Allah said,

(But whosoever cannot afford (that), then he should fast for three days.) Ubayy bin Ka`b and Ibn Mas`ud and his students read this Ayah as follows, "Then he should fast three consecutive days." Even if this statement was not narrated to us as a part of the Qur'an through Mutawatir narration, it would still be an explanation of the Qur'an by the Companions that has the ruling of being related from the Prophet . Allah's statement,

(That is the expiation for the oaths when you have sworn.)(5:89) means, this is the legal way to atone for deliberate oaths,

(And protect your oaths.) Do not leave your broken oaths without paying the expiation for them, according to the meaning given by Ibn Jarir.

(Thus Allah makes clear to you His Ayat) and explains them to you,

(that you may be grateful.)

Surah 5: Ayah: 90, Ayah: 91, Ayah: 92 & Ayah: 93

﴿ يَـٰٓأَيُّهَا ٱلَّذِينَ ءَامَنُوٓاْ إِنَّمَا ٱلْخَمْرُ وَٱلْمَيْسِرُ وَٱلْأَنصَابُ وَٱلْأَزْلَـٰمُ رِجْسٌ مِّنْ عَمَلِ ٱلشَّيْطَـٰنِ فَٱجْتَنِبُوهُ لَعَلَّكُمْ تُفْلِحُونَ ﴾

90. O you who believe! Intoxicants (all kinds of alcoholic drinks), and gambling, and Al-Ansâb, and Al-Azlâm (arrows for seeking luck or decision) are an abomination of Shaitân's (Satan) handiwork. So avoid (strictly all) that (abomination) in order that you may be successful.

﴿ إِنَّمَا يُرِيدُ ٱلشَّيْطَـٰنُ أَن يُوقِعَ بَيْنَكُمُ ٱلْعَدَٰوَةَ وَٱلْبَغْضَآءَ فِى ٱلْخَمْرِ وَٱلْمَيْسِرِ وَيَصُدَّكُمْ عَن ذِكْرِ ٱللَّهِ وَعَنِ ٱلصَّلَوٰةِ ۖ فَهَلْ أَنتُم مُّنتَهُونَ ﴾

91. Shaitân (Satan) wants only to excite enmity and hatred between you with intoxicants (alcoholic drinks) and gambling, and hinder you from the remembrance of Allâh and from As-Salât (the prayer). So, will you not then abstain?

﴿ وَأَطِيعُواْ ٱللَّهَ وَأَطِيعُواْ ٱلرَّسُولَ وَٱحْذَرُواْ ۚ فَإِن تَوَلَّيْتُمْ فَٱعْلَمُوٓاْ أَنَّمَا عَلَىٰ رَسُولِنَا ٱلْبَلَـٰغُ ٱلْمُبِينُ ﴾

92. And obey Allâh and the Messenger (Muhammad (peace be upon him)) and beware (of even coming near to drinking or gambling or Al-Ansâb, or Al-Azlâm, etc.) and fear Allâh. Then if you turn away, you should know that it is Our Messenger's duty to convey (the Message) in the clearest way.

﴿ لَيْسَ عَلَى ٱلَّذِينَ ءَامَنُواْ وَعَمِلُواْ ٱلصَّـٰلِحَـٰتِ جُنَاحٌ فِيمَا طَعِمُوٓاْ إِذَا مَا ٱتَّقَواْ وَّءَامَنُواْ وَعَمِلُواْ ٱلصَّـٰلِحَـٰتِ ثُمَّ ٱتَّقَواْ وَّءَامَنُواْ ثُمَّ ٱتَّقَواْ وَّأَحْسَنُواْ ۗ وَٱللَّهُ يُحِبُّ ٱلْمُحْسِنِينَ ﴾

93. Those who believe and do righteous good deeds, there is no sin on them for what they ate (in the past), if they fear Allâh (by keeping away from His

forbidden things), and believe and do righteous good deeds, and again fear Allâh and believe, and once again fear Allâh and do good deeds with Ihsân (perfection). And Allâh loves the good-doers.

Transliteration

90. Ya ayyuha allatheena amanoo innama alkhamru waalmaysiru waal-ansabu waal-azlamu rijsun min AAamali alshshaytani faijtaniboohu laAAallakum tuflihoona 91. Innama yureedu alshshaytanu an yooqiAAa baynakumu alAAadawata waalbaghdaa fee alkhamri waalmaysiri wayasuddakum AAan thikri Allahi waAAani alssalati fahal antum muntahoona 92. WaateeAAoo Allaha waateeAAoo alrrasoola waihtharoo fa-in tawallaytum faiAAlamoo annama AAala rasoolina albalaghu almubeenu 93. Laysa AAala allatheena amanoo waAAamiloo alssalihati junahun feema taAAimoo itha ma ittaqaw waamanoo waAAamiloo alssalihati thumma ittaqaw waamanoo thumma ittaqaw waahsanoo waAllahu yuhibbu almuhsineena

Tafsir Ibn Kathir

Prohibiting Khamr (Intoxicants) and Maysir (Gambling)

Allah forbids His believing servants from consuming Khamr and Maysir which is gambling. Ibn Abi Hatim recorded that `Ali bin Abi Talib, the Leader of the Faithful, said that chess is a type of gambling. Ibn Abi Hatim recorded that `Ata', Mujahid and Tawus, or , two of them, said that every type of gambling, including children's playing with (a certain type of) nuts, is Maysir. Ibn `Umar said that Al-Maysir means gambling, and this is the same statement that Ad-Dahhak reported from Ibn `Abbas, who added, "They used to gamble during the time of Jahiliyyah, until Islam came. Allah then forbade them from this evil behavior."

Meaning of Ansab and Azlam

Al-Ansab were altar stones, in whose vicinity sacrifices were offered (during the time of Jahiliyyah), according to Ibn `Abbas, Mujahid, `Ata', Sa`id bin Jubayr and Al-Hasan. They also said that Al-Azlam were arrows that they used for lotteries to make decisions, as Ibn Abi Hatim narrated. Allah said,

(A Rijs of Shaytan's handiwork) meaning, abomination of Shaytan's handiwork, according to `Ali bin Abi Talhah who reported it from Ibn `Abbas. Sa`id bin Jubayr said that Rijs means `sin' while Zayd bin Aslam said; "An evil handiwork of Shaytan."

(So avoid that) avoid all of these abominations,

(in order that you may be successful.) and this is a statement of encouragement. Allah said next,

(Shaytan wants only to excite enmity and hatred between you with Khamr (intoxicants) and Maysir (gambling), and hinder you from the remembrance of Allah and from the Salah (the prayer). So, will you not then abstain) This is a threat and a warning.

Hadiths that Prohibit Khamr (Intoxicants)

Imam Ahmad recorded that Abu Hurayrah said, "There were three stages to prohibiting Khamr (intoxicants). When the Messenger of Allah migrated to Al-Madinah, the people were consuming alcohol and gambling, so they asked the Messenger of Allah about these things, Allah revealed,

(They ask you about alcoholic drink and gambling. Say: "In them is a great sin, and (some) benefit for men.")(2:219), until the end of the Ayah. The people said, `They (intoxicants and gambling) were not prohibited for us. Allah only said,

(In them is a great sin, and (some) benefit for men.)' So they went on drinking Khamr until one day, one of the emigrants lead his companions in the Maghrib prayer and mixed up the Ayat in his recitation. Thereafter, Allah sent down a tougher statement,

(O you who believe! Approach not the Salah (the prayer) when you are in a drunken state until you know (the meaning of) what you utter.)(4:43) xThen, the people would drink before the time of the prayer so that they would attend the prayer while sober. A firmer Ayah was later revealed,

(O you who believe! Khamr, Maysir, Ansab, and Azlam are an abomination of Shaytan's handiwork. So avoid that in order that you may be successful.)(5:90-91) So they said, `We abstained, O Lord!' Later, some people said, `O Allah's Messenger! Some people died in the cause of Allah, while some others died in their beds, but they used to drink alcohol and indulge in gambling, which Allah has made a Rijs of the work of Shaytan.' So Allah sent down,

(Those who believe and do righteous good deeds, there is no sin on them for what they ate...) (5:93), until the end of the Ayah. The Prophet said,

«لَوْ حُرِّمَ عَلَيْهِمْ لَتَرَكُوهُ كَمَا تَرَكْتُمْ»

(Had they been made impermissible for them, they would have abandoned them as you have abandoned them.) Ahmad recorded this Hadith. Imam Ahmad recorded that `Umar bin Al-Khattab said, "O Allah! Explain the verdict about Khamr to us clearly." The Ayah in Surat Al-Baqarah was revealed,

(They ask you about alcoholic drink and gambling. Say: "In them is a great sin.")(2:219) `Umar was summoned and this Ayah was recited to him, but he still said, "O Allah! Make the verdict of Khamr clear to us." Then the Ayah in Surat An-Nisa' was revealed,

(O you who believe! Do not approach the Salah when you are in a drunken state.)(4:43) Thereafter, the Prophet had someone herald when it was time to pray, "Those in a drunken state are not to approach the prayer." `Umar was again summoned and the Ayah was recited to him, but he still said, "O Allah! Make the verdict concerning Khamr clear to us." Then, the Ayah in Surat Al-Ma'idah (5:91) was revealed, and `Umar was summoned and it was recited to him. When he reached the part of the Ayah that reads,

(So, will you not then abstain)(5:91), `Umar said, "We abstained, we abstained." Abu Dawud, At-Tirmidhi, and An-Nasa'i recorded this Hadith. `Ali bin Al-Madini and At-Tirmidhi graded it Sahih. It is recorded in the Two Sahihs, that `Umar bin Al-Khattab said in a speech; while standing on the Minbar of the Messenger of Allah (in the Prophet's Masjid in Al-Madinah) "O people! The prohibition of Khamr was revealed; and Khamr was extracted from five things: From grapes, dates, honey, wheat and barley. Khamr is what intoxicates the mind." Al-Bukhari recorded that Ibn `Umar said, "The prohibition of Khamr was revealed when there were five kinds of intoxicants in Al-Madinah, besides what was produced from grapes."

Another Hadith

Imam Ahmad recorded that Anas said, "I once was giving an alcoholic beverage to Abu `Ubaydah bin Al-Jarrah, `Ubayy bin Ka`b, Suhayl bin Bayda' and several of their friends meeting at Abu Talhah's house. When they were almost intoxicated, some Muslims came and said, `Did you not know that Khamr has been prohibited' They said, `We'll wait and ask.' They then said, `O Anas! Spill the remaining alcohol out of your container.' By Allah! They never drank it again, and their Khamr at that time was made from unripe and normal dates.'" This is also recorded in the Two Sahihs. In another narration by Anas, "I was the butler of the people in the house of Abu Talhah when Khamr was prohibited, and in those days alcohol was made from unripe and normal dates. A caller then heralded, and Abu Talhah ordered me to see what it was about. So I found that a person was announcing that alcoholic drinks had been prohibited. Abu Talhah ordered me to go out and spill the wine. I went out and spilled it, and it flowed in the streets of Al-Madinah. Some people said, `Some people were killed and wine was still in their stomachs.' Later on, Allah's revelation came,

(Those who believe and do righteous good deeds, there is no sin on them for what they ate...)(5:93)." Ibn Jarir recorded that Anas bin Malik said, "I was serving Abu Talhah, Abu `Ubaydah bin Al-Jarrah, Abu Dujanah, Mu`adh bin Jabal and Suhayl bin Bayda', until they became intoxicated from an alcoholic drink made of mixed unripe and normal dates. Then I heard someone herald, `Khamr has been made illegal.' So no one went in or out until we spilled the alcohol and broke its barrels. Some of us then performed ablution and others took a shower, and we wore some perfume. We then went out to the Masjid while the Messenger of Allah was reciting,

(O you who believe! Khamr, Maysir, Ansab, and Azlam are only an abomination of Shaytan's handiwork. So avoid that...)(5:90), until,

(So, will you not then abstain)(5:91). A man asked, `O Allah's Messenger! What about those who died drinking it' Allah sent down the verse,

(Those who believe and do righteous good deeds, there is no sin on them for what they ate.)(5:93)."

Another Hadith

Imam Ahmad recorded that Ibn `Umar said that the Messenger of Allah said,

«لُعِنَتِ الْخَمْرُ عَلَى عَشْرَةِ أَوْجُهٍ: لُعِنَتِ الْخَمْرُ بِعَيْنِهَا، وَشَارِبُهَا، وَسَاقِيهَا، وَبَائِعُهَا، وَمُبْتَاعُهَا، وَعَاصِرُهَا، وَمُعْتَصِرُهَا، وَحَامِلُهَا، وَالْمَحْمُولَةُ إِلَيْهِ، وَآكِلُ ثَمَنِهَا»

(Ten matters related to Khamr were cursed. Khamr itself was cursed, whoever drinks it, its server, seller, buyer, brewer, who asks for it to be brewed, whoever carries it, whomever it is carried to and whoever consumes its price.) Abu Dawud and Ibn Majah recorded this Hadith. Ahmad recorded that Ibn `Umar said, "Once, the Messenger of Allah went out and I went out with him. I walked to his right, but Abu Bakr came along and I gave way to him, and Abu Bakr was walking on the Prophet's right, while I was walking on his left. Then `Umar came along and he was walking on the Prophet's left, since I gave way to him. The Messenger of Allah then found a leather skin hanging containing alcohol, so he asked for a knife and ordered that the skin be cut open. He then said,

«لُعِنَتِ الْخَمْرُ وَشَارِبُهَا، وَسَاقِيهَا، وَبَائِعُهَا، وَمُبْتَاعُهَا، وَحَامِلُهَا، وَالْمَحْمُولَةُ إِلَيْهِ، وَعَاصِرُهَا وَمُعْتَصِرُهَا، وَآكِلُ ثَمَنِهَا»

(Khamr was cursed, and so are those who drink it, serve it, sell it, buy it, carry it, have it carried to them, brew it, have it brewed and consume its price.)"

Another Hadith

Al-Hafiz Abu Bakr Al-Bayhaqi recorded that Sa`d said, "There were four Ayat revealed about Khamr..." He then said, "A man from Al-Ansar made some food and invited us. We drank Khamr before it was prohibited and became intoxicated, and thus started to boast about our status. The Ansar said that they were better, while Quraysh (the Muhajirin) said that they were better. So a man from the Ansar took a bone and struck Sa`d's nose with it and made a flesh wound on it. Ever since that happened, Sa`d's nose had a scar from that wound. The Ayah,

(Intoxicants, gambling,) until,

(So, will you not then abstain) was later revealed." Muslim recorded this Hadith.

Another Hadith

Ibn Abi Hatim recorded that `Abdullah bin `Amr said, "This Ayah in the Qur'an,

(O you who believe! Khamr, Maysir, Ansab, and Azlam are only an abomination of Shaytan's handiwork. So avoid that in order that you may be successful.)(5:90), was also in the Tawrah; `Allah has sent down truth to eradicate falsehood, joyful play, flute or wind instruments, Zafan (dances) and Kibarat (refering to cabarets using the lute and bagpipe), tambourine, guitar, harp and lyric and love poetry. And Khamr is bitter for those who taste it. Allah has vowed by His grace and power, `Whoever drinks it after I prohibited it, I will make him thirsty on the Day of Resurrection. Whoever abandons it after I prohibited it, I will let him taste it in the residence of Grace (Paradise).'" Its chain of narration is Sahih

Another Hadith

Ash-Shafi`i narrated that Malik narrated that Nafi` said that Ibn `Umar said that the Messenger of Allah said,

«مَنْ شَرِبَ الْخَمْرَ فِي الدُّنْيَا ثُمَّ لَمْ يَتُبْ مِنْهَا حُرِمَهَا فِي الْآخِرَةِ»

(Whoever drinks Khamr in the life of this world and does not repent from it, will be deprived of it in the Hereafter.) Al-Bukhari and Muslim recorded this Hadith. Muslim recorded that Ibn `Umar said that the Messenger of Allah said,

«كُلُّ مُسْكِرٍ خَمْرٌ، وَكُلُّ مُسْكِرٍ حَرَامٌ، وَمَنْ شَرِبَ الْخَمْرَ فَمَاتَ وَهُوَ يُدْمِنُهَا وَلَمْ يَتُبْ مِنْهَا، لَمْ يَشْرَبْهَا فِي الْآخِرَةِ»

(Every intoxicant is Khamr, and every intoxicant is unlawful. Whoever drinks Khamr and dies while addicted to it, without repenting from drinking it, will not drink it in the Hereafter.) `Abdur-Rahman bin Al-Harith bin Hisham said that he heard `Uthman bin `Affan saying, "Avoid Khamr, for it is the mother of all sins. There was a man before your time who used to worship Allah secluded from the people. Later, an evil woman loved him and sent her female servant to him saying that they wanted him to witness something. So he went with the servant. Whenever they went through the door, she locked it behind them, until he reached a beautiful woman with a young servant boy and some alcohol. She said to him, `By Allah! I did not invite you to be a witness for anything, but called you to have sex with me, kill this boy or drink this alcohol.' So she gave him some alcohol, and he kept asking for more until he (became intoxicated and) had sex with her and killed the boy. Therefore, avoid Khamr, because it is never combined with faith, but one of them is bound to expel the other (from the heart)." This was recorded by Al-Bayhaqi. This statement has an authentic chain of narration. Abu Bakr bin Abi Ad-Dunya recorded this statement in his book on the prohibition of intoxicants, but he related it from the Prophet. Relating it from `Uthman is more authentic, and Allah knows best. Ahmad bin Hanbal recorded that Ibn `Abbas said, "When Khamr was prohibited, some people said, `O Allah's Messenger! What about our brethren who died while still drinking Khamr' Allah sent down the Ayah

(Those who believe and do righteous good deeds, there is no sin on them for what they ate,) until the end of the Ayah. When the Qiblah (direction of the prayer) was changed (from Jerusalem to Makkah), some people asked, `O Allah's Messenger! What about our brethren who died while still praying toward Jerusalem' Allah sent down,

(And Allah would never make your faith to be lost.)"(2:143) `Abdullah bin Mas`ud said that the Prophet said when the Ayah,

(Those who believe and do righteous good deeds, there is no sin on them for what they ate, if they have Taqwa, and believe...) was revealed,

《قِيلَ لِي: أَنْتَ مِنْهُم》

(I was told, that you are among them.) This is the narration that Muslim, At-Tirmidhi and An-Nasa'i collected.

Surah 5: Ayah: 94 & Ayah: 95

﴿يَـٰٓأَيُّهَا ٱلَّذِينَ ءَامَنُوا۟ لَيَبْلُوَنَّكُمُ ٱللَّهُ بِشَىْءٍ مِّنَ ٱلصَّيْدِ تَنَالُهُۥٓ أَيْدِيكُمْ وَرِمَاحُكُمْ لِيَعْلَمَ ٱللَّهُ مَن يَخَافُهُۥ بِٱلْغَيْبِ ۚ فَمَنِ ٱعْتَدَىٰ بَعْدَ ذَٰلِكَ فَلَهُۥ عَذَابٌ أَلِيمٌ ۞﴾

94. O you who believe! Allâh will certainly make a trial of you with something in (the matter of) the game that is well within the reach of your hands and your lances, that Allâh may test him who fears Him unseen. Then whoever transgresses thereafter, for him there is a painful torment.

﴿يَـٰٓأَيُّهَا ٱلَّذِينَ ءَامَنُوا۟ لَا تَقْتُلُوا۟ ٱلصَّيْدَ وَأَنتُمْ حُرُمٌ ۚ وَمَن قَتَلَهُۥ مِنكُم مُّتَعَمِّدًا فَجَزَآءٌ مِّثْلُ مَا قَتَلَ مِنَ ٱلنَّعَمِ يَحْكُمُ بِهِۦ ذَوَا عَدْلٍ مِّنكُمْ هَدْيًا بَـٰلِغَ ٱلْكَعْبَةِ أَوْ كَفَّـٰرَةٌ طَعَامُ مَسَـٰكِينَ أَوْ عَدْلُ ذَٰلِكَ صِيَامًا لِّيَذُوقَ وَبَالَ أَمْرِهِۦ ۗ عَفَا ٱللَّهُ عَمَّا سَلَفَ ۚ وَمَنْ عَادَ فَيَنتَقِمُ ٱللَّهُ مِنْهُ ۗ وَٱللَّهُ عَزِيزٌ ذُو ٱنتِقَامٍ ۞﴾

95. O you who believe! Kill not the game while you are in a state of Ihrâm (for Hajj or 'Umrah (pilgrimage)) and whosoever of you kills it intentionally, the penalty is an offering, brought to the Ka'bah, of an eatable animal (i.e. sheep, goat, cow) equivalent to the one he killed, as adjudged by two just men among you; or, for expiation, he should feed Masâkin (poor persons), or its equivalent in Saum (fasting), that he may taste the heaviness (punishment) of his deed. Allâh has forgiven what is past, but whosoever commits it again, Allâh will take retribution from him. And Allâh is All-Mighty, All-Able of Retribution.

Transliteration

94. Ya ayyuha allatheena amanoo layabluwannakumu Allahu bishay-in mina alssaydi tanaluhu aydeekum warimahukum liyaAAlama Allahu man yakhafuhu bialghaybi famani iAAtada baAAda thalika falahu AAathabun aleemun 95. Ya ayyuha allatheena amanoo la taqtuloo alssayda waantum hurumun waman qatalahu minkum mutaAAammidan fajazaon mithlu ma qatala mina alnnaAAami yahkumu bihi thawa AAadlin minkum hadyan baligha alkaAAbati aw kaffaratun taAAamu masakeena aw AAadlu thalika siyaman liyathooqa wabala amrihi AAafa Allahu AAamma salafa waman AAada fayantaqimu Allahu minhu waAllahu AAazeezun thoo intiqamin .

Tafsir Ibn Kathir

Prohibiting Hunting Game in the Sacred Area and During the State of Ihram

`Ali bin Abi Talhah) Al-Walibi said that Ibn `Abbas said that Allah's statement,

(Allah will certainly make a trial for you with something in (the matter of) the game that is well within reach of your hands and your lances,)(5:94), refers to, "The weak and young game. Allah tests His servants with such game during their Ihram, that if they wish, they would be able to catch it with their hands. Allah has commanded them to avoid catching it." Mujahid said that,

(well within reach of your hands) refers to the young game and chicks, while

(and your lances,) refers to mature game. Muqatil bin Hayyan said that this Ayah was revealed during the `Umrah of Al-Hudaybiyyah, when wild game and birds were coming to the Muslim camping area, which they had never seen the likes of before. Allah prohibited them from hunting the game while in the state of Ihram,

(that Allah may test who fears Him in the unseen.) Therefore, Allah tests His servants with the game that comes near their camping area, for if they wish, they can catch it with their hands and spears in public and secret. This is how the obedience of those who obey Allah in public and secret becomes apparent and tested. In another Ayah, Allah said;

(Verily! Those who fear their Lord in the unseen, theirs will be forgiveness and a great reward (i.e. Paradise).) Allah said next,

(Then whoever transgresses thereafter.) after this warning and threat, according to As-Suddi, then,

(for him there is a painful torment.) for his defiance of Allah's command and what He has decreed. Allah said next,

(O you who believe! Kill not game while you are in a state of Ihram,) This Ayah prohibits killing the game in the state of Ihram, except what is exempt from this as mentioned in the Two Sahihs; `A'ishah narrated that the Messenger of Allah said,

»خَمْسٌ فَوَاسِقُ يُقْتَلْنَ فِي الْحِلِّ وَالْحَرَمِ: الْغُرَابُ، وَالْحِدَأَةُ، وَالْعَقْرَبُ، وَالْفَأْرَةُ، وَالْكَلْبُ الْعَقُورُ«

(Five are Fawasiq, they may be killed while in Ihram or not; the crow, the kite, the scorpion, the mouse and the rabid dog.) Ibn `Umar narrated that the Messenger of Allah said,

»خَمْسٌ مِنَ الدَّوَابِّ لَيْسَ عَلَى الْمُحْرِمِ فِي قَتْلِهِنَّ جُنَاحٌ: الْغُرَابُ، وَالْحِدَأَةُ، وَالْعَقْرَبُ، وَالْفَأْرَةُ، وَالْكَلْبُ الْعَقُورُ«

(It is not harmful in a state of Ihram to kill five kinds of animals: the crow, the kite, the scorpion, the mouse and the rabid dog.) This Hadith was recorded in the Two Sahihs. Ayyub narrated that Nafi` narrated similar wordings for this Hadith from Ibn `Umar. Ayyub said, "So I said to Nafi`, `What about the snake' He said, `There is no doubt that killing the snake is allowed.'" The ruling concerning the rabid dog also includes the wolf, lion, leopard, tiger and their like, since they are more dangerous than the rabid dog, or because the term Kalb (dog) covers them. Allah knows best. Abu Sa`id narrated that the Prophet was asked about the animals that the Muhrim is allowed to kill and he said,

»الْحَيَّةُ، وَالْعَقْرَبُ، وَالْفُوَيْسِقَةُ، وَيَرْمِي الْغُرَابَ وَلَا يَقْتُلُهُ، وَالْكَلْبُ الْعَقُورُ، وَالْحِدَأَةُ، وَالسَّبُعُ الْعَادِي«

(The snake, the scorpion, the mouse, and the crow - which is shot at but not killed -- the rabid dog, the kite and wild beasts of prey.) Abu Dawud recorded this Hadith, as did At-Tirmidhi, who said, "Hasan", and Ibn Majah.

The Penalty of Killing Game in the Sacred Area or in the State of Ihram

Allah said,

(And whosoever of you kills it intentionally, the penalty is (an offering of) livestock equivalent to the one he killed.) Mujahid bin Jabr said, "The meaning of `intentionally' here is that one intends to kill the game while forgetting that he is in the state of Ihram. Whoever intentionally kills the game while aware that he is in the state of Ihram, then this offense is more grave than to make an expiation, and he also loses his Ihram." This statement is odd, and the view of majority is that they have to pay the expiation for killing the game whether they forgot that they are in Ihram or not. Az-Zuhri said, "The Book (the Qur'an) asserts the expiation for intentional killing, and the Sunnah included those who forget, as well." The meaning of this statement is that the Qur'an mentioned the expiation and sin of those who intentionally kill game, (that he may taste the heaviness (punishment) of his deed. Allah has forgiven what is past, but whosoever commits it again, Allah will take retribution from him.) the Sunnah that includes the rulings issued by the Prophet and his Companions, indicated the necessity of expiation in cases of unintentional killing of game, just as the Book legislated expiation for intentional killing. Killing game is a form of waste, which requires expiation in intentional and unintentional cases, although those who intend it have sinned, rather than those who made an honest error. Allah's statement,

(The penalty is (an offering of) livestock equivalent to the one he killed.) indicates the necessity of offering an equivalent animal to the one the Muhrim killed. The Companions gave rulings that the camel, for instance, is the equivalent of the ostrich, the cow is the equivalent of wild cattle, and the goat for the deer. As for the cases when there is no equivalent for the killed animal, Ibn `Abbas said that one should spend its amount in Makkah (i.e. charity), as Al-Bayhaqi recorded. Allah's statement,

(As adjudged by two just men among you;) means, two just Muslim men should determine an animal equivalent to the game killed, or the amount of its price. Ibn Jarir recorded that Abu Jarir Al-Bajali said, "I killed a deer when I was in the state of Ihram and mentioned this fact to `Umar, who said, `Bring two of your brethren and let them judge you.' So I went to `Abdur-Rahman and Sa`d and they said that I should offer a male sheep." Ibn Jarir recorded that Tariq said, "Arbad killed a deer while in the state of Ihram and he went to `Umar to judge him. `Umar said to him, `Let us both judge,' and they judged that Arbad should offer a goat that was fed on abundant water and grass. `Umar commented,

(As adjudged by two just men among you;)." Allah's statement,

(...an offering brought to the Ka`bah.) indicates that this equivalent animal should be brought to the Ka`bah, meaning, the Sacred Area, where it should be slaughtered and its meat divided between the poor of the Sacred Area. There is a consensus on this ruling. Allah said,

(or, for expiation, he should feed the poor, or its equivalent in fasting,) that is, if the Muhrim does not find an equivalent to what he killed, or the animal hunted is not comparable to anything else. `Ali bin Abi Talhah said that Ibn `Abbas commented on the Ayah,

(...an offering brought to the Ka`bah, or, for expiation, he should feed the poor, or its equivalent in fasting.) "If the Muhrim killed game, then his judgement is its equivalent. If he kills an antelope, he offers a sheep slaughtered in Makkah. If he cannot, then he feeds six poor people, otherwise he should fast for three days. If he kills a deer, he offers a cow. If unable, he feeds twenty poor people, or otherwise if unable, he fasts for twenty days. If he kills an ostrich or zebra, he offers a camel, or he feeds thirty poor people, or fasts thirty days." Ibn Abi Hatim and Ibn Jarir recorded this statement, and in Ibn Jarir's narration, the food measurement is a Mudd (4 handfuls of food) each that suffices for the poor. Allah's statement,

(that he may taste the heaviness (punishment) of his deed.) means, We have required him to pay this expiation so that he tastes the punishment of his error,

(Allah has forgiven what is past.) during the time of Jahiliyyah, provided that one becomes good in Islam and follows Allah's Law, all the while avoiding the sin. Allah then said,

(but whosoever commits it again, Allah will take retribution from him.) meaning, whoever does this after it has been prohibited in Islam and having knowledge that it is prohibited,

(Allah will take retribution from him. And Allah is Almighty, All-Able of retribution.) Ibn Jurayj said, "I said to `Ata', `What is the meaning of,

(Allah has forgiven what is past.)' He said, `Meaning, during the time of Jahiliyyah.' I asked about,

(but whosoever commits it again, Allah will take retribution from him.) He said, `Whoever commits this offense again in Islam, then Allah will take retribution from him and he also has to pay the expiation.' I asked, `Is there any punishment for repeating this offense that you know of' He said, `No.' I said, `Do you think that the authorities should punish him' He said, `No, for it is a sin that he committed between him and Allah. He should pay the expiation.'" Ibn Jarir recorded this statement. It was said that the `Allah will take retribution' refers to the expiation, according to Sa`id bin Jubayr, `Ata', and the majority among the earlier and later generations. They stated that when the Muhrim kills game, the expiation becomes necessary, regardless of whether it was the first, second or third offense, and whether intentional or by error. Ibn Jarir commented on Allah's statement;

(And Allah is Almighty, All-Able of retribution.) "Allah says that He is invincible in His control, none can resist Him, prevent Him from exacting retribution from anyone, or stop Him from punishing anyone. This is because all creation is His creation and the decision is His, His is the might, and His is the control. His statement, (All-Able of retribution.) meaning, He punishes those who disobey Him for their disobedience of Him."

Surah 5: Ayah: 96, Ayah: 97, Ayah: 98 & Ayah: 99

﴿أُحِلَّ لَكُمْ صَيْدُ ٱلْبَحْرِ وَطَعَامُهُ مَتَـٰعًا لَّكُمْ وَلِلسَّيَّارَةِ وَحُرِّمَ عَلَيْكُمْ صَيْدُ ٱلْبَرِّ مَا دُمْتُمْ حُرُمًا وَٱتَّقُوا۟ ٱللَّهَ ٱلَّذِىٓ إِلَيْهِ تُحْشَرُونَ ۝﴾

96. Lawful to you is (the pursuit of) water-game and its use for food - for the benefit of yourselves and those who travel, but forbidden is (the pursuit of) land-game as long as you are in a state of Ihrâm (for Hajj or 'Umrah). And fear Allâh to Whom you shall be gathered back.

﴿ ۞ جَعَلَ ٱللَّهُ ٱلْكَعْبَةَ ٱلْبَيْتَ ٱلْحَرَامَ قِيَـٰمًا لِّلنَّاسِ وَٱلشَّهْرَ ٱلْحَرَامَ وَٱلْهَدْىَ وَٱلْقَلَـٰٓئِدَ ۚ ذَٰلِكَ لِتَعْلَمُوٓا۟ أَنَّ ٱللَّهَ يَعْلَمُ مَا فِى ٱلسَّمَـٰوَٰتِ وَمَا فِى ٱلْأَرْضِ وَأَنَّ ٱللَّهَ بِكُلِّ شَىْءٍ عَلِيمٌ ۝ ﴾

97. Allâh has made the Ka'bah, the Sacred House, an asylum of security and benefits (e.g. Hajj and 'Umrah) for mankind, and also the Sacred Month and the animals of offerings and the garlanded (people or animals marked with the garlands on their necks made from the outer part of the stem of the Makkah trees for their security), that you may know that Allâh has knowledge of all that is in the heavens and all that is in the earth, and that Allâh is the All-Knower of each and everything.

﴿ ٱعْلَمُوٓا۟ أَنَّ ٱللَّهَ شَدِيدُ ٱلْعِقَابِ وَأَنَّ ٱللَّهَ غَفُورٌ رَّحِيمٌ ۝ ﴾

98. Know that Allâh is Severe in punishment and that Allâh is Oft-Forgiving, Most Merciful.

﴿ مَّا عَلَى ٱلرَّسُولِ إِلَّا ٱلْبَلَـٰغُ ۗ وَٱللَّهُ يَعْلَمُ مَا تُبْدُونَ وَمَا تَكْتُمُونَ ۝ ﴾

99. The duty of the Messenger (i.e. Our Messenger Muhammad (peace be upon him) whom We have sent to you, (O mankind)) is nothing but to convey (the Message). And Allâh knows all that you reveal and all that you conceal.

Transliteration

96. Ohilla lakum saydu albahri wataAAamuhu mataAAan lakum walilssayyarati wahurrima AAalaykum saydu albarri ma dumtum huruman waittaqoo Allaha allathee ilayhi tuhsharoona   97. JaAAala Allahu alkaAAbata albayta alharama qiyaman lilnnasi waalshshahra alharama waalhadya waalqala-ida thalika litaAAlamoo anna Allaha yaAAlamu ma fee alssamawati wama fee al-ardi waanna Allaha bikulli shay-in AAaleemun   98. IAAlamoo anna Allaha shadeedu alAAiqabi waanna Allaha ghafoorun raheemun   99. Ma AAala alrrasooli illa albalaghu waAllahu yaAAlamu ma tubdoona wama taktumoona

Tafsir Ibn Kathir

Water Game is Allowed for the Muhrim

Sa`id bin Al-Musayyib, Sa`id bin Jubayr and others commented on Allah's statement;

(Lawful to you is (the pursuit of) water game...) that it means, what one eats fresh from it, while,

(And its use for food) what is eaten dry and salted. Ibn `Abbas said that `water game' refers to what is taken from water while still alive, while, (and its use for food) refers to what the water throws ashore dead. Similar statements were reported from Abu Bakr As-Siddiq, Zayd bin Thabit, `Abdullah bin `Amr, Abu Ayyub Al-Ansari, `Ikrimah, Abu Salamah bin `Abdur-Rahman, Ibrahim An-Nakha`i and Al-Hasan Al-Basri. Allah's statement,

(for the benefit of yourselves and those who travel,) as food and provision for you,

(and those who travel,) those who are in the sea and traveling along the sea, according to `Ikrimah. Other scholars said that water game is allowed for those who fish it from the sea, as well as, when it is salted and used as food for travelers inland. A similar statement was reported from Ibn `Abbas, Mujahid and As-Suddi and others. Imam Malik bin Anas recorded that Jabir bin `Abdullah said, "Allah's Messenger sent an army towards the east coast and appointed Abu `Ubaydah bin Al-Jarrah as their commander, and the army consisted of three hundred men, including myself. We marched on until we reached a place where our food was about to finish. Abu `Ubaydah ordered us to collect all the food for our journey, and it was collected in two bags of dates. Abu `Ubaydah kept on giving us our daily ration in small amounts from it, until it was exhausted. The share of each of us used to be one date only." I (one of the narrators from Jabir) said, "How could one date suffice for you" Jabir replied, "We came to know its value when even that finished." Jabir added, "When we reached the seashore, we saw a huge fish which was like a small mountain. The army ate from it for eighteen days. Then Abu `Ubaydah ordered that two of its ribs be affixed in the ground. Then he ordered that a she-camel be ridden, and it passed under the two ribs (forming an arch) without touching them." This Hadith was also collected in the Two Sahihs. eMalik recorded that Abu Hurayrah said, "A man asked Allah's Messenger, `O Allah's Messenger! We go to sea and carry little water with us. If we use it for Wudu', we get thirsty, so should we use seawater for Wudu" The Messenger of Allah said,

«هُوَ الطَّهُورُ مَاؤُهُ الْحِلُّ مَيْتَتُهُ»

(Its water is pure and its dead are lawful)." The two Imams, Ash-Shafi`i and Ahmad bin Hanbal, recorded this Hadith, along with the Four Sunan compilers. Al-Bukhari, At-Tirmidhi and Ibn Hibban graded it Sahih. This Hadith was also recorded from the Prophet by several other Companions.

Hunting Land Game is Prohibited During Ihram

Allah said,

(but forbidden is land game as long as you are in a state of Ihram.) Therefore, hunting land game during Ihram is not allowed, and if someone who is in the state of Ihram hunts, he will have to pay expiation, along with the sin he earns if he does it intentionally. If he hunts by mistake, he will have to pay the expiation and is not allowed to eat from it, because this type of game is just like dead animals, be he a Muhrim or a non-Muhrim. If someone who is not in the state of Ihram hunts and gives the food to a Muhrim, the Muhrim is not allowed to eat from its meat if it was killed for him in particular. As-Sa`b bin Jaththamah said that he gave a zebra as a gift to the Prophet in the area of Waddan or Abwa', the Prophet gave it back. When the Prophet saw the effect of his returning the gift on As-Sa`b's face, he said,

«إِنَّا لَمْ نَرُدَّهُ عَلَيْكَ إِلَّا أَنَّا حُرُمٌ»

(We only gave it back to you because we are in a state of Ihram.) This Hadith was collected in the Two Sahihs. The Prophet thought that As-Sa`b hunted the zebra for him, and this is why he refused to take it. Otherwise, the Muhrim is allowed to eat from the game if one who is not in Ihram hunts it. For when Abu Qatadah hunted a zebra when he was not a Muhrim and offered it to those who were in the state of Ihram, they hesitated to eat from it. They asked the Messenger of Allah and he said,

«هَلْ كَانَ مِنْكُمْ أَحَدٌ أَشَارَ إِلَيْهَا أَوْ أَعَانَ فِي قَتْلِهَا؟»

(Did any of you point at it or help kill it) They said, "No." He said,

«فَكُلُوا»

(Then eat,) and he also ate from it. This Hadith is also in the Two Sahihs with various wordings. (Ibn Kathir only mentioned Ayat 96 to 99 here and explained the better part of Ayah number 96, but he did not mention the explanation of the rest of that Ayah or the other Ayat (97 to 99). This is the case in all of the copies of his Tafsir in existence, and he might have forgotten to do that, for it is less likely that all who copied this book forgot to copy only this part. So we used a summary of the Tafsir of these Ayat from the Imam of Tafsir, Ibn Jarir At-Tabari. We tried to summarize At-Tabari's eloquent words to the best of our ability, by Allah's help and leave.)

(And have Taqwa of Allah to Whom you shall be gathered back.) Allah says, fear Allah, O people, and beware of His might, by obeying what He commands you and avoiding what He prohibits for you in these Ayat revealed to your Prophet . These Ayat forbid Khamr, gambling, Al-Ansab and Al-Azlam, along with hunting land game and killing it while in the state of Ihram. To Allah will be your return and destination, and He will punish you for disobeying Him and will reward you for obeying Him.

(Allah has made the Ka`bah, the Sacred House, an asylum of security and benefits for mankind,) Allah says, Allah made the Ka`bah, the Sacred House, an asylum of safety for the people who have no chief to prevent the strong from transgressing against the weak, the evil from the good-doers, and the oppressors from the oppressed.

(And also the Sacred Month and the animals of offerings and the garlanded.) Allah says that He made these symbols an asylum of safety for the people, just as He made the Ka`bah an asylum of safety for them, so that He distinguishes them from each other, for this is their asylum and symbol for their livelihood and religion. Allah made the Ka`bah, the Sacred Month, the Hady, the garlanded animals and people an asylum of safety for the Arabs who used to consider these symbols sacred. Thus, these symbols were just like the chief who is obeyed by his followers, and who upholds harmony and public safety. As for the Ka`bah, it includes the entire sacred boundary. Allah termed it "Haram" because He prohibited hunting its game and cutting its trees or grass. Similarly, the Ka`bah, the Sacred Month, the animals of offerings and the garlands were the landmarks of existing Arabs. These symbols were sacred during the time of Jahiliyyah and the people's affairs were guided and protected by them. With Islam they became the symbols of their Hajj, their rituals, and the direction of the prayer. (i.e., the Ka`bah in Makkah.)

(that you may know that Allah has knowledge of all that is in the heavens and all that is in the earth, and that Allah is the All-Knower of each and everything.) Allah says; O people, I made these symbols an asylum for you, so that you know that He Who made these symbols that benefit your life and provide you with security, also knows everything in the heavens and earth that brings about your immediate or eventual benefit. Know that He has perfect knowledge of everything and that none of your deeds or affairs ever escapes His observation; and He will count them for you so that He rewards those who do good with the same and those who do evil in kind.

(Know that Allah is severe in punishment and that Allah is Oft-Forgiving, Most Merciful.) Allah says, know that your Lord, Who has perfect knowledge of whatever is in the heavens and earth, and Who is never unaware of your deeds - public or secret - is severe in punishment for those who disobey and defy Him. He also pardons the sins of those who obey and repent to Him, more Merciful than to punish them for the sins that they repented from.

(The Messenger's duty is but to convey. And Allah knows all that you reveal and all that you conceal.) This is a warning from Allah for His servants in which He says: Our Messenger, whom We sent to you, has only to convey Our Message and then the reward for the obedience, and punishment for the disobedience is on Us. The obedience of those who accept Our Message never escapes Our knowledge, just as in the case of those who disobey and defy Our Message. We know what one of you does, demonstrates physically, announces, and utters with his tongue, and what you hide in your hearts, be it of faith, disbelief, certainty, doubt or hypocrisy. He Who is so capable, then nothing that the hearts conceal, nor any of the apparent acts of the souls in the heavens and earth could escape His knowledge. In His Hand, alone, is the reward and punishment, and He is worthy to be feared, obeyed and never disobeyed.

Surah 5: Ayah: 100, Ayah: 101 & Ayah: 102

﴿ قُل لَّا يَسْتَوِي ٱلْخَبِيثُ وَٱلطَّيِّبُ وَلَوْ أَعْجَبَكَ كَثْرَةُ ٱلْخَبِيثِ ۚ فَٱتَّقُواْ ٱللَّهَ يَـٰٓأُوْلِي ٱلْأَلْبَـٰبِ لَعَلَّكُمْ تُفْلِحُونَ ۝ ﴾

100. Say (O Muhammad (peace be upon him)) "Not equal are Al-Khabîth (all that is evil and bad as regards things, deeds, beliefs, persons, foods) and At-Taiyyib (all that is good as regards things, deeds, beliefs, persons, foods), even though the abundance of Al-Khabîth may please you." So fear Allâh O men of understanding in order that you may be successful.

﴿ يَٰٓأَيُّهَا ٱلَّذِينَ ءَامَنُواْ لَا تَسْـَٔلُواْ عَنْ أَشْيَآءَ إِن تُبْدَ لَكُمْ تَسُؤْكُمْ وَإِن تَسْـَٔلُواْ عَنْهَا حِينَ يُنَزَّلُ ٱلْقُرْءَانُ تُبْدَ لَكُمْ عَفَا ٱللَّهُ عَنْهَا ۗ وَٱللَّهُ غَفُورٌ حَلِيمٌ ﴾ ۞ ١٠١

101. O you who believe! Ask not about things which, if made plain to you, may cause you trouble. But if you ask about them while the Qur'ân is being revealed, they will be made plain to you. Allâh has forgiven that, and Allâh is Oft-Forgiving, Most Forbearing.

﴿ قَدْ سَأَلَهَا قَوْمٌ مِّن قَبْلِكُمْ ثُمَّ أَصْبَحُواْ بِهَا كَٰفِرِينَ ﴾ ۞ ١٠٢

102. Before you, a community asked such questions, then on that account they became disbelievers.

Transliteration

100. Qul la yastawee alkhabeethu waalttayyibu walaw aAAjabaka kathratu alkhabeethi faittaqoo Allaha ya olee al-albabi laAAallakum tuflihoona 101. Ya ayyuha allatheena amanoo la tas-aloo AAan ashyaa in tubda lakum tasu/kum wa-in tas-aloo AAanha heena yunazzalu alqur-anu tubda lakum AAafa Allahu AAanha waAllahu ghafoorun haleemun 102. Qad saalaha qawmun min qablikum thumma asbahoo biha kafireena

Tafsir Ibn Kathir

Allah says to His Messenger ,

(Say,) O Muhammad ,

(Not equal are the bad things and the good things, even though they may please you) O human,

(the abundance of bad.) This Ayah means, the little permissible is better than the abundant evil.

(have Taqwa of Allah, O men of understanding...) who have sound minds, avoid and abandon the impermissible, and let the permissible be sufficient for you,

(in order that you may be successful.) in this life and the Hereafter. " So have Taqwa of Allah, O men of understanding in order that you may be successful.) (101. O you who believe! Ask not about things which, if made plain to you, may cause you trouble. But if you ask about them while the Qur'an is being revealed, they will be made plain to you. Allah has forgiven that, and Allah is Oft-Forgiving, Most Forbearing.) (102. Before you, a community asked such questions, then on that account they became disbelievers.) Allah says to His Messenger ,

(Say,) O Muhammad ,

(Not equal are the bad things and the good things, even though they may please you) O human,

(the abundance of bad.) This Ayah means, the little permissible is better than the abundant evil.

(have Taqwa of Allah, O men of understanding...) who have sound minds, avoid and abandon the impermissible, and let the permissible be sufficient for you,

(in order that you may be successful.) in this life and the Hereafter.

Unnecessary Questioning is Disapproved of

Allah said next,

(O you who believe! Ask not about things which, if made plain to you, may cause you trouble.) This Ayah refers to good conduct that Allah is teaching His believing servants, by forbidding them from asking about useless things. Since if they get the answers they sought, they might be troublesome for them and difficult on their ears. Al-Bukhari recorded that Anas bin Malik said, "The Messenger of Allah gave a speech unlike anything I heard before. In this speech, he said,

«لَو تَعْلَمُونَ مَا أَعْلَمُ، لَضَحِكْتُمْ قَلِيلًا، وَلَبَكَيْتُمْ كَثِيرًا»

(If you but know what I know, you will laugh little and cry a lot.) The companions of Allah's Messenger covered their faces and the sound of crying was coming out of their chests. A man asked, `Who is my father' The Prophet said, `So-and-so'. This Ayah was later revealed,

(Ask not about things...)." Muslim, Ahmad, At-Tirmidhi and An-Nasa'i recorded this Hadith. Ibn Jarir recorded that Qatadah said about Allah's statement,

(O you who believe! Ask not about things which, if made plain to you, may cause you trouble.) Anas bin Malik narrated that once, the people were questioning the Messenger of Allah until they made him angry. So he ascended the Minbar and said,

«لَا تَسْأَلُونِي الْيَوْمَ عَنْ شَيْءٍ إِلَّا بَيَّنْتُهُ لَكُم»

(You will not ask me about anything today but I will explain it to you.) So the Companions of the Messenger of Allah feared that it was the commencement of a momentous event, and I looked to my right and left and found only people who covered their faces, crying. An argumentative man who was said to be the son of someone other than his true father asked, "O Allah's Messenger! Who is my father The Prophet said, `Your father is Hudhafah." `Umar stood up (when he saw anger on the Prophet's face) and said, "We accept Allah as our Lord, Islam as our religion and Muhammad as our Messenger, I seek refuge with Allah from the evil of the Fitan (trials in life and religion)." The Messenger of Allah said,

Chapter 5: Al-Maidah (The Table, The Table Spread), Verses 082-120

«لَمْ أَرَ فِي الْخَيْرِ وَالشَّرِّ كَالْيَوْمِ قَطُّ، صُوِّرَتْ لِي الْجَنَّةُ وَالنَّارُ حَتَّى رَأَيْتُهُمَا دُونَ الْحَائِطِ»

(I have never witnessed both goodness and evil like I have today. Paradise and the Fire were shown to me and I saw them before that wall.) This Hadith was recorded in the Two Sahihs from Sa`id. Al-Bukhari recorded that Ibn `Abbas said, "Some people used to question the Messenger of Allah to mock him. One of them would ask, `Who is my father,' while another would ask, `Where is my camel,' when he lost his camel. Allah sent down this Ayah about them,

(O you who believe! Ask not about things which, if made plain to you, may cause you trouble...)." Imam Ahmad recorded that `Ali said, "When this Ayah was revealed,

(And Hajj to the House is a duty that mankind owes to Allah, those who can bear the journey.)(3:97), they asked, `O Allah's Messenger! Is it required every year' He did not answer them, and they asked again, `Is it every year' He still did not answer them, so they asked, `Is it every year' He said,

(No, and had I said `yes', it would have become obligated, and had it become obligated, you would not be able to bear it.) Allah sent down,

(O you who believe! Ask not about things which, if made plain to you, may cause you trouble.)." At-Tirmidhi and Ibn Majah also recorded this Hadith. The apparent wording of this Ayah indicates that we are forbidden to ask about things that if one has knowledge of, he would be sorry he had asked. Consequently, it is better to avoid such questions. rAllah's statement,

(But if you ask about them while the Qur'an is being revealed, they will be made plain to you.) means, if you ask about things that you are prohibited from asking about, then when the revelation about them comes to the Messenger , they will be made plain for you,

(Verily! That is easy for Allah.) Allah said next,

(Allah has forgiven that,) what you did before this,

(and Allah is Oft-Forgiving, Most Forbearing.) Do not ask about things that do not have a ruling yet, for because of your questions, a difficult ruling may be ordained. A Hadith states,

«أَعْظَمُ الْمُسْلِمِينَ جُرْمًا مَنْ سَأَلَ عَنْ شَيْءٍ لَمْ يُحَرَّمْ، فَحُرِّمَ مِنْ أَجْلِ مَسْأَلَتِهِ»

(The worst criminal among the Muslims is he who asks if a matter is unlawful (or not), and it becomes unlawful because of his asking about it.) It is recorded in the Sahih that the Messenger of Allah said,

«ذَرُونِي مَا تَرَكْتُكُمْ، فَإِنَّمَا أَهْلَكَ مَنْ كَانَ قَبْلَكُمْ كَثْرَةُ سُؤَالِهِمْ وَاخْتِلَافُهُمْ عَلَى أَنْبِيَائِهِم»

(Leave me as I have left you, those before you were destroyed because of many questions and disputing with their Prophets.) An authentic Hadith also states,

«أَنَّ اللهَ تَعَالَى فَرَضَ فَرَائِضَ فَلَا تُضَيِّعُوهَا، وَحَدَّ حُدُودًا فَلَا تَعْتَدُوهَا، وَحَرَّمَ أَشْيَاءَ فَلَا تَنْتَهِكُوهَا، وَسَكَتَ عَنْ أَشْيَاءَ رَحْمَةً بِكُمْ غَيْرَ نِسْيَانٍ فَلَا تَسْأَلُوا عَنْهَا»

(Allah, the Most Honored, has ordained some obligations, so do not ignore them; has set some limits, so do not trespass them; has prohibited some things, so do not commit them; and has left some things without rulings, out of mercy for you, not that He forgot them, so do not ask about them.) Allah said next,

(Before you, a community asked such questions, then on that account they became disbelievers.) meaning, some people before your time asked such questions and they were given answers. They did not believe the answers, so they became disbelievers because of that. This occurred because these rulings were made plain to them, yet they did not benefit at all from that, for they asked about these things not to gain guidance, but only to mock and defy.

Surah 5: Ayah: 103 & Ayah: 104

﴿ مَا جَعَلَ ٱللَّهُ مِنۢ بَحِيرَةٍ وَلَا سَآئِبَةٍ وَلَا وَصِيلَةٍ وَلَا حَامٍ وَلَٰكِنَّ ٱلَّذِينَ كَفَرُوا۟ يَفْتَرُونَ عَلَى ٱللَّهِ ٱلْكَذِبَ وَأَكْثَرُهُمْ لَا يَعْقِلُونَ ۝ ﴾

103. Allâh has not instituted things like Bahîrah, or Sâ'ibah, or Wasîlah, or Hâm, (all these animals were liberated in honor of idols as practiced by pagan Arabs in the pre-Islâmic period). But those who disbelieve invent lies against Allâh, and most of them have no understanding.

﴿ وَإِذَا قِيلَ لَهُمْ تَعَالَوْا۟ إِلَىٰ مَآ أَنزَلَ ٱللَّهُ وَإِلَى ٱلرَّسُولِ قَالُوا۟ حَسْبُنَا مَا وَجَدْنَا عَلَيْهِ ءَابَآءَنَآ ۚ أَوَلَوْ كَانَ ءَابَآؤُهُمْ لَا يَعْلَمُونَ شَيْـًٔا وَلَا يَهْتَدُونَ ۝ ﴾

104. And when it is said to them: "Come to what Allâh has revealed and unto the Messenger (Muhammad (peace be upon him) for the verdict of that which you have made unlawful)." They say: "Enough for us is that which we found our

fathers following," even though their fathers had no knowledge whatsoever and no guidance.

Transliteration

103. Ma jaAAala Allahu min baheeratin wala sa-ibatin wala waseelatin wala hamin walakinna allatheena kafaroo yaftaroona AAala Allahi alkathiba waaktharuhum la yaAAqiloona   104. Wa-itha qeela lahum taAAalaw ila ma anzala Allahu wa-ila alrrasooli qaloo hasbuna ma wajadna AAalayhi abaana awa law kana abaohum la yaAAlamoona shay-an wala yahtadoona

Tafsir Ibn Kathir

The Meaning of Bahirah, Sa'ibah, Wasilah and Ham

Al-Bukhari recorded that Sa`id bin Al-Musayyib said, "The Bahirah is a female camel whose milk was spared for the idols and no one was allowed to milk it. The Sa'ibah is a female camel let loose for free pasture for the idols, and nothing was allowed to be carried on it. Abu Hurayrah said that the Messenger of Allah said,

«رَأَيْتُ عَمْرُو بْنَ عَامِرٍ الْخُزَاعِيَّ يَجُرُّ قُصْبَهُ فِي النَّارِ، وَكَانَ أَوَّلَ مَنْ سَيَّبَ السَّوَائِبَ»

(I saw `Amr bin `Amir Al-Khuza`i pulling his intestines behind him in the Fire, and he was the first to start the practice of Sa'ibah.) As for the Wasilah, it is a female camel set free for the idols, because it had given birth to a she-camel in its first delivery and then another she-camel at its second delivery. They used to set such camel free if she gave birth to two females without a male between them. As for the Ham, it is a male camel which would be freed from work for the idols, after it had finished a number of copulations assigned for it. The male camel freed from work in this case is called a Hami." Muslim and An-Nasa'i recorded this Hadith. Imam Ahmad recorded that `Abdullah bin Mas`ud said that the Prophet said,

«إِنَّ أَوَّلَ مَنْ سَيَّبَ السَّوَائِبَ وَعَبَدَ الْأَصْنَامَ أَبُو خُزَاعَةَ عَمْرُو بْنُ عَامِرٍ، وَإِنِّي رَأَيْتُهُ يَجُرُّ أَمْعَاءَهُ فِي النَّارِ»

(The first to start the practice of Sa'ibah and worshipping idols was Abu Khuza`ah, `Amr bin `Amir. I saw him pulling his intestines behind him in the Fire.) The `Amr mentioned in the above Hadith is the son of Luhay bin Qam`ah, one of the chiefs of the tribe of Khuza`ah who were the caretakers of the House of Allah after the tribe of Jurhum, (and before the Prophet's tribe, Quraysh). He was the first to change the religion of Ibrahim (Al-Khalil in Makkah) bringing idol worshipping to the area of Hijaz (Western Arabia). He also called the foolish people to worship idols and offer sacrifices to them and started these ignorant rituals concerning the animals as well as other rituals of Jahiliyyah. Allah said in Surat Al-An`am,

(And they assign to Allah a share of the tilth and cattle which He has created...)(3:136). As for the Bahirah, `Ali bin Abi Talhah said that Ibn `Abbas said, "It is the female camel that has given delivery five times. After that, they looked at the fifth delivery, if it were a male, they would slaughter it and give it to the men only and not the women. If it were a female, they would cut off its ears and proclaim, `This is a Bahirah (no one is allowed to milk it).'" As-Suddi and others mentioned a similar statement. As for the Sa'ibah, Mujahid said that it is for sheep, and mentioned a similar meaning as for Bahirah. He said that it delivers six females and then a male, female or two males, and that they then would slaughter it (the newly born sheep) and feed its meat to the men, but not to the woman. Muhammad bin Ishaq said that the Sa'ibah is the female camel that delivers ten females, without giving birth to a single male between them. They would then set it free and no one was allowed to ride it, cut its wool or milk it, except for a guest. Abu Rawq said, "The Sa'ibah was made as such when one goes out for some of his affairs and succeeds in whatever he intended to do. So he would designate a Sa'ibah from his property, a female camel or another type, and would set it free for the idols (in appreciation for his success). Then, whatever this camel gave birth to was set free for the idols too." As-Suddi said, "When one's affair was successful, or if he was cured from an illness, or if his wealth increased, he would set some of his wealth free for the idols. Those who would try to acquire any of the Sa'ibah property were punished in this world." As for the Wasilah, `Ali bin Abi Talhah said that Ibn `Abbas said, "It is the sheep that gives birth seven times, if she gives birth to a male or a female stillborn at its seventh delivery, the men, but not the women, would eat from it. If she gave birth to a female, or a female and a male, they would set them free, proclaiming (about the male in this case), His sister Wasalat (literally, `connected him to being forbidden on us')." Ibn Abi Hatim recorded this statement. `Abdur-Razzaq narrated that Ma`mar said that Az-Zuhri said that Sa`id bin Al-Musayyib said that,

(Or a Wasilah) "It is the female camel that gives delivery to a female and then another female at its second delivery. They would call such a camel a Wasilah, proclaiming that she has Wasalat (connected) between two females without giving birth to a male between them. So they used to cut off the ears of the Wasilah and let it roam free to pasture for their idols." A similar explanation was reported from Imam Malik bin Anas. Muhammad bin Ishaq said, "The Wasilah sheep is the ewe that gives birth to ten females in five deliveries, giving birth to two females at each delivery. This sheep would be called Wasilah and would be set free. Whatever this sheep delivers afterwards, male or female, would be given to the men, but not the women, but if it delivers a stillborn, men and women would share it!" As for the Ham, Al-`Awfi said that Ibn `Abbas said, "If a man's camel performs ten copulations, they would call him a Ham, `So set him free.," Similar was reported from Abu Rawq and Qatadah. `Ali bin Abi Talhah said that Ibn `Abbas said, "The Ham is the male camel whose offspring gave birth to their own offspring; they would then proclaim, `This camel has Hama (protected) its back.' Therefore, they would not carry anything on this male camel, cut his wool, prevent him from grazing wherever he likes or drinking from any pool, even if the pool did not belong to its owner." Ibn Wahb said, "I heard Malik saying, `As for the Ham, it is the male camel who is assigned a certain number of copulations, and when having finished what was assigned to him, would have peacock feathers placed on him and be set free.''' Other opinions were also mentioned to explain this Ayah. There is a Hadith on this subject that Ibn Abi Hatim collected from Abu Ishaq As-Subay`i from Al-Ahwas Al-Jushami from his father Malik bin Nadlah who said, "I came to the Prophet wearing old clothes. So he said to me,

«هَلْ لَكَ مِنْ مَالٍ؟»

(Do you have any property) I said, `Yes.' He asked,

«مِنْ أَيِّ الْمَالِ؟»

(What type) I said, `All types; camels, sheep, horses and slaves.' He said,

«فَإِذَا آتَاكَ اللهُ مَالًا فَلْيُرَ عَلَيْكَ»

(If Allah gives you wealth, then let it show on you.) He then asked,

«تُنْتِجُ إِبِلُكَ وَافِيَةً آذَانُهَا؟»

(Do your camels deliver calves that have full ears) I said, `Yes, and do camels give birth but to whole calves' He said,

«فَلَعَلَّكَ تَأْخُذُ الْمُوسَى فَتَقْطَعُ آذَانَ طَائِفَةٍ مِنْهَا وَتَقُولَ: هَذِهِ بَحِيرَةٌ، تَشُقَّ آذَانَ طَائِفَةٍ مِنْهَا وَتَقُولَ: هَذِهِ حُرُّمٌ»

(Do you take the knife and cut off the ears of some of them saying, `This is a Bahirah,' and tear the ears of some of them and proclaim, `This is Sacred') I said, `Yes.' He said,

«فَلَا تَفْعَلْ إِنَّ كُلَّ مَا آتَاكَ اللهُ لَكَ حِلٌّ»

(Then do not do that, for all the wealth that Allah has given you is allowed for you.) Then he said;

[مَا جَعَلَ اللَّهُ مِن بَحِيرَةٍ وَلاَ سَآئِبَةٍ وَلاَ وَصِيلَةٍ وَلاَ حَامٍ]

(Allah has not instituted things like Bahirah or a Sa'ibah or a Wasilah or a Ham.) As for the Bahirah, it is the animal whose ears were cut, one would not allow his wife, daughters, or any of his household to benefit from its wool, hair or milk. But, if it died, they would share it. As for the Sa'ibah, they used to set it free for their idols and announce this fact in the vicinity of the idols. As for the Wasilah, it is the sheep that gives birth to six offspring. When she delivered for the seventh time, they would cut its ears and horns, saying, `It has Wasalat (connected deliveries),' and they would not slaughter it, hit it or prevent it from drinking from any pool." This Hadith was narrated with the addition of the explanation of these words in it. In another narration for this Hadith from Abu Ishaq from Abu Al-Ahwas, `Awf bin Malik used his own words (i.e., he explained these words not as a part of the Hadith itself) and this is more sound. Imam Ahmad recorded this Hadith from Sufyan bin `Uyaynah, from Abu Az-Za`ra' `Amr bin `Amr, from his uncle Abu Al-Ahwas `Awf bin Malik bin Nadlah from his father, Malik bin Nadlah. This narration also does not contain the explanation of Bahirah, Ham etc., that is added to the Hadith above, and Allah knows best. Allah's statement,

(But those who disbelieve invent lies against Allah, and most of them have no understanding.) means, Allah did not legislate these invented rituals and He does not consider them acts of obedience. Rather, it is the idolators who made them into rituals and acts of worship that they used to draw near to Allah. But they did not and will not help them to draw near to Him, rather, these innovations will only harm them.

(And when it is said to them: "Come to what Allah has revealed and to the Messenger." They say: "Enough for us is that which we found our fathers following,") imeaning, if they are called to Allah's religion, Law and commandments and to avoiding what He prohibited, they say, `The ways and practices that we found our fathers and forefathers following are good enough for us.` Allah said,

(even though their fathers had no knowledge whatsoever...) That is, even though their fathers did not understand or recognize the truth or find its way. Therefore, who would follow their forefathers, except those who are even more ignorant and misguided than they were

Surah 5: Ayah: 105

﴿ يَٰٓأَيُّهَا ٱلَّذِينَ ءَامَنُواْ عَلَيْكُمْ أَنفُسَكُمْ ۖ لَا يَضُرُّكُم مَّن ضَلَّ إِذَا ٱهْتَدَيْتُمْ ۚ إِلَى ٱللَّهِ مَرْجِعُكُمْ جَمِيعًا فَيُنَبِّئُكُم بِمَا كُنتُمْ تَعْمَلُونَ ﴾

105. O you who believe! Take care of your own selves. If you follow the (right) guidance

Transliteration

105. Ya ayyuha allatheena amanoo AAalaykum anfusakum la yadurrukum man dalla itha ihtadaytum ila Allahi marjiAAukum jameeAAan fayunabbi-okum bima kuntum taAAmaloona

Chapter 5: Al-Maidah (The Table, The Table Spread), Verses 082-120

Tafsir Ibn Kathir

One is Required to Reform Himself First

Allah commands His believing servants to reform themselves and to do as many righteous deeds as possible. He also informs them that whoever reforms himself, he would not be affected by the wickedness of the wicked, whether they were his relatives or otherwise. Imam Ahmad recorded that Qays said, "Abu Bakr As-Siddiq stood up, thanked Allah and praised Him and then said, `O people! You read this Ayah,

(O you who believe! Take care of yourselves. If you follow the right guidance, no hurt can come to you from those who are in error.) You explain it the wrong way. I heard the Messenger of Allah say,

《إِنَّ النَّاسَ إِذَا رَأَوُا الْمُنْكَرَ وَلَا يُغَيِّرُونَهُ، يُوشِكُ اللهُ عَزَّ وَجَلَّ أَنْ يَعُمَّهُمْ بِعِقَابِهِ》

(If the people witness evil and do not change it, then Allah is about to send His punishment to encompass them.) I (Qays) also heard Abu Bakr say, `O people! Beware of lying, for lying contradicts faith.'"

Surah 5: Ayah: 106, Ayah: 107 & Ayah: 108

﴿ يَٰٓأَيُّهَا ٱلَّذِينَ ءَامَنُواْ شَهَٰدَةُ بَيۡنِكُمۡ إِذَا حَضَرَ أَحَدَكُمُ ٱلۡمَوۡتُ حِينَ ٱلۡوَصِيَّةِ ٱثۡنَانِ ذَوَا عَدۡلٍ مِّنكُمۡ أَوۡ ءَاخَرَانِ مِنۡ غَيۡرِكُمۡ إِنۡ أَنتُمۡ ضَرَبۡتُمۡ فِي ٱلۡأَرۡضِ فَأَصَٰبَتۡكُم مُّصِيبَةُ ٱلۡمَوۡتِۚ تَحۡبِسُونَهُمَا مِنۢ بَعۡدِ ٱلصَّلَوٰةِ فَيُقۡسِمَانِ بِٱللَّهِ إِنِ ٱرۡتَبۡتُمۡ لَا نَشۡتَرِي بِهِۦ ثَمَنٗا وَلَوۡ كَانَ ذَا قُرۡبَىٰۙ وَلَا نَكۡتُمُ شَهَٰدَةَ ٱللَّهِ إِنَّآ إِذٗا لَّمِنَ ٱلۡءَاثِمِينَ ﴾

106. O you who believe! When death approaches any of you, and you make a bequest, then take the testimony of two just men of your own folk or two others from outside, while you are travelling through the land and death befalls on you. Detain them both after As-Salât (the prayer), (then) if you are in doubt (about their truthfulness), let them both swear by Allâh (saying): "We wish not for any worldly gain in this, even though he (the beneficiary) be our near relative. We shall not hide Testimony of Allâh, for then indeed we should be of the sinful."

﴿ فَإِنْ عُثِرَ عَلَىٰ أَنَّهُمَا ٱسْتَحَقَّآ إِثْمًا فَـَٔاخَرَانِ يَقُومَانِ مَقَامَهُمَا مِنَ ٱلَّذِينَ ٱسْتَحَقَّ عَلَيْهِمُ ٱلْأَوْلَيَـٰنِ فَيُقْسِمَانِ بِٱللَّهِ لَشَهَـٰدَتُنَآ أَحَقُّ مِن شَهَـٰدَتِهِمَا وَمَا ٱعْتَدَيْنَآ إِنَّآ إِذًا لَّمِنَ ٱلظَّـٰلِمِينَ ۝ ﴾

107. If then it gets known that these two had been guilty of sin, let two others stand forth in their places, nearest in kin from among those who claim a lawful right. Let them swear by Allâh (saying): "We affirm that our testimony is truer than that of both of them, and that we have not trespassed (the truth), for then indeed we should be of the wrong-doers."

﴿ ذَٰلِكَ أَدْنَىٰٓ أَن يَأْتُوا۟ بِٱلشَّهَـٰدَةِ عَلَىٰ وَجْهِهَآ أَوْ يَخَافُوٓا۟ أَن تُرَدَّ أَيْمَـٰنٌۢ بَعْدَ أَيْمَـٰنِهِمْ ۗ وَٱتَّقُوا۟ ٱللَّهَ وَٱسْمَعُوا۟ ۗ وَٱللَّهُ لَا يَهْدِى ٱلْقَوْمَ ٱلْفَـٰسِقِينَ ۝ ﴾

108. That should make it closer (to the fact) that their testimony would be in its true shape (and thus accepted), or else they would fear that (other) oaths would be admitted after their oaths. And fear Allâh and listen (with obedience to Him). And Allâh guides not the people who are Al-Fâsiqûn (the rebellious and disobedient).

Transliteration

106. Ya ayyuha allatheena amanoo shahadatu baynikum itha hadara ahadakumu almawtu heena alwasiyyati ithnani thawa AAadlin minkum aw akharani min ghayrikum in antum darabtum fee al-ardi faasabatkum museebatu almawti tahbisoonahuma min baAAdi alssalati fayuqsimani biAllahi ini irtabtum la nashtaree bihi thamanan walaw kana tha qurba wala naktumu shahadata Allahi inna ithan lamina al-athimeena 107. Fa-in AAuthira AAala annahuma istahaqqa ithman faakharani yaqoomani maqamahuma mina allatheena istahaqqa AAalayhimu al-awlayani fayuqsimani biAllahi lashahadatuna ahaqqu min shahadatihima wama iAAtadayna inna ithan lamina alththalimeena 108. Thalika adna an ya/too bialshshahadati AAala wajhiha aw yakhafoo an turadda aymanun baAAda aymanihim waittaqoo Allaha waismaAAoo waAllahu la yahdee alqawma alfasiqeena

Tafsir Ibn Kathir

Testimony of Two Just Witnesses for the Final Will and Testament

This honorable Ayah contains a glorious ruling from Allah. Allah's statement,

(O you who believe! When death approaches any of you, and you make a bequest, then take the testimony of two...) meaning that there should be two witnesses in such cases,

(just men...) thus, describing them as just,

(of your own folk) Muslims.

(or two others from outside) non-Muslims, meaning the People of the Book, according to Ibn `Abbas as Ibn Abi Hatim recorded. Allah said next,

(if you are traveling through the land) on a journey,

(and the calamity of death befalls you.) These are two conditions that permit using non-Muslims from among the Dhimmis for witnesses when there are no Muslims present: When one is traveling and needs to write a will, as Sharih Al-Qadi said. Ibn Jarir recorded that Sharih said, "The witness of the Jews and Christians is not allowed except while traveling, and even then only to witness the dictation of the will." Allah's statement,

(Detain them both after the Salah (the prayer),) refers to the `Asr prayer, according to Al-`Awfi who reported it from Ibn `Abbas. This is the same explanation reported from Sa`id bin Jubayr, Ibrahim An-Nakha`i, Qatadah, `Ikrimah and Muhammad bin Sirin. As for Az-Zuhri, he said that they are detained after Muslim prayer (i.e., in congregation). Therefore, these two witnesses will be detained after a congregational prayer,

(let them both swear by Allah if you are in doubt.) meaning, if you are in doubt that they might have committed treachery or theft, then they should swear by Allah,

(We wish not in this) in our vows, according to Muqatil bin Hayyan,

(for any worldly gain) of this soon to end life,

(even though he be our near relative.) meaning, if the beneficiary be our near relative, we will still not compromise on the truth.

(We shall not hide the testimony of Allah,) thus stating that the testimony is Allah's, as a way of respecting it and valuing its significance,

(for then indeed we should be of the sinful.) if we distort the testimony, change, alter or hide it entirely. Allah said next,

(If it then becomes known that these two had been guilty of sin...) if the two witnesses were found to have cheated or stolen from the money that the will is being written about,

(let two others stand forth in their places, nearest in kin from among those who claim a lawful right.) This Ayah indicates that if the two witnesses were found to have committed treachery, then two of the nearest rightful inheritors should stand for witness in their place,

(Let them swear by Allah (saying): "We affirm that our testimony is truer than that of both of them...") Meaning, our testimony that they have cheated is more truthful than the testimony that they have offered,

(and that we have not trespassed (the truth),) when we accused them of treachery, (for then indeed we should be of the wrongdoers.) if we had lied about them. This is the oath of the heirs, and preference is to be given to their saying. Just as in the case with the oath of relative of a murdered person if he attempts to tarnish the case of the murdered person. So his family takes an oath in defense of his honor. This is discussed in the studies of the oaths in the books of Ahkam. Allah's statement,

(That should make it closer (to the fact) that their testimony would be in its true nature and shape (and thus accepted),) means, the ruling requiring the two Dhimmi witnesses to swear, if there is a doubt that they were not truthful, might compel them to admit to the testimony in its true form. Allah's statement,

(or else they would fear that (other) oaths would be admitted after their oaths.) means, requiring them to swear by Allah might encourage them to admit to the true testimony because they respect swearing by Allah and they glorify and revere Him. They also fear exposure if the heirs of the deceased are required to swear instead of them. In this case, the heirs would swear and earn the rightful inheritance that the two witnesses failed to declare. This is why Allah said,

(or else they would fear that (other) oaths would be admitted after their oaths.), then,

(And have Taqwa of Allah) in all of your affairs,

(and listen.) and obey,

(And Allah guides not the rebellious people.) who do not obey Him or follow His Law.

Surah 5: Ayah: 109

﴿ ۞ يَوْمَ يَجْمَعُ ٱللَّهُ ٱلرُّسُلَ فَيَقُولُ مَاذَآ أُجِبْتُمْ ۖ قَالُواْ لَا عِلْمَ لَنَآ ۖ إِنَّكَ أَنتَ عَلَّٰمُ ٱلْغُيُوبِ ۱۰۹ ﴾

109. On the Day when Allâh will gather the Messengers together and say to them: "What was the response you received (from men to your teaching)?" They will say: "We have no knowledge, verily, only You are the All-Knower of all that is hidden (or unseen)."

Transliteration

109. Yawma yajmaAAu Allahu alrrusula fayaqoolu matha ojibtum qaloo la AAilma lana innaka anta AAallamu alghuyoobi

Tafsir Ibn Kathir

The Messengers Will be Asked About Their Nations

Allah states that on the Day of Resurrection, He will ask the Messengers about how their nations, to whom He sent them, answered and responded to their teachings. Allah said in other Ayat,

(Then surely, We shall question those (people) to whom it (the Book) was sent and verily, We shall question the Messengers.) (7:6), and,

(So, by your Lord, We shall certainly call all of them to account. For all that they used to do.) (15:92-93). The statement of the Messengers here,

(We have no knowledge) is the result of the horror of that Day, according to Mujahid, Al-Hasan Al-Basri and As-Suddi. `Abdur-Razzaq narrated that Ath-Thawri said that Al-A`mash said that Mujahid said about the Ayah,

(On the Day when Allah will gather the Messengers together and say to them: "What was the response you received") They will become afraid and reply,

(We have no knowledge. ..) Ibn Jarir and Ibn Abi Hatim also recorded this explanation. `Ali bin Abi Talhah said that Ibn `Abbas commented on the Ayah,

(On the Day when Allah will gather the Messengers together and say to them: "What was the response you received (from men to your teaching)" They will say: "We have no knowledge, verily, only You are the Knower of all that is hidden.") "They will say to the Lord, Most Honored, `We have no knowledge beyond what we know, and even that, You have more knowledge of them than us." This response is out of respect before the Lord, Most Honored, and it means, we have no knowledge compared to Your encompassing knowledge. Therefore, our knowledge only grasped the visible behavior of these people, not the secrets of their hearts. You are the Knower of everything, Who has encompassing knowledge of all things, and our knowledge compared to Your knowledge is similar to not having any knowledge at all, for

(only You are the Knower of all that is hidden.)

Surah 5: Ayah: 110 & Ayah: 111

﴿ إِذْ قَالَ ٱللَّهُ يَٰعِيسَى ٱبْنَ مَرْيَمَ ٱذْكُرْ نِعْمَتِى عَلَيْكَ وَعَلَىٰ وَٰلِدَتِكَ إِذْ أَيَّدتُّكَ بِرُوحِ ٱلْقُدُسِ تُكَلِّمُ ٱلنَّاسَ فِى ٱلْمَهْدِ وَكَهْلًا وَإِذْ عَلَّمْتُكَ ٱلْكِتَٰبَ وَٱلْحِكْمَةَ وَٱلتَّوْرَىٰةَ وَٱلْإِنجِيلَ وَإِذْ تَخْلُقُ مِنَ ٱلطِّينِ كَهَيْـَٔةِ ٱلطَّيْرِ بِإِذْنِى فَتَنفُخُ فِيهَا فَتَكُونُ طَيْرًۢا بِإِذْنِى وَتُبْرِئُ ٱلْأَكْمَهَ وَٱلْأَبْرَصَ بِإِذْنِى وَإِذْ تُخْرِجُ ٱلْمَوْتَىٰ بِإِذْنِى وَإِذْ كَفَفْتُ بَنِىٓ إِسْرَٰٓءِيلَ عَنكَ إِذْ جِئْتَهُم بِٱلْبَيِّنَٰتِ فَقَالَ ٱلَّذِينَ كَفَرُوا۟ مِنْهُمْ إِنْ هَٰذَآ إِلَّا سِحْرٌ مُّبِينٌ ۝ ﴾

110. (Remember) when Allâh will say (on the Day of Resurrection). "O 'Isâ (Jesus), son of Maryam (Mary)! Remember My Favor to you and to your mother when I supported you with Rûh-ul-Qudus (Jibrîl (Gabriel)) so that you spoke to the people in the cradle and in maturity; and when I taught you writing, Al-Hikmah (the power of understanding), the Taurât (Torah) and the Injeel (Gospel); and

when you made out of the clay a figure like that of a bird, by My Permission, and you breathed into it, and it became a bird by My Permission, and you healed those born blind, and the lepers by My Permission, and when you brought forth the dead by My Permission; and when I restrained the Children of Israel from you (when they resolved to kill you) as you came unto them with clear proofs, and the disbelievers among them said: 'This is nothing but evident magic.' "

﴿ وَإِذْ أَوْحَيْتُ إِلَى ٱلْحَوَارِيِّنَ أَنْ ءَامِنُواْ بِى وَبِرَسُولِى قَالُوٓاْ ءَامَنَّا وَٱشْهَدْ بِأَنَّنَا مُسْلِمُونَ ﴿١١١﴾ ﴾

111. And when I (Allâh) revealed to Al-Hawârîeen (the disciples) (of 'Isâ (Jesus)) to believe in Me and My Messenger, they said: "We believe. And bear witness that we are Muslims."

Transliteration

110. Ith qala Allahu ya AAeesa ibna maryama othkur niAAmatee AAalayka waAAala walidatika ith ayyadtuka biroohi alqudusi tukallimu alnnasa fee almahdi wakahlan wa-ith AAallamtuka alkitaba waalhikmata waalttawrata waal-injeela wa-ith takhluqu mina altteeni kahay-ati alttayri bi-ithnee fatanfukhu feeha fatakoonu tayran bi-ithnee watubri-o al-akmaha waal-abrasa bi-ithnee wa-ith tukhrijualmawta bi-ithnee wa-ith kafaftu banee isra-eela AAanka ith ji/tahum bialbayyinati faqala allatheena kafaroo minhum in hatha illa sihrun mubeenun 111. Wa-ith awhaytu ila alhawariyyeena an aminoo bee wabirasoolee qaloo amanna waishhad bi-annana muslimoona

Tafsir Ibn Kathir

Reminding `Isa of the Favors that Allah Granted him

Allah mentions how He blessed His servant and Messenger, `Isa, son of Maryam, and the miracles and extraordinary acts He granted him. Allah said,

(Remember My favor to you) when I created you from your mother, without male intervention, and made you a sign and clear proof of My perfect power over all things.
d

(And to your mother) when I made you testify to her chastity and you thus absolved her from the sin that the unjust, ignorant liars accused her of,

(when I supported you with Ruh - il-Qudus) the angel Jibril, and made you a Prophet, calling to Allah in the cradle and manhood. I made you speak in the cradle, and you testified that your mother was free from any immoral behavior, and you proclaimed that you worship Me. You also conveyed the news of My Message and invited them to worship Me.

(so that you spoke to the people in the cradle and in maturity;) Meaning you called the people to Allah in childhood and in maturity. And the word Tukallim means invited, because his speaking to people while a child is nothing strange by itself. Allah's statement,

(And when I taught you the Book and the Hikmah,) the power of writing and understanding,

(and the Tawrah,) which was revealed to Musa, son of `Imran, who spoke to Allah directly. Allah's statement,

(and when you made out of the clay, as it were, the figure of a bird, by My permission,) means: `you shaped it in the figure of a bird by My permission, and it became a bird with My permission, after you blew into it'. Then, it became a flying bird with a soul by Allah's permission. Allah said;

(and you healed those born blind, and the lepers by My permission,) This was explained before in Surah Al `Imran (chapter 3) and we do not need to repeat it here. Allah's statement,

(And when you brought forth the dead by My permission,) meaning, you called them and they rose from their graves by Allah's leave, power, Intent and will. Allah said next,

(and when I restrained the Children of Israel from you since you came unto them with clear proofs, and the disbelievers among them said: "This is nothing but evident magic.") Meaning: `remember My favor, when I stopped the Children of Israel from harming you, when you brought them the clear proofs and evidence, testifying to your prophethood and Message from Me to them. They rejected you and accused you of being a magician and tried to kill you by crucifixion, but I saved you, raised you to Me, purified you from their vulgarity and protected you from their harm.' The wording of this Ayah indicates that `Isa will be reminded of these favors on the Day of Resurrection. Allah used the past tense in these Ayat indicating that it is a forgone matter that will certainly occur. This Ayah also contains some of the secrets of the Unseen that Allah revealed to His Messenger Muhammad . Allah said,

(And when I (Allah) Awhaytu Al-Hawariyyin to believe in Me and My Messenger.) This is also a reminder of Allah's favor on `Isa, by making discples and companions for him. It is also said that Awhaytu in the Ayah means, `inspired', just as in another Ayah, Allah said;

(And We inspired the mother of Musa (saying): Suckle him...) (28:7). Allah said in other Ayat,

(And your Lord Awha (inspired) the bee, saying: "Take habitations in the mountains and in the trees and in what they erect. Then, eat of all fruits, and follow the ways of your Lord made easy (for you).") (16:68-69) Al-Hasan Al-Basri commented about the Hawariyyun, "Allah inspired them", while As-Suddi said, "`He put in their hearts," and the Hawariyyun said,

(We believe. And bear witness that we are Muslims.)

Surah 5: Ayah: 112, Ayah: 113, Ayah: 114 & Ayah: 115

﴿ إِذْ قَالَ ٱلْحَوَارِيُّونَ يَـٰعِيسَى ٱبْنَ مَرْيَمَ هَلْ يَسْتَطِيعُ رَبُّكَ أَن يُنَزِّلَ عَلَيْنَا مَآئِدَةً مِّنَ ٱلسَّمَآءِ قَالَ ٱتَّقُوا۟ ٱللَّهَ إِن كُنتُم مُّؤْمِنِينَ ﴾

112. (Remember) when Al-Hawâriyyûn (the disciples) said: "O 'Isâ (Jesus), son of Maryam (Mary)! Can your Lord send down to us a table spread (with food) from heaven?" 'Isâ (Jesus) said: "Fear Allâh, if you are indeed believers."

﴿ قَالُوا۟ نُرِيدُ أَن نَّأْكُلَ مِنْهَا وَتَطْمَئِنَّ قُلُوبُنَا وَنَعْلَمَ أَن قَدْ صَدَقْتَنَا وَنَكُونَ عَلَيْهَا مِنَ ٱلشَّـٰهِدِينَ ﴾

113. They said: "We wish to eat thereof and to satisfy our hearts (to be stronger in Faith), and to know that you have indeed told us the truth and that we ourselves be its witnesses."

﴿ قَالَ عِيسَى ٱبْنُ مَرْيَمَ ٱللَّهُمَّ رَبَّنَآ أَنزِلْ عَلَيْنَا مَآئِدَةً مِّنَ ٱلسَّمَآءِ تَكُونُ لَنَا عِيدًا لِّأَوَّلِنَا وَءَاخِرِنَا وَءَايَةً مِّنكَ وَٱرْزُقْنَا وَأَنتَ خَيْرُ ٱلرَّٰزِقِينَ ﴾

114. 'Isâ (Jesus), son of Maryam (Mary), said: "O Allâh, our Lord! Send us from the heaven a table spread (with food) that there may be for us - for the first and the last of us - a festival and a sign from You; and provide us sustenance, for You are the Best of sustainers."

﴿ قَالَ ٱللَّهُ إِنِّى مُنَزِّلُهَا عَلَيْكُمْ فَمَن يَكْفُرْ بَعْدُ مِنكُمْ فَإِنِّىٓ أُعَذِّبُهُۥ عَذَابًا لَّآ أُعَذِّبُهُۥٓ أَحَدًا مِّنَ ٱلْعَـٰلَمِينَ ﴾

115. Allâh said: "I am going to send it down unto you, but if any of you after that disbelieves, then I will punish him with a torment such as I have not inflicted on anyone among (all) the 'Alamîn (mankind and jinn)."

Transliteration

112. Ith qala alhawariyyoona ya AAeesa ibna maryama hal yastateeAAu rabbuka an yunazzila AAalayna ma-idatan mina alssama-i qala ittaqoo Allaha in kuntum mu/mineena   113. Qaloo nureedu an na/kula minha watatma-inna quloobuna wanaAAlama an qad sadaqtana wanakoona AAalayha mina alshshahideena   114. Qala AAeesa ibnu maryama allahumma rabbana anzil AAalayna ma-idatan mina alssama-i takoonu lana AAeedan li-awwalina waakhirina waayatan minka waorzuqna waanta khayru alrraziqeena   115. Qala Allahu innee munazziluha AAalaykum faman yakfur baAAdu minkum fa-innee oAAaththibuhu AAathaban la oAAaththibuhu ahadan mina alAAalameena

Tafsir Ibn Kathir

Sending Down the Ma'idah

This is the story of the Ma'idah, the name of which this Surah bears, Surat Al-Ma'idah. This is also among the favors that Allah granted His servant and Messenger, `Isa, accepting his request to send the Ma'idah down, and doing so as clear proof and unequivocal evidence. Allah said,

((Remember) when Al-Hawaryun said...) the disciples of `Isa said,

(O `Isa, son of Maryam! Can your Lord send down to us a Ma'idah from heaven) The Ma'idah is the table that has food on it. Some scholars said that the disciples requested this table because they were poor and deprived. So they asked `Isa to supplicate to Allah to send a table of food down to them that they could eat from every day and thus be more able to perform the acts of worship.

(`Isa said: "Have Taqwa of Allah, if you are indeed believers.") `Isa answered them by saying, `Have Taqwa of Allah! And do not ask for this, for it may become a trial for you, but trust in Allah for your provisions, if you are truly believers. '

(They said: "We wish to eat thereof.") we need to eat from it,

(and to be stronger in faith,) when we witness it descending from heaven as sustenance for us,

(and to know that you have indeed told us the truth,) of your Message and our faith in you increases and also our knowledge,

(and that we ourselves be its witnesses.) testifying that it is a sign from Allah, as proof and evidence that you are a Prophet, and attesting to the truth of what you brought us,

(`Isa, son of Maryam, said: "O Allah, our Lord! Send us from heaven a table spread (with food) that there may be for us -- for the first and the last of us -- a festival...") As-Suddi commented that the Ayah means, "We will take that day on which the table was sent down as a day of celebration, that we and those who come after us would consider sacred." Sufyan Ath-Thawri said that it means, "A day of prayer."

(and a sign from You.) proving that You are able to do all things and to accept my supplication, so that they accept what I convey to them from You,

(and provide us sustenance,) a delicious food from You that does not require any effort or hardship,

("For You are the Best of sustainers." Allah said: "I am going to send it down unto you, but if any of you after that disbelieves...") by denying this sign and defying its implication, O `Isa,

(then I will punish him with a torment such as I have not inflicted on anyone among the `Alamin.) among the people of your time. Allah said in similar Ayat,

(And on the Day when the Hour will be established (it will be said to the angels): "Cause Fir'awn's people to enter the severest torment!") (40:46), and,

(Verily, the hypocrites will be in the lowest depths of the Fire.) (4:145) Ibn Jarir said that `Abdullah bin `Amr said, "Those who will receive the severest torment on the Day of Resurrection are three: The hypocrites, those from the people of Al-Ma'idah who disbelieved in it, and the people of Fir`awn." Ibn Abi Hatim recorded that Ibn `Abbas said, "They said to `Isa, son of Maryam, `Supplicate to Allah to send down to us from heaven, a table spread with food.' He also said, `So the angels brought the table down containing seven fish and seven pieces of bread and placed it before them. So the last group of people ate as the first group did." Ibn Jarir recorded that Ishaq bin `Abdullah said that the table was sent down to `Isa son of Maryam having seven pieces of bread and seven fish, and they ate from it as much as they wished. But when some of them stole food from it, saying, "It might not come down tomorrow," the table ascended. These statements testify that the table was sent down to the Children of Israel during the time of `Isa, son of Maryam, as a result of Allah's accepting his supplication to Him. The apparent wording of this Ayah also states so,

(Allah said: "I am going to send it down unto you...") (5:115).

Surah 5: Ayah: 116, Ayah: 117 & Ayah: 118

﴿ وَإِذْ قَالَ ٱللَّهُ يَٰعِيسَى ٱبْنَ مَرْيَمَ ءَأَنتَ قُلْتَ لِلنَّاسِ ٱتَّخِذُونِي وَأُمِّيَ إِلَٰهَيْنِ مِن دُونِ ٱللَّهِ قَالَ سُبْحَٰنَكَ مَا يَكُونُ لِي أَنْ أَقُولَ مَا لَيْسَ لِي بِحَقٍّ إِن كُنتُ قُلْتُهُ فَقَدْ عَلِمْتَهُۥ تَعْلَمُ مَا فِي نَفْسِى وَلَآ أَعْلَمُ مَا فِي نَفْسِكَ إِنَّكَ أَنتَ عَلَّٰمُ ٱلْغُيُوبِ ﴾

116. And (remember) when Allâh will say (on the Day of Resurrection): "O 'Isâ (Jesus), son of Maryam (Mary)! Did you say unto men: 'Worship me and my mother as two gods besides Allâh?' " He will say: "Glory be to You! It was not for me to say what I had no right (to say). Had I said such a thing, You would surely have known it. You know what is in my inner-self though I do not know what is in Yours; truly, You, only You, are the All-Knower of all that is hidden (and unseen).

﴿ مَا قُلْتُ لَهُمْ إِلَّا مَآ أَمَرْتَنِى بِهِۦٓ أَنِ ٱعْبُدُواْ ٱللَّهَ رَبِّى وَرَبَّكُمْ وَكُنتُ عَلَيْهِمْ شَهِيدًا مَّا دُمْتُ فِيهِمْ فَلَمَّا تَوَفَّيْتَنِى كُنتَ أَنتَ ٱلرَّقِيبَ عَلَيْهِمْ وَأَنتَ عَلَىٰ كُلِّ شَىْءٍ شَهِيدٌ ﴾

117. "Never did I say to them aught except what You (Allâh) did command me to say: 'Worship Allâh, my Lord and your Lord.' And I was a witness over them while I dwelt amongst them, but when You took me up, You were the Watcher over them; and You are a Witness to all things. (This is a great admonition and warning to the Christians of the whole world).

Chapter 5: Al-Maidah (The Table, The Table Spread), Verses 082-120

﴿ إِن تُعَذِّبْهُمْ فَإِنَّهُمْ عِبَادُكَ ۖ وَإِن تَغْفِرْ لَهُمْ فَإِنَّكَ أَنتَ ٱلْعَزِيزُ ٱلْحَكِيمُ ۝ ﴾

118. "If You punish them, they are Your slaves, and if You forgive them, verily You, only You are the All-Mighty, the All-Wise."

Transliteration

116. Wa-ith qala Allahu ya AAeesa ibna maryama aanta qulta lilnnasi ittakhithoonee waommiya ilahayni min dooni Allahi qala subhanaka ma yakoonu lee an aqoola ma laysa lee bihaqqin in kuntu qultuhu faqad AAalimtahu taAAlamu ma fee nafsee wala aAAlamu ma fee nafsika innaka anta AAallamu alghuyoobi 117. Ma qultu lahum illa ma amartanee bihi ani oAAbudoo Allaha rabbee warabbakum wakuntu AAalayhim shaheedan ma dumtu feehim falamma tawaffaytanee kunta anta alrraqeeba AAalayhim waanta AAala kulli shay-in shaheedun 118. In tuAAaththibhum fa-innahum AAibaduka wa-in taghfir lahum fa-innaka anta alAAazeezu alhakeemu

Tafsir Ibn Kathir

`Isa Rejects Shirk and Affirms Tawhid

Allah will also speak to His servant and Messenger, `Isa son of Maryam, peace be upon him, saying to him on the Day of Resurrection in the presence of those who worshipped `Isa and his mother as gods besides Allah,

(O `Isa, son of Maryam! Did you say unto men: `Worship me and my mother as two gods besides Allah') This is a threat and a warning to Christians, chastising them in public, as Qatadah and others said, and Qatadah mentioned this Ayah as evidence,

("This is a Day on which the truthful will profit from their truth.") (5:119) Allah's statement,

(Glory be to You! It was not for me to say what I had no right (to say)...) contains Allah's direction for `Isa to utter the perfect answer. Ibn Abi Hatim recorded that Abu Hurayrah said, "`Isa will be taught his argument in reply to what Allah will ask him,

(And (remember) when Allah will say (on the Day of Resurrection): "O `Isa, son of Maryam! Did you say unto men: `Worship me and my mother as two gods besides Allah') (5:116)." Abu Hurayrah then narrated that the Prophet said that Allah taught `Isa to say,

(Glory be to You! It was not for me to say what I had no right (to say)...) Ath-Thawri narrated this Hadith from Ma`mar from Ibn Tawus from Tawus. `Isa's statement,

(Had I said such a thing, You would surely have known it.) means, had I said it, You, my Lord, would have known it, for nothing escapes Your knowledge. Rather, I have not said these words nor did the thought even cross my mind, this why he said,

(You know what is in my inner self though I do not know what is in Yours, truly, You, only You, are the Knower of all that is hidden and unseen. Never did I say to them ought except what You (Allah) did command me to say...) and convey,

(Worship Allah, my Lord and your Lord.) I only called them to what You sent me with and commanded me to convey to them,

(Worship Allah, my Lord and your Lord) and this is what I conveyed to them,

(And I was a witness over them while I dwelled amongst them,) I was a witness over what they did when I was amongst them,

(but when You took me (up), You were the Watcher over them, and You are a Witness to all things.) Abu Dawud At-Tayalisi recorded that Ibn `Abbas said, "The Messenger of Allah stood up once and gave us a speech in which he said,

«يَا أَيُّهَا النَّاسُ إِنَّكُمْ مَحْشُورُونَ إِلَى اللهِ عَزَّ وَجَلَّ حُفَاةً، عُرَاةً، غُرْلاً»

(O people! You will be gathered to Allah while barefooted, naked and uncircumcised;

[كَمَا بَدَأْنَا أَوَّلَ خَلْقٍ نُعِيدُهُ]

(As We began the first creation, We shall repeat it.)

«وَإِنَّ أَوَّلَ الْخَلَائِقِ يُكْسَى يَوْمَ الْقِيَامَةِ إِبْرَاهِيمُ، أَلَا وَإِنَّهُ يُجَاءُ بِرِجَالٍ مِنْ أُمَّتِي فَيُؤْخَذُ بِهِمْ ذَاتَ الشِّمَالِ، فَأَقُولُ: أَصْحَابِي، فَيُقَالُ: إِنَّكَ لَا تَدْرِي مَا أَحْدَثُوا بَعْدَكَ، فَأَقُولُ كَمَا قَالَ الْعَبْدُ الصَّالِحُ»

The first among the creation who will be covered with clothes will be Ibrahim. Some men from my Ummah will be brought and taken to the left (to the Fire) and I will yell, `They are my followers!' It will be said, `You do not know what they innvovated after you (in religion).' So I will say just as the righteous servant (`Isa) said,

[مَا قُلْتُ لَهُمْ إِلَّا مَا أَمَرْتَنِي بِهِ أَنِ اعْبُدُواْ اللَّهَ رَبِّي وَرَبَّكُمْ وَكُنتُ عَلَيْهِمْ شَهِيداً مَّا دُمْتُ فِيهِمْ فَلَمَّا تَوَفَّيْتَنِي كُنتَ أَنتَ الرَّقِيبَ عَلَيْهِمْ وَأَنتَ عَلَى كُلِّ شَىْءٍ شَهِيدٌ - إِن تُعَذِّبْهُمْ فَإِنَّهُمْ عِبَادُكَ وَإِن تَغْفِرْ لَهُمْ فَإِنَّكَ أَنتَ الْعَزِيزُ الْحَكِيمُ]

(And I was a witness over them while I dwelled amongst them, but when You took me (up), You were the Watcher over them, and You are a Witness to all things. If You punish them, they are Your servants, and if You forgive them, verily You, only You are the Almighty, the All-Wise.)

«فَيُقَالُ: إِنَّ هَؤُلَاءِ لَمْ يَزَالُوا مُرْتَدِّينَ عَلَى أَعْقَابِهِمْ مُنْذُ فَارَقْتَهُمْ»

(It will further be said, `These people kept reverting back on their heels after you left them.')" Al-Bukhari also recorded this Hadith in the explanation of this Ayah. Allah said;

(If You punish them, they are Your servants, and if You forgive them, verily You, only You are the Almighty, the All-Wise.) All matters refer back to Allah, for He does what He Wills and none can question Him about what He does, while He will question them. This Ayah also shows the crime of the Christians who invented a lie against Allah and His Messenger, thus making a rival, wife and son for Allah. Allah is glorified in that He is far above what they attribute to Him. So this Ayah (5:118) has tremendous value and delivers unique news.

Surah 5: Ayah: 119 & Ayah: 120

﴿ قَالَ ٱللَّهُ هَٰذَا يَوْمُ يَنفَعُ ٱلصَّٰدِقِينَ صِدْقُهُمْ لَهُمْ جَنَّٰتٌ تَجْرِى مِن تَحْتِهَا ٱلْأَنْهَٰرُ خَٰلِدِينَ فِيهَآ أَبَدًا رَّضِىَ ٱللَّهُ عَنْهُمْ وَرَضُوا۟ عَنْهُ ذَٰلِكَ ٱلْفَوْزُ ٱلْعَظِيمُ ﴾

119. Allâh will say: "This is a Day on which the truthful will profit from their truth: theirs are Gardens under which rivers flow (in Paradise) - they shall abide therein forever. Allâh is pleased with them and they with Him. That is the great success (Paradise).

﴿ لِلَّهِ مُلْكُ ٱلسَّمَٰوَٰتِ وَٱلْأَرْضِ وَمَا فِيهِنَّ وَهُوَ عَلَىٰ كُلِّ شَىْءٍ قَدِيرٌ ﴾

120. To Allâh belongs the dominion of the heavens and the earth and all that is therein, and He is Able to do all things.

Transliteration

119. Qala Allahu hatha yawmu yanfaAAu alssadiqeena sidquhum lahum jannatun tajree min tahtiha al-anharu khalideena feeha abadan radiya Allahu AAanhum waradoo AAanhu thalika alfawzu alAAatheemu 120. Lillahi mulku alssamawati waal-ardi wama feehinna wahuwa AAala kulli shay-in qadeerun

Tafsir Ibn Kathir

Only Truth will be of Benefit on the Day of Resurrection

Allah answers His servant and Messenger `Isa, son of Maryam, after he disowns the disbelieving Christians who lied about Allah and His Messenger, and when `Isa refers their end to the will of his Lord, (This is a Day on which the truthful will profit from their truth.) Ad-Dahhak said that Ibn `Abbas commented, "This is the Day when Tawhid will benefit those who believed in it."

(Theirs are Gardens under which rivers flow (in Paradise) -- they shall abide therein forever.) and they will never be removed from it, (Allah is pleased with them and they with Him.)

(But the greatest bliss is the good pleasure of Allah.) (9:72) We will mention the Hadiths about this Ayah (9:72) later on. Allah's statement,

(That is the great success.) means, this is the great success, other than which there is no greater success. Allah said in another Ayat,

(For the like of this let the workers work.) (37:61), and, (And for this let (all) those strive who want to strive.) (83:26) Allah's statement, (To Allah belongs the dominion of the heavens and the earth and all that is therein, and He is able to do all things.) means, He created everything, owns everything, controls the affairs of everything and is able to do all things. Therefore, everything and everyone are in His domain and under His power and will. There is none like Him, nor is there rival, ancestor, son, or wife for Him, nor a lord or god besides Him. Ibn Wahb said that he heard Huyay bin `Abdullah saying that Abu `Abdur-Rahman Al-Habli said that `Abdullah bin `Amr said, "The last revealed Surah was Surat Al-Ma'idah."

INTRODUCTION TO CHAPTER (SURAH) 6: AL-AN'AM (CATTLE, LIVESTOCK)

Ibn kathir's Introduction

The Virtue of Surat Al-An`am and When it Was Revealed

Al-`Awfi, `Ikrimah and `Ata' said that Ibn `Abbas said, "Surat Al-An`am was revealed in Makkah" At-Tabarani recorded that Ibn `Abbas said, "All of Surat Al-An`am was revealed in Makkah at night, accompanied by seventy thousand angels, raising their voices in glorification of Allah" As-Suddi said that Murrah said that `Abdullah said, "Surat Al-An`am was revealed in the company of seventy thousand angels."

CHAPTER (SURAH) 6: AL-AN'AM (CATTLE, LIVESTOCK), VERSES 001-110

﴿بِسْمِ ٱللَّهِ ٱلرَّحْمَٰنِ ٱلرَّحِيمِ ۝﴾

In the Name of Allâh, the Most Gracious, the Most Merciful.

Surah: 6 Ayah: 1, Ayah: 2 & Ayah: 3

﴿ٱلْحَمْدُ لِلَّهِ ٱلَّذِى خَلَقَ ٱلسَّمَٰوَٰتِ وَٱلْأَرْضَ وَجَعَلَ ٱلظُّلُمَٰتِ وَٱلنُّورَ ثُمَّ ٱلَّذِينَ كَفَرُواْ بِرَبِّهِمْ يَعْدِلُونَ ۝﴾

1. All praises and thanks are to Allâh, Who (Alone) created the heavens and the earth, and originated the darkness and the light; yet those who disbelieve hold others as equal with their Lord.

﴿ هُوَ ٱلَّذِى خَلَقَكُم مِّن طِينٍ ثُمَّ قَضَىٰٓ أَجَلاً ۖ وَأَجَلٌ مُّسَمًّى عِندَهُۥ ۖ ثُمَّ أَنتُمْ تَمْتَرُونَ ﴾

2. He it is Who has created you from clay, and then has decreed a (stated) term (for you to die). And there is with Him another determined term (for you to be resurrected), yet you doubt (in the Resurrection.)

﴿ وَهُوَ ٱللَّهُ فِى ٱلسَّمَـٰوَٰتِ وَفِى ٱلْأَرْضِ ۖ يَعْلَمُ سِرَّكُمْ وَجَهْرَكُمْ وَيَعْلَمُ مَا تَكْسِبُونَ ﴾

3. And He is Allâh (to be worshipped Alone) in the heavens and on the earth; He knows what you conceal and what you reveal, and He knows what you earn (good or bad). (See V. 43:84)

Transliteration

1. Alhamdu lillahi allathee khalaqa alssamawati waal-arda wajaAAala aluththulumati waalnnoora thumma allatheena kafaroo birabbihim yaAAdiloona 2. Huwa allathee khalaqakum min teenin thumma qada ajalan waajalun musamman AAindahu thumma antum tamtaroona 3. Allatheena yuqeemoona alssalata wamimma razaqnahum yunfiqoona

Tafsir Ibn Kathir

All Praise is Due to Allah for His Glorious Ability and Great Power

Allah praises and glorifies His Most Honorable Self for creating the heavens and earth, as a dwelling for His servants, and for making the darkness and the light to benefit them in the night and the day. In this Ayah, Allah describes darkness in the plural, Zulumat (where Zulmah is singular for darkness), while describing the light in the singular, An-Nur, because An-Nur is more honored. In other Ayat, Allah said,

(To the right and to the lefts.) (16:48) Near the end of this Surah (chapter 6), Allah also said;

(And verily, this is my straight path, so follow it, and follow no (other) ways, for they will separate you away from His way.) (6:153) Allah said next,

(Yet those who disbelieve hold others as equal with their Lord.) meaning, in spite of all this, some of Allah's servants disbelieve in Him and hold others as partners and rivals with Him. Some of Allah's servants claimed a wife and a son for Allah, hallowed be He far above what they attribute to Him. Allah's statement,

(He it is Who has created you from clay,) refers to the father of mankind, Adam, from whom mankind originated, multiplied in numbers and spread about, east and west. Allah said,

(Then has decreed a stated term. And there is with Him another determined term...) His saying;

(Then has decreed a stated term,) refers to death, while,

(And there is with Him another determined term...) refers to the Hereafter, according to Sa`id bin Jubayr who reported this from Ibn `Abbas. Similar statements were narrated from Mujahid, `Ikrimah, Sa`id bin Jubayr, Al-Hasan, Qatadah, Ad-Dahhak, Zayd bin Aslam, `Atiyyah, As-Suddi, Muqatil bin Hayyan and others. Ibn `Abbas and Mujahid said that,

(And then has decreed a stated term,) is the term of this earthly life, while,

(And there is with Him another determined term) refers to man's extent of life until he dies as mentioned in Allah's statement;

(It is He, Who takes your souls by night (when you are asleep), and has knowledge of all that you have done by day, then He raises (wakes) you up again that a term appointed (life) be fulfilled.) (6:60) The meaning of Allah's statement,

(With Him) is that none but Him knows when it will occur. Allah said in other Ayat,

(The knowledge thereof is with my Lord. None can reveal its time but He.) (7:187), and,

(They ask you about the Hour -- when will be its appointed time You have no knowledge to say anything about it. To your Lord belongs (the knowledge of) the term thereof.) (79:42-44) Allah said,

(Yet you doubt.) the coming of the (last) Hour, according to As-Suddi. Allah said next,

(And He is Allah in the heavens and the earth, He knows what you conceal and what you reveal, and He knows what you earn.) Meaning, it is He Who is called Allah, throughout the heavens and the earth, that is, it is He who is worshipped, singled out, whose divinity is believed in by the inhabitants of the heavens and the earth. They call Him Allah, and they supplicate to Him in fear and hope, except those who disbelieve among the Jinns and mankind. In another Ayah, Allah said;

(It is He Who is God in the heavens and the earth.)(43:84) meaning, He is the God of those in heaven and those on earth, and He knows all affairs, public and secret.

(And He knows what you earn) all the good and bad deeds that you perform.

Surah: 6 Ayah: 4, Ayah: 5 & Ayah: 6

﴿ وَمَا تَأْتِيهِم مِّنْ ءَايَةٍ مِّنْ ءَايَـٰتِ رَبِّهِمْ إِلَّا كَانُوا۟ عَنْهَا مُعْرِضِينَ ۝ ﴾

4. And never an Ayah (sign) comes to them from the Ayât (proofs, evidences, verses, lessons, signs, revelations, etc.) of their Lord, but that they have been turning away from it.

﴿ فَقَدْ كَذَّبُوا۟ بِٱلْحَقِّ لَمَّا جَآءَهُمْ ۖ فَسَوْفَ يَأْتِيهِمْ أَنۢبَـٰٓؤُا۟ مَا كَانُوا۟ بِهِۦ يَسْتَهْزِءُونَ ۝ ﴾

5. Indeed, they rejected the truth (the Qur'ân and Muhammad (peace be upon him)) when it came to them, but there will come to them the news of that (the torment) which they used to mock at.

﴿ أَلَمْ يَرَوْا۟ كَمْ أَهْلَكْنَا مِن قَبْلِهِم مِّن قَرْنٍ مَّكَّنَّـٰهُمْ فِى ٱلْأَرْضِ مَا لَمْ نُمَكِّن لَّكُمْ وَأَرْسَلْنَا ٱلسَّمَآءَ عَلَيْهِم مِّدْرَارًا وَجَعَلْنَا ٱلْأَنْهَـٰرَ تَجْرِى مِن تَحْتِهِمْ فَأَهْلَكْنَـٰهُم بِذُنُوبِهِمْ وَأَنشَأْنَا مِنۢ بَعْدِهِمْ قَرْنًا ءَاخَرِينَ ۝ ﴾

6. Have they not seen how many a generation before them We have destroyed whom We had established on the earth such as We have not established you? And We poured out on them rain from the sky in abundance, and made the rivers flow under them. Yet We destroyed them for their sins, and created after them other generations.

Transliteration

4. Wama ta/teehim min ayatin min ayati rabbihim illa kanoo AAanha muAArideena 5. Faqad kaththaboo bialhaqqi lamma jaahum fasawfa ya/teehim anbao ma kanoo bihi yastahzi-oona 6. Alam yaraw kam ahlakna min qablihim min qarnin makkannahum fee al-ardi ma lam numakkin lakum waarsalna alssamaa AAalayhim midraran wajaAAalna al-anhara tajree min tahtihim faahlaknahum bithunoobihim waansha/na min baAAdihim qarnan akhareena

Tafsir Ibn Kathir

Threatening the Idolators for their Stubbornness

Allah states that the rebellious, stubborn polytheists will turn away from every Ayah, meaning, sign, miracle and proof that is evidence of Allah's Uniqueness and the truth of His honorable Messengers. They will not contemplate about these Ayat or care about them. Allah said,

(Indeed, they rejected the truth when it came to them, but there will come to them the news of that which they used to mock at.) This Ayah contains a warning and a stern threat for the disbelievers' rejection of the truth, stating that the disbelievers will surely know the truth of what they used to deny and taste the evil end of their behavior. Allah advises and warns the disbelievers, that they should avoid the torments and afflictions of this life, similar to what befell their likes from previous nations, who were stronger, wealthier, had more offspring, and were more exploitive on the earth. Allah said,

(Have they not seen how many a generation before them We have destroyed whom We had established on the earth such as We have not established you) meaning, they had more wealth, children, buildings, abundant provision, riches and soldiers. Allah said next,

(and We poured out on them rain from the sky in abundance,) in reference to rain that comes often,

(And made the rivers flow under them.) as rain was abundant and the springs were plentiful, so that We deceived them.

(Yet We destroyed them for their sins) meaning the mistakes and errors that they committed,

(and created after them other generations,) for, these generations of old perished and became as legends and stories,

(And created after them other generations.) so that We test the new generations, as well. Yet, they committed similar errors and were destroyed, as their ancestors were destroyed. Therefore, beware of the same end that might befall you, for you are not dearer to Allah than these previous nations, but the Messenger whom you defied is dearer to Allah than the Messengers they defied. Thus, you are more liable than them to receive torment, if it was not for Allah's mercy and kindness.

Surah: 6 Ayah: 7, Ayah: 8, Ayah: 9, Ayah: 10 & Ayah: 11

﴿ وَلَوْ نَزَّلْنَا عَلَيْكَ كِتَٰبًا فِى قِرْطَاسٍ فَلَمَسُوهُ بِأَيْدِيهِمْ لَقَالَ ٱلَّذِينَ كَفَرُوٓا۟ إِنْ هَٰذَآ إِلَّا سِحْرٌ مُّبِينٌ ۝ ﴾

7. And even if We had sent down unto you (O Muhammad (peace be upon him)) a Message written on paper so that they could touch it with their hands, the disbelievers would have said: "This is nothing but obvious magic!"

﴿ وَقَالُوا۟ لَوْلَآ أُنزِلَ عَلَيْهِ مَلَكٌ وَلَوْ أَنزَلْنَا مَلَكًا لَّقُضِىَ ٱلْأَمْرُ ثُمَّ لَا يُنظَرُونَ ۝ ﴾

8. And they say: "Why has not an angel been sent down to him?" Had We sent down an angel, the matter would have been judged at once, and no respite would be granted to them.

﴿ وَلَوْ جَعَلْنَٰهُ مَلَكًا لَّجَعَلْنَٰهُ رَجُلًا وَلَلَبَسْنَا عَلَيْهِم مَّا يَلْبِسُونَ ۝ ﴾

9. And had We appointed him an angel, We indeed would have made him a man, and We would have certainly confused them in which they are already confused (i.e. the Message of Prophet Muhammad (peace be upon him))

﴿ وَلَقَدِ ٱسْتُهْزِئَ بِرُسُلٍ مِّن قَبْلِكَ فَحَاقَ بِٱلَّذِينَ سَخِرُواْ مِنْهُم مَّا كَانُواْ بِهِۦ يَسْتَهْزِءُونَ ۝ ﴾

10. And indeed (many) Messengers were mocked before you, but their scoffers were surrounded by the very thing that they used to mock at.

﴿ قُلْ سِيرُواْ فِى ٱلْأَرْضِ ثُمَّ ٱنظُرُواْ كَيْفَ كَانَ عَٰقِبَةُ ٱلْمُكَذِّبِينَ ۝ ﴾

11. Say (O Muhammad (peace be upon him)) "Travel in the land and see what was the end of those who rejected truth."

Transliteration

7. Walaw nazzalna AAalayka kitaban fee qirtasin falamasoohu bi-aydeehim laqala allatheena kafaroo in hatha illa sihrun mubeenun   8. Waqaloo lawla onzila AAalayhi malakun walaw anzalna malakan laqudiya al-amru thumma la yuntharoona   9. Walaw jaAAalnahu malakan lajaAAalnahu rajulan walalabasna AAalayhim ma yalbisoona   10. Walaqadi istuhzi-a birusulin min qablika fahaqa biallatheena sakhiroo minhum ma kanoo bihi yastahzi-oona   11. Qul seeroo fee al-ardi thumma onthuroo kayfa kana AAaqibatu almukaththibeena

Tafsir Ibn Kathir

Censuring the Rebellious and their Refusal to Accept Human Messengers

Allah describes the rebellion and stubbornness of the idolators in defying the truth and arguing against it,

(And even if We had sent down unto you a Message written on paper so that they could touch it with their hands,) meaning, if they saw this Message's descent and were eye-witnesses to that,

(the disbelievers would have said: "This is nothing but obvious magic!") This is similar to Allah's description of the disbelievers' defiance of facts and truth,

(And even if We opened to them a gate from the heaven and they were to continue ascending thereto. They would surely say: "Our eyes have been (as if) dazzled. Nay, we are a people bewitched.") (15:14-15), and,

(And if they were to see a piece of the heaven falling down, they would say, "Clouds gathered in heaps!") (52:44).

(And they say: "Why has not an angel been sent down to him") to convey the Message with admonition along with him. Allah replied,

(Had We sent down an angel, the matter would have been judged at once, and no respite would be granted to them.) Consequently, even if the angels descend, while the disbelievers still had the same attitude, then the torment will surely befall them from Allah as a consequence. Allah said in other Ayat,

(We send not the angels down except with the truth (i.e. for torment, etc.), and in that case, they (the disbelievers) would have no respite!) (15:8), and,

(On the Day they will see the angels, no glad tidings will there be for the criminals that day.) (25:22) Allah's statement,

(And had We appointed him an angel, We indeed would have made him a man, and We would have certainly caused them confusion in a matter which they have already covered with confusion.) meaning, if We send an angel along with the human Messenger, or if We send an angel as a Messenger to mankind, he would be in the shape of a man so that they would be able to speak to him and benefit from his teachings. In this case, the angel (in the shape of a human) will also cause confusion for them, just as the confusion they caused themselves over accepting humans as Messengers! Allah said,

(Say: "If there were on the earth, angels walking about in peace and security, We should certainly have sent down for them from the heaven an angel as a Messenger.") (17:95) It is a mercy from Allah to His creation that He sends every type of creation, Messengers from among their kind, so that they are able to call their people to Allah, and their people able to talk to them, ask them and benefit from them. In another Ayah, Allah said;

(Indeed Allah conferred a great favor on the believers when He sent among them a Messenger from among themselves, reciting unto them His verses (the Qur'an), and purifying them.) (3:164) Ad-Dahhak said that Ibn `Abbas said about the Ayah (6:9 above), "If an angel was sent to them, he would come in the shape of a man. This is because they will not be able to look at the angel due to light."

(... and We would have certainly caused them confusion in a matter which they have already covered with confusion.) meaning, We would confuse them over their confusion. And Al-Walibi reported Ibn `Abbas saying; "We brought doubts around them." Allah's statement,

(And indeed Messengers were mocked before you, but their scoffers were surrounded by the very thing that they used to mock at.) comforts the Messenger concerning the denial of him by his people. The Ayah also promises the Messenger , and his believers, of Allah's victory and the good end in this life and the Hereafter. Allah said next,

(Say: "Travel in the land and see what was the end of those who rejected truth.") meaning, contemplate about yourselves and think about the afflictions Allah struck the previous nations with, those who defied His Messengers and denied them. Allah sent torment, afflictions and punishment on them in this life, as well as the painful torment in the Hereafter, while saving His Messengers and believing servants.

Chapter 6: Al-An'am (Cattle, Livestock), Verses 001-110

Surah: 6 Ayah: 12, Ayah: 13, Ayah: 14, Ayah: 15 & Ayah: 16

﴿ قُل لِّمَن مَّا فِى ٱلسَّمَٰوَٰتِ وَٱلۡأَرۡضِ ۖ قُل لِّلَّهِ ۚ كَتَبَ عَلَىٰ نَفۡسِهِ ٱلرَّحۡمَةَ ۚ لَيَجۡمَعَنَّكُمۡ إِلَىٰ يَوۡمِ ٱلۡقِيَٰمَةِ لَا رَيۡبَ فِيهِ ۚ ٱلَّذِينَ خَسِرُوٓاْ أَنفُسَهُمۡ فَهُمۡ لَا يُؤۡمِنُونَ ۝ ﴾

12. Say (O Muhammad (peace be upon him)) "To whom belongs all that is in the heavens and the earth?" Say: "To Allâh. He has prescribed Mercy for Himself. Indeed He will gather you together on the Day of Resurrection, about which there is no doubt. Those who have lost themselves will not believe (in Allâh as being the only Ilâh (God), and Muhammad (peace be upon him) as being one of His Messengers, and in Resurrection).

﴿ ۞ وَلَهُۥ مَا سَكَنَ فِى ٱلَّيۡلِ وَٱلنَّهَارِ ۚ وَهُوَ ٱلسَّمِيعُ ٱلۡعَلِيمُ ۝ ﴾

13. And to Him belongs whatsoever exists in the night and the day, and He is the All-Hearing, the All-Knowing."

﴿ قُلۡ أَغَيۡرَ ٱللَّهِ أَتَّخِذُ وَلِيّٗا فَاطِرِ ٱلسَّمَٰوَٰتِ وَٱلۡأَرۡضِ وَهُوَ يُطۡعِمُ وَلَا يُطۡعَمُ ۗ قُلۡ إِنِّىٓ أُمِرۡتُ أَنۡ أَكُونَ أَوَّلَ مَنۡ أَسۡلَمَ ۖ وَلَا تَكُونَنَّ مِنَ ٱلۡمُشۡرِكِينَ ۝ ﴾

14. Say (O Muhammad (peace be upon him)) "Shall I take as a Walî (Helper, Protector, Lord or God) any other than Allâh, the Creator of the heavens and the earth? And it is He Who feeds but is not fed." Say: "Verily, I am commanded to be the first of those who submit themselves to Allâh (as Muslims)." And be not you (O Muhammad (peace be upon him)) of the Mushrikûn (polytheists, pagans, idolaters and disbelievers in the Oneness of Allâh).

﴿ قُلۡ إِنِّىٓ أَخَافُ إِنۡ عَصَيۡتُ رَبِّى عَذَابَ يَوۡمٍ عَظِيمٖ ۝ ﴾

15. Say: "I fear, if I disobey my Lord, the torment of a Mighty Day."

﴿ مَّن يُصۡرَفۡ عَنۡهُ يَوۡمَئِذٖ فَقَدۡ رَحِمَهُۥ ۚ وَذَٰلِكَ ٱلۡفَوۡزُ ٱلۡمُبِينُ ۝ ﴾

16. He who is averted from (such a torment) on that Day, (Allâh) has surely been Merciful to him. And that would be the obvious success.

Transliteration

12. Qul liman ma fee alssamawati waal-ardi qul lillahi kataba AAala nafsihi alrrahmata layajmaAAannakum ila yawmi alqiyamati la rayba feehi allatheena khasiroo anfusahum fahum la yu/minoona   13. Walahu ma sakana fee allayli waalnnahari wahuwa alssameeAAu alAAaleemu   14. Qul aghayra Allahi attakhithu waliyyan fatiri alssamawati waal-ardi wahuwa yutAAimu wala yutAAamu qul innee omirtu an akoona awwala man aslama wala takoonanna mina almushrikeena   15. Qul innee akhafu in

AAasaytu rabbee AAathaba yawmin AAatheemin 16. Man yusraf AAanhu yawma-ithin faqad rahimahu wathalika alfawzu almubeenu

Tafsir Ibn Kathir

Allah is the Creator and the Sustainer

Allah states that He is the King and Owner of the heavens and earth and all of what is in them, and that He has written mercy on His Most Honorable Self. It is recorded in the Two Sahihs, that Abu Hurayrah said that the Prophet said,

«إِنَّ اللهَ لَمَّا خَلَقَ الْخَلْقَ، كَتَبَ كِتَابًا عِنْدَهُ فَوْقَ الْعَرْشِ، إِنَّ رَحْمَتِي تَغْلِبُ غَضَبِي»

(When Allah created the creation, He wrote in a Book that He has with Him above the Throne; `My mercy overcomes My anger.') Allah said;

(Indeed He will gather you together on the Day of Resurrection, about which there is no doubt.) swearing by His Most Honored Self that He will gather His servants,

(For appointed meeting of a known Day.) (56:50), the Day of Resurrection that will certainly occur, and there is no doubt for His believing servants in this fact. As for those who deny and refuse, they are in confusion and disarray. Allah's statement,

(Those who destroy themselves) on the Day of Resurrection,

(will not believe.) in the Return and thus do not fear the repercussions of that Day. Allah said next,

(And to Him belongs whatsoever exists in the night and the day.) meaning, all creatures in the heavens and earth are Allah's servants and creatures, and they are all under His authority, power and will; there is no deity worthy of worship except Him,

(and He is the All-Hearing, the All-Knowing.) He hears the statements of His servants and knows their actions, secrets and what they conceal. Allah then said to His servant and Messenger Muhammad , whom He sent with the pure Tawhid and the straight religion, commanding him to call the people to Allah's straight path;

(Say: "Shall I take as a guardian any other than Allah, the Creator of the heavens and the earth") Similarly, Allah said,

(Say: "Do you order me to worship other than Allah, O you fools") (39:64). The meaning here is, I will not take a guardian except Allah, without partners, for He is the Creator of the heavens and earth Who orignated them without precedent,

(And it is He Who feeds but is not fed.) For He sustains His creatures without needing them. Allah also said;

(And I created not the Jinn and humans except that they should worship Me (Alone).) (51:56) Some scholars read it, "And it is He Who feeds but He does not eat." meaning, Allah does not eat. Abu Hurayrah narrated, "A man from Al-Ansar from the area of Quba' invited the Prophet to eat some food, and we went along with the Prophet. When the Prophet ate and washed his hands, he said,

«الْحَمْدُ لِلَّهِ الَّذِي يُطْعِمُ وَلَا يُطْعَمُ، وَمَنَّ عَلَيْنَا فَهَدَانَا وَأَطْعَمَنَا، وَسَقَانَا مِنَ الشَّرَابِ، وَكَسَانَا مِنَ الْعُرْيِ، وَكُلَّ بَلَاءٍ حَسَنٍ أَبْلَانَا، الْحَمْدُ لِلَّهِ غَيْرَ مُوَدَّعٍ رَبِّي وَلَا مُكَافَأً وَلَا مَكْفُورٍ، وَلَا مُسْتَغْنًى عَنْهُ، الْحَمْدُ لِلَّهِ الَّذِي أَطْعَمَنَا مِنَ الطَّعَامِ، وَسَقَانَا مِنَ الشَّرَابِ، وَكَسَانَا مِنَ الْعُرْيِ، وَهَدَانَا مِنَ الضَّلَالِ، وَبَصَّرَنَا مِنَ الْعَمَى، وَفَضَّلَنَا عَلَى كَثِيرٍ مِمَّنْ خَلَقَ تَفْضِيلًا، الْحَمْدُ لِلَّهِ رَبِّ الْعَالَمِين»

(All praise is due to Allah, Who feeds but is never fed, He bestowed bounty unto us, Who gave us guidance and fed us, gave us something to drink, covered our nakedness; and for every favor He has given us. All praise is due to Allah, praise that should not be neglected, my Lord, all the while affirming that we will never be able to duly thank Him; nor be appreciative enough of Him, nor be free of needing Him. All thanks and praises are due to Allah Who fed us the food, gave us the drink, covered our nudity, guided us from misguidance, gave us sight from blindness, and honored us above many of His creaturers. All praise is due to Allah, Lord of all that exists.")

(Say: "Verily, I am commanded to be the first of those who submit themselves to Allah as (Muslims).") from this Ummah,

(And be not you of the idolaters. Say: "I fear, if I disobey my Lord, the torment of a Mighty Day.") (6:14-15), the Day of Resurrection,

(Who is averted from) such a torment,

(on that Day, He has surely been Merciful to him) meaning, Allah will have been merciful to him,

(And that would be the obvious success.) Allah also said,

(And whoever is moved away from the Fire and admitted to Paradise, he indeed is successful.) (3:185), success here indicates acquiring profit and negates loss.

Surah: 6 Ayah: 17, Ayah: 18, Ayah: 19, Ayah: 20 & Ayah: 21

﴿ وَإِن يَمْسَسْكَ ٱللَّهُ بِضُرٍّ فَلَا كَاشِفَ لَهُۥ إِلَّا هُوَۖ وَإِن يَمْسَسْكَ بِخَيْرٍ فَهُوَ عَلَىٰ كُلِّ شَىْءٍ قَدِيرٌ ﴾

17. And if Allâh touches you with harm, none can remove it but He, and if He touches you with good, then He is Able to do all things.

﴿ وَهُوَ ٱلْقَاهِرُ فَوْقَ عِبَادِهِۦۚ وَهُوَ ٱلْحَكِيمُ ٱلْخَبِيرُ ﴾

18. And He is the Irresistible, (Supreme) above His slaves, and He is the All-Wise, Well-Acquainted with all things.

﴿ قُلْ أَىُّ شَىْءٍ أَكْبَرُ شَهَٰدَةًۖ قُلِ ٱللَّهُۖ شَهِيدٌۢ بَيْنِى وَبَيْنَكُمْۚ وَأُوحِىَ إِلَىَّ هَٰذَا ٱلْقُرْءَانُ لِأُنذِرَكُم بِهِۦ وَمَنۢ بَلَغَۚ أَئِنَّكُمْ لَتَشْهَدُونَ أَنَّ مَعَ ٱللَّهِ ءَالِهَةً أُخْرَىٰۚ قُل لَّآ أَشْهَدُۚ قُلْ إِنَّمَا هُوَ إِلَٰهٌ وَٰحِدٌ وَإِنَّنِى بَرِىٓءٌ مِّمَّا تُشْرِكُونَ ﴾

19. Say (O Muhammad (peace be upon him)) "What thing is the most great in witness?" Say: "Allâh (the Most Great!) is Witness between me and you; this Qur'ân has been revealed to me that I may therewith warn you and whomsoever it may reach. Can you verily bear witness that besides Allâh there are other alihâ (gods)?" Say "I bear no (such) witness!" Say: "But in truth He (Allâh) is the only one Ilâh (God). And truly I am innocent of what you join in worship with Him."

﴿ ٱلَّذِينَ ءَاتَيْنَٰهُمُ ٱلْكِتَٰبَ يَعْرِفُونَهُۥ كَمَا يَعْرِفُونَ أَبْنَآءَهُمُۘ ٱلَّذِينَ خَسِرُوٓا۟ أَنفُسَهُمْ فَهُمْ لَا يُؤْمِنُونَ ﴾

20. Those to whom We have given the Scripture (Jews and Christians) recognize him (i.e. Muhammad (peace be upon him) as a Messenger of Allâh, and they also know that there is no Ilah (God) but Allâh and Islâm is Allâh's Religion), as they recognize their own sons. Those who have lost (destroyed) themselves will not believe. (Tafsir At-Tabarî)

﴿ وَمَنْ أَظْلَمُ مِمَّنِ ٱفْتَرَىٰ عَلَى ٱللَّهِ كَذِبًا أَوْ كَذَّبَ بِـَٔايَٰتِهِۦٓۗ إِنَّهُۥ لَا يُفْلِحُ ٱلظَّٰلِمُونَ ﴾

21. And who does more aggression and wrong than he who invents a lie against Allâh or rejects His Ayât (proofs, evidences, verses, lessons, revelations)? Verily, the Zâlimûn (polytheists and wrong-doers) shall never be successful.

Transliteration

17. Wa-in yamsaska Allahu bidurrin fala kashifa lahu illa huwa wa-in yamsaska bikhayrin fahuwa AAala kulli shay-in qadeerun   18. Wahuwa alqahiru fawqa AAibadihi wahuwa alhakeemu alkhabeeru 19. Qul ayyu shay-in akbaru shahadatan quli Allahu shaheedun baynee wabaynakum waoohiya ilayya hatha alqur-anu li-onthirakum bihi waman balagha a-innakum latashhadoona anna maAAa Allahi alihatan okhra qul la ashhadu qul innama huwa ilahun wahidun wa-innanee baree-on mimma tushrikoona 20. Allatheena ataynahumu alkitaba yaAArifoonahu kama yaAArifoona abnaahum allatheena khasiroo anfusahum fahum la yu/minoona 21. Waman athlamu mimmani iftara AAala Allahi kathiban aw kaththaba bi-ayatihi innahu la yuflihu alththalimoona

Tafsir Ibn Kathir

Allah is the Irresistible, Able to Bring Benefit and Protect from Harm

Allah states that He Alone brings benefit or harm, and that He does what He wills with His creatures, none can resist His judgment or prevent what He decrees,

(And if Allah touches you with harm, none can remove it but He, and if He touches you with good, then He is able to do all things.) Similarly, Allah said,

(Whatever mercy, Allah may grant to mankind, none can withhold it, and whatever He may withhold, none can grant it thereafter) (35:2). It is recorded in the Sahih that the Messenger of Allah used to supplicate,

«اللَّهُمَّ لَا مَانِعَ لِمَا أَعْطَيْتَ وَلَا مُعْطِيَ لِمَا مَنَعْتَ، وَلَا يَنْفَعُ ذَا الْجَدِّ مِنْكَ الْجَدُّ»

(O Allah, there is none Who can avert what You grant or give what You deprive, and no fortune ever helps the fortunate against You.) This is why Allah said,

(And He is the Irresistible, above His servants,) meaning, to Him the necks are subservient, the tyrants humble before Him and He has complete control over all things. The creatures have all bowed to Allah and are humbled before His grace, honor, pride, greatness, highness and ability over all things. The creatures are insignificant before Him, for they are all under His irresistible decision and power,

(and He is the All-Wise,) in all His actions,

(Well-Acquainted with all things.) Who places everything in its rightful place, grants and favors whomever deserves His favor. Allah said next,

(Say: "What thing is the most great in witness") or what is the greatest witness,

(Say: "Allah (the Most Great!) is Witness between you and I") for He knows what I brought you and what you will answer me with, (this Qur'an has been revealed to me that I may therewith warn you and whomsoever it may reach.) Therefore, this Qur'an is a warner for all those who hear of it. In another Ayah, Allah said,

(But those of the sects that reject it, the Fire will be their promised meeting place.) (11:17) Ar-Rabi` bin Anas said, "Those who follow the Messenger of Allah ought to call to what the Messenger of Allah called to and warn against what he warned against." Allah said next,

("Can you verily bear witness...") O idolators,

("that besides Allah there are other gods" Say, "I bear no (such) witness!") Similarly, in another Ayah, Allah said;

(Then if they testify, testify not you with them.) (6:150) Allah said next,

(Say: "Only He is God, alone, and truly I am innocent of what you join in worship with Him.")

People of the Book Recognize the Prophet Just as They Recognize Their Own Children

Allah says, the People of the Book know what you brought them, O Muhammad , as they know their own children. This is because they received good news from the previous Messengers and Prophets about the coming of Muhammad , his attributes, homeland, his migration, and the description of his Ummah. Allah said next,

(Those who have lost (destroyed) themselves) and thus incurred the ultimate loss,

(will not believe.) in this clear matter. A matter about which the previous Prophets gave good news, and a matter extolled about in ancient and modern times. Allah said next,

(And who does more wrong than he who invents a lie against Allah or rejects His Ayat) meaning, there is no person more unjust than he who lies about Allah and claims that Allah has sent him, while Allah did not send him. There is no person more unjust than he who denies Allah's proofs, signs and evidences,

(Verily, the wrongdoers shall never be successful.) Surely, both of these people will never acquire success, whoever falsely claims that Allah sent him and whoever refuses Allah's Ayat.

Surah: 6 Ayah: 22, Ayah: 23, Ayah: 24, Ayah: 25 & Ayah: 26

﴿ وَيَوْمَ نَحْشُرُهُمْ جَمِيعًا ثُمَّ نَقُولُ لِلَّذِينَ أَشْرَكُواْ أَيْنَ شُرَكَآؤُكُمُ ٱلَّذِينَ كُنتُمْ تَزْعُمُونَ

22. And on the Day when We shall gather them all together, then We shall say to those who joined partners in worship (with Us): "Where are your partners (false deities) whom you used to assert (as partners in worship with Allâh)?"

﴿ ثُمَّ لَمْ تَكُن فِتْنَتُهُمْ إِلَّا أَن قَالُوا وَاللَّهِ رَبِّنَا مَا كُنَّا مُشْرِكِينَ ۝ ﴾

23. There will then be (left) no Fitnah (excuses or statements or arguments) for them but to say: "By Allâh, our Lord, we were not those who joined others in worship with Allâh."

﴿ ٱنظُرْ كَيْفَ كَذَبُوا عَلَىٰ أَنفُسِهِمْ وَضَلَّ عَنْهُم مَّا كَانُوا يَفْتَرُونَ ۝ ﴾

24. Look! How they lie against themselves! But the (lie) which they invented will disappear from them.

﴿ وَمِنْهُم مَّن يَسْتَمِعُ إِلَيْكَ وَجَعَلْنَا عَلَىٰ قُلُوبِهِمْ أَكِنَّةً أَن يَفْقَهُوهُ وَفِىٓ ءَاذَانِهِمْ وَقْرًا وَإِن يَرَوْا كُلَّ ءَايَةٍ لَّا يُؤْمِنُوا بِهَا حَتَّىٰ إِذَا جَآءُوكَ يُجَٰدِلُونَكَ يَقُولُ ٱلَّذِينَ كَفَرُوٓا إِنْ هَٰذَآ إِلَّآ أَسَٰطِيرُ ٱلْأَوَّلِينَ ۝ ﴾

25. And of them there are some who listen to you; but We have set veils on their hearts, so they understand it not, and deafness in their ears; and even if they see every one of the Ayât (proofs, evidences, verses, lessons, signs, revelations, etc.) they will not believe therein; to the point that when they come to you to argue with you, the disbelievers say: "These are nothing but tales of the men of old."

﴿ وَهُمْ يَنْهَوْنَ عَنْهُ وَيَنْـَٔوْنَ عَنْهُ وَإِن يُهْلِكُونَ إِلَّآ أَنفُسَهُمْ وَمَا يَشْعُرُونَ ۝ ﴾

26. And they prevent others from him (from following Prophet Muhammad (peace be upon him)) and they themselves keep away from him, and (by doing so) they destroy not but their own selves, yet they perceive (it) not.

Transliteration

22. Wayawma nahshuruhum jameeAAan thumma naqoolu lillatheena ashrakoo ayna shurakaokumu allatheena kuntum tazAAumoona   23. Thumma lam takun fitnatuhum illa an qaloo waAllahi rabbina ma kunna mushrikeena   24. Onthur kayfa kathaboo AAala anfusihim wadalla AAanhum ma kanoo yaftaroona   25. Waminhum man yastamiAAu ilayka wajaAAalna AAala quloobihim akinnatan an yafqahoohu wafee athanihim waqran wa-in yaraw kulla ayatin la yu/minoo biha hatta itha jaooka yujadiloonaka yaqoolu allatheena kafaroo in hatha illa asateeru al-awwaleena   26. Wahum yanhawna AAanhu wayan-awna AAanhu wa-in yuhlikoona illa anfusahum wama yashAAuroona

Tafsir Ibn Kathir

The Polythiests Shall be Questioned About the Shirk They Committed

About the polytheists, Allah said:

(And on the Day when We shall gather them all together,) This is on the Day of Resurrection, when He will ask them about the idols and rivals that they worshipped instead of Him. Allah will say to them,

(Where are your partners (false deities) whom you used to assert (as partners in worship with Allah)) Allah said in Surat Al-Qasas,

(And (remember) the Day when He will call to them, and say, "Where are My (so-called) partners whom you used to assert") (28:62). Allah's statement,

(There will then be (left) no Fitnah for them) means, argument. `Ata' Al-Khurasani said that,

(There will then be (left) no Fitnah for them) in the face of the affliction that will be placed on them,

(but to say: "By Allah, our Lord, we were not those who joined others (in worship with Allah).") Allah said next,

(Look! How they lie against themselves! But the (lie) which they invented will disappear from them.) which is similar to His other statement,

(Then it will be said to them: "Where are (all) those whom you used to join in worship as partners. Besides Allah" They will say, "They have vanished from us: Nay, we did not invoke (worship) anything before." Thus Allah leads astray the disbelievers.) (40:73-74)

The Miserable Do Not Benefit from the Qur'an

Allah's statement,

(And of them there are some who listen to you; but We have set veils on their hearts, so they understand it not, and deafness in their ears; if they see every one of the Ayat they will not believe therein;) means, they come to you, (O Muhammad), so that they hear you recite the Qur'an, but its recitation does not benefit them, because Allah has set veils on their hearts, and so they do not understand the Qur'an,

(and (set) deafness in their ears;) that prevents them from hearing what benefits them. In another Ayah, Allah said;

(And the example of those who disbelieve, is as that of him who shouts at one who hears nothing but calls and cries.) (2:171) Allah said next, (if they see every one of the Ayat they will not believe therein;) meaning, they will not believe in any of the Ayat, proofs, clear evidences and signs they witness because they do not have sound comprehension or fair judgment. In another Ayah, Allah said,

(Had Allah known of any good in them, He would indeed have made them listen.) (8:23) Allah said,

(to the point that when they come to you to argue with you...) using falsehood against truth,

(those who disbelieve say: "These are nothing but tales of the men of old.") The disbelievers say, what you (O Muhammad) brought us was taken from the books of those who were before us, meaning plagiarized,

(And they prevent others from him and they themselves keep away from him,) They discourage people from following the truth, believing in Muhammad and obeying the Qur'an,

(and they themselves keep away from him,) They thus combine both evil acts, for they neither benefit themselves, nor let others benefit from the Prophet . `Ali bin Abi Talhah said that Ibn `Abbas said that the Ayah,

(And they prevent others from him.) means, they hinder people from believing in Muhammad . Muhammad bin Al-Hanafiyyah said, "The disbelievers of Quraysh used to refrain from meeting Muhammad and they discouraged people from coming to him." Similar was reported from Qatadah, Mujahid and Ad-Dahhak and several others.

(and (by doing so) they destroy not but themselves, yet they perceive (it) not.) They destroy themselves by committing this evil action, and its harm will only touch them. Yet, they do not perceive this fact!

Surah: 6 Ayah: 27, Ayah: 28, Ayah: 29 & Ayah: 30

﴿ وَلَوْ تَرَىٰ إِذْ وُقِفُوا۟ عَلَى ٱلنَّارِ فَقَالُوا۟ يَٰلَيْتَنَا نُرَدُّ وَلَا نُكَذِّبَ بِـَٔايَٰتِ رَبِّنَا وَنَكُونَ مِنَ ٱلْمُؤْمِنِينَ ﴿٢٧﴾ ﴾

27. If you could but see when they will be held over the (Hell) Fire! They will say: "Would that we were but sent back (to the world)! Then we would not deny the Ayât (proofs, evidences, verses, lessons, revelations, etc.) of our Lord, and we would be of the believers!"

﴿ بَلْ بَدَا لَهُم مَّا كَانُوا۟ يُخْفُونَ مِن قَبْلُ ۖ وَلَوْ رُدُّوا۟ لَعَادُوا۟ لِمَا نُهُوا۟ عَنْهُ وَإِنَّهُمْ لَكَٰذِبُونَ ﴿٢٨﴾ ﴾

28. Nay, it has become manifest to them what they had been concealing before. But if they were returned (to the world), they would certainly revert to that which they were forbidden. And indeed they are liars.

$$﴿ وَقَالُواْ إِنْ هِىَ إِلَّا حَيَاتُنَا ٱلدُّنْيَا وَمَا نَحْنُ بِمَبْعُوثِينَ ۝ ﴾$$

29. And they said: "There is no (other life) but our (present) life of this world, and never shall we be resurrected (on the Day of Resurrection)."

$$﴿ وَلَوْ تَرَىٰٓ إِذْ وُقِفُواْ عَلَىٰ رَبِّهِمْ قَالَ أَلَيْسَ هَـٰذَا بِٱلْحَقِّ قَالُواْ بَلَىٰ وَرَبِّنَا قَالَ فَذُوقُواْ ٱلْعَذَابَ بِمَا كُنتُمْ تَكْفُرُونَ ۝ ﴾$$

30. If you could but see when they will be held (brought and made to stand) in front of their Lord! He will say: "Is not this (Resurrection and the taking of the accounts) the truth?" They will say: "Yes, by our Lord!" He will then say: "So taste you the torment because you used not to believe."

Transliteration

27. Walaw tara ith wuqifoo AAala alnnari faqaloo ya laytana nuraddu wala nukaththiba bi-ayati rabbina wanakoona mina almu/mineena 28. Bal bada lahum ma kanoo yukhfoona min qablu walaw ruddoo laAAadoo lima nuhoo AAanhu wa-innahum lakathiboona 29. Waqaloo in hiya illa hayatuna alddunya wama nahnu bimabAAootheena 30. Walaw tara ith wuqifoo AAala rabbihim qala alaysa hatha bialhaqqi qaloo bala warabbina qala fathooqoo alAAathaba bima kuntum takfuroona

Tafsir Ibn Kathir

Wishes and Hopes Do Not Help One When He Sees the Torment

Allah mentions the condition of the disbelievers when they are made to stand before the Fire on the Day of Resurrection and witness its chains and restraints, along with seeing the horrible, momentous conditions in the Fire with their own eyes. This is when the disbelievers will say,

("Would that we were but sent back (to the world)! Then we would not deny the Ayat of our Lord, and we would be of the believers!") They wish that they would be sent back to the life of the world so that they could perform righteous deeds, refrain from disbelieving in the Ayat of their Lord and be among the believers. Allah said,

(Nay, what they had been concealing before has become manifest to them.) meaning, the disbelief, denial and rebellion that they used to hide in their hearts will then be uncovered, even though they will try to hide this fact in this life and the Hereafter. Earlier, Allah said,

(There will then be (left) no trial for them but to say: "By Allah, our Lord, we were not those who joined others in worship with Allah." Look! How they lie against themselves! But the (lie) which they invented will disappear from them.) It is also possible that the meaning here is that the disbelievers will realize the truth that they knew all along in their hearts, that is, that what the Messengers brought them in this life is true, although they used to deny his Message before their followers. Allah said that Musa said to Fir`awn,

("Verily, you know that these signs have clearly been sent down by none but the Lord of the heavens and the earth as eye-opening evidence.") (17:102) Allah said about Fir`awn and his people,

(And they belied them (those Ayat) wrongfully and arrogantly, though they were themselves convinced thereof.) (27:14)

(Nay, it has become manifest to them what they had been concealing before.) (6:28) When this occurs, and the disbelievers ask to be returned to this life, they will not do so because they truly wish to embrace the faith. Rather, they ask to be returned to this life for fear of the torment that they are witnessing before them, as punishment for the disbelief they committed, and to try and avoid the Fire that they see before their eyes.

(But if they were returned, they would certainly revert to that which they were forbidden. And indeed they are liars.) meaning, they lie when they say they wish to go back to this life so that they can embrace the faith. Allah states that even if they were sent back to the life of this world, they will again commit the disbelief and defiance that they were prohibited.

(And indeed they are liars.) in their statement that,

("Would that we were but sent back! Then we would not deny the Ayat of our Lord, and we would be of the believers!" Nay, what they had been concealing before has become manifest to them. But if they were returned, they would certainly revert to that which they were forbidden. And indeed they are liars. And they said: "There is no (other life) but our (present) life of this world, and never shall we be resurrected.") Therefore, they will revert to their old behavior and say,

(There is no life but our life of this world) and there is no Hereafter,

(and never shall we be resurrected.) Allah said,

(If you could but see when they will stand before their Lord!) in front of Him,

("Is not this the truth") meaning, is not Resurrection true, contarary to what you thought,

(They will say: "Yes, by our Lord!" He will then say: "So taste you the torment because you used not to believe.") and because you today denied Resurrection. Therefore, taste the torment,

("Is this magic, or do you not see") (52:15)

Surah: 6 Ayah: 31 & Ayah: 32

﴿ قَدْ خَسِرَ ٱلَّذِينَ كَذَّبُواْ بِلِقَآءِ ٱللَّهِ ۖ حَتَّىٰٓ إِذَا جَآءَتْهُمُ ٱلسَّاعَةُ بَغْتَةً قَالُواْ يَٰحَسْرَتَنَا عَلَىٰ مَا فَرَّطْنَا فِيهَا وَهُمْ يَحْمِلُونَ أَوْزَارَهُمْ عَلَىٰ ظُهُورِهِمْ ۚ أَلَا سَآءَ مَا يَزِرُونَ ﴿٣١﴾

31. They indeed are losers who denied their Meeting with Allâh, until all of a sudden, the Hour (signs of death) is on them, and they say: "Alas for us that we gave no thought to it," while they will bear their burdens on their backs; and evil indeed are the burdens that they will bear!

﴿ وَمَا ٱلْحَيَوٰةُ ٱلدُّنْيَآ إِلَّا لَعِبٌ وَلَهْوٌ وَلَلدَّارُ ٱلْأَخِرَةُ خَيْرٌ لِّلَّذِينَ يَتَّقُونَ أَفَلَا تَعْقِلُونَ ﴿٣٢﴾ ﴾

32. And the life of this world is nothing but play and amusement. But far better is the house in the Hereafter for those who are Al-Muttaqûn (the pious - see V.2:2). Will you not then understand?

Transliteration

31. Qad khasira allatheena kaththaboo biliqa-i Allahi hatta itha jaat-humu alssaAAatu baghtatan qaloo ya hasratana AAala ma farratna feeha wahum yahmiloona awzarahum AAala thuhoorihim ala saa ma yaziroona 32. Wama alhayatu alddunya illa laAAibun walahwun walalddaru al-akhirati khayrun lillatheena yattaqoona afala taAAqiloona

Tafsir Ibn Kathir

Allah describes the regret of the disbelievers when facing Him, and their disappointment at the commencement, along with their sorrow for not performing good deeds and for their evil deeds.

This is why Allah said,

(until all of a sudden, the Hour (signs of death) is upon them, and they say: "Alas for us that we gave no thought to it.") `It' here refers to either the life of this world, or the affairs of the Hereafter. Allah's statement,

(while they will bear their burdens on their backs; and evil indeed are the burdens that they will bear!) Asbat said that As-Suddi said, "Upon entering his grave, every unjust person will meet a man with an ugly face, dark skin, awful odor, wearing dirty clothes, who will enter his grave with him. When the unjust person sees him, he will say, `How ugly is your face!' He will reply, `So was your work, it was ugly.' The unjust person will say, `How foul is the odor coming from you!' He will reply, `Such was the case with your work, it stunk.' The unjust person will say, `How dirty are your clothes!' He will reply, `And your work too was dirty.' The unjust person will ask, `Who are you' He will reply, `I am your deeds.' So he will remain with the unjust person in his grave, and when he is resurrected on the Day of Resurrection, his companion will say to him, `In the life of the world, I used to carry you because you followed desire and lust. Today, you carry me.' So he will ride on the unjust person's back and lead him until he enters the Fire. So Allah said,

(while they will bear their burdens on their backs; and evil indeed are the burdens that they will bear!) (6:31)" Allah's statement,

(And the life of this world is nothing but play and amusement.) means, most of it is play and amusement,

(But far better is the abode of the Hereafter for those who have Taqwa. Will you not then understand)

Surah: 6 Ayah: 33, Ayah: 34, Ayah: 35 & Ayah: 36

﴿ قَدْ نَعْلَمُ إِنَّهُ لَيَحْزُنُكَ ٱلَّذِى يَقُولُونَ ۖ فَإِنَّهُمْ لَا يُكَذِّبُونَكَ وَلَٰكِنَّ ٱلظَّٰلِمِينَ بِـَٔايَٰتِ ٱللَّهِ يَجْحَدُونَ ۝ ﴾

33. We know indeed the grief which their words cause you (O Muhammad (peace be upon him)) it is not you that they deny, but it is the Verses (the Qur'ân) of Allâh that the Zâlimûn (polytheists and wrong-doers) deny.

﴿ وَلَقَدْ كُذِّبَتْ رُسُلٌ مِّن قَبْلِكَ فَصَبَرُوا۟ عَلَىٰ مَا كُذِّبُوا۟ وَأُوذُوا۟ حَتَّىٰٓ أَتَىٰهُمْ نَصْرُنَا وَلَا مُبَدِّلَ لِكَلِمَٰتِ ٱللَّهِ ۚ وَلَقَدْ جَآءَكَ مِن نَّبَإِى۟ ٱلْمُرْسَلِينَ ۝ ﴾

34. Verily, (many) Messengers were denied before you (O Muhammad (peace be upon him)) but with patience they bore the denial, and they were hurt; till Our Help reached them, and none can alter the Words (Decisions) of Allâh. Surely there has reached you the information (news) about the Messengers (before you).

﴿ وَإِن كَانَ كَبُرَ عَلَيْكَ إِعْرَاضُهُمْ فَإِنِ ٱسْتَطَعْتَ أَن تَبْتَغِىَ نَفَقًا فِى ٱلْأَرْضِ أَوْ سُلَّمًا فِى ٱلسَّمَآءِ فَتَأْتِيَهُم بِـَٔايَةٍ ۚ وَلَوْ شَآءَ ٱللَّهُ لَجَمَعَهُمْ عَلَى ٱلْهُدَىٰ ۚ فَلَا تَكُونَنَّ مِنَ ٱلْجَٰهِلِينَ ۝ ﴾

35. If their aversion (from you, O Muhammad (peace be upon him) and from that with which you have been sent) is hard on you, (and you cannot be patient of their harm to you), then if you were able to seek a tunnel in the earth or a ladder to the sky, so that you may bring them a sign (and you cannot do it, so be patient). And had Allâh willed, He could have gathered them together (all) on true guidance, so be not you one of those who are Al-Jâhilûn (the ignorant).

﴿ ۞ إِنَّمَا يَسْتَجِيبُ ٱلَّذِينَ يَسْمَعُونَ ۘ وَٱلْمَوْتَىٰ يَبْعَثُهُمُ ٱللَّهُ ثُمَّ إِلَيْهِ يُرْجَعُونَ ۝ ﴾

36. It is only those who listen (to the Message of Prophet Muhammad (peace be upon him)) will respond (benefit from it), but as for the dead (disbelievers), Allâh will raise them up, then to Him they will be returned (for their recompense).

Transliteration

33. Qad naAAlamu innahu layahzunuka allathee yaqooloona fa-innahum la yukaththiboonaka walakinna alththalimeena bi-ayati Allahi yajhadoona 34. Walaqad kuththibat rusulun min qablika fasabaroo AAala ma kuththiboo waoothoo hatta atahum nasruna wala mubaddila likalimati Allahi walaqad jaaka min naba-i almursaleena 35. Wa-in kana kabura AAalayka iAAraduhum fa-ini istataAAta an tabtaghiya nafaqan fee al-ardi aw sullaman fee alssama-i fata/tiyahum bi-ayatin walaw shaa Allahu lajamaAAahum AAala alhuda fala takoonanna mina aljahileena 36. Innama yastajeebu allatheena yasmaAAoona waalmawta yabAAathuhumu Allahu thumma ilayhi yurjaAAoona

Tafsir Ibn Kathir

Comforting the Prophet

Allah comforts the Prophet in his grief over his people's denial and defiance of him,

(We know indeed the grief which their words cause you;) meaning, We know about their denial of you and your sadness and sorrow for them. Allah said in other Ayat,

(So destroy not yourself in sorrow for them.) (35:8), and

(It may be that you are going to kill yourself with grief, that they do not become believers.) (26:3), and,

(Perhaps, you, would kill yourself in grief, over their footsteps (for their turning away from you), because they believe not in this narration.) (18:6) Allah's statement,

(it is not you that they deny, but it is the verses of Allah that the wrongdoers deny.) means, they do not accuse you of being a liar,

(but it is the Verses of Allah that the wrongdoers deny.) It is only the truth that they reject and refuse. Muhammad bin Ishaq mentioned that Az-Zuhri said that Abu Jahl, Abu Sufyan Sakhr bin Harb and Al-Akhnas bin Shurayq once came to listen to the Prophet reciting the Qur'an at night, but these three men were not aware of the presence of each other. So they listened to the Prophet's recitation until the morning, and then left. They met each other on their way back and each one of them asked the others, "What brought you" So they mentioned to each other the reason why they came. They vowed not to repeat this incident so that the young men of Quraysh would not hear of what they did and imitate them. On the second night, each one of the three came back thinking that the other two would not come because of the vows they made to each other. In the morning, they again met each other on their way back and criticized each other, vowing not to repeat what they did. On the third night, they again went to listen to the Prophet and in the morning they again vowed not to repeat this incident. During that day, Al-Akhnas bin Shurayq took his staff and went to Abu Sufyan bin Harb in his house saying, "O Abu Hanzalah! What is your opinion concerning what you heard from Muhammad." Abu Sufyan said, "O Abu Tha`labah! By Allah, I have heard some things that I recognize and know their implications. I also heard some things whose meaning and implications were unknown to me." Al-Akhnas said, "And I the same, by He Whom you swore by!" Al-Akhnas left Abu Sufyan and went to Abu Jahl and asked him, "O Abu Al-Hakam! What is your opinion about what you heard from Muhammad. " Abu Jahl said, "We competed with Bani `Abd Manaf (the Prophet's subtribe) and so we fed as they fed and gave away as they gave away. So, when we were neck and neck with them, just as two horses in a race, they said, `There is a Prophet from among us, to whom revelation from the heaven comes.' So how can we ever beat them at that By Allah we will never believe in him or accept what he says.' This is when Al-Akhnas left Abu Jahl and went away." Allah's statement,

(Verily, (many) Messengers were denied before you, but with patience they bore the denial, and they were hurt, till Our help reached them,) This comforts the Prophet's concern for those who denied and rejected him. Allah also commands the Prophet to be patient, just as the mighty Messengers before him were. He also promised him victory, just as the previous Messengers were victorious and the good end was theirs, after the denial and harm their people placed on them. Then, victory came to them in this life, just as victory is theirs in the Hereafter. Allah said,

(and none can alter the Words of Allah.) This refers to His decision that victory in this life and the Hereafter is for His believing servants. Allah said in other Ayat,

(And, verily, Our Word has gone forth of old for Our servants, the Messengers. That they verily would be made triumphant. And that Our hosts, they verily would be the victors.) (37:171-173), and,

(Allah has decreed: "Verily! It is I and My Messengers who shall be the victorious." Verily, Allah is All-Powerful, Almighty.) (58:21) Allah said;

(Surely, there has reached you the information about the Messengers (before you).) who were given victory and prevailed over the people who rejected them. And you (O Muhammad), have a good example in them. Allah said next,

(If their aversion is hard on you,) and you cannot be patient because of their aversion,

(then if you were able to seek a tunnel in the ground or a ladder to the sky...) `Ali bin Abi Talhah reported that Ibn `Abbas commented, "If you were able to seek a tunnel and bring them an Ayah, or go up a ladder in the sky and bring a better Ayah than the one I (Allah) gave them, then do that." Similar was reported from Qatadah, As-Suddi and others. Allah's statement,

(And had Allah willed, He could have gathered them together upon true guidance, so be not you one of the ignorant.) is similar to His statement,

(And had your Lord willed, those on earth would have believed, all of them together) `Ali bin Abi Talhah reported that Ibn `Abbas said about Allah's statement,

(And had Allah willed, He could have gathered them together upon true guidance,) "The Messenger of Allah was eager that all people believe and be guided to follow him. Allah told him that only those whose happiness Allah has written in the first Dhikr will believe." Allah's statement,

(It is only those who listen, that will respond,) means, only those who hear the speech, comprehend and understand it, will accept your call, O Muhammad ! In another Ayah, Allah said;

(That it may give warning to him who is living, and that the Word may be justified against the disbelievers.) (36:70). Allah's statement,

(but as for the dead, Allah will raise them up, then to Him they will be returned.) refers to the disbelievers because their hearts are dead. Therefore, Allah resembled them to dead corpses as a way of mocking and belittling them, saying,

(but as for the dead (disbelievers), Allah will raise them up, then to Him they will be returned (for their recompense).)

Surah: 6 Ayah: 37, Ayah: 38 & Ayah: 39

﴿ وَقَالُواْ لَوْلَا نُزِّلَ عَلَيْهِ ءَايَةٌ مِّن رَّبِّهِۦ ۚ قُلْ إِنَّ ٱللَّهَ قَادِرٌ عَلَىٰٓ أَن يُنَزِّلَ ءَايَةً وَلَٰكِنَّ أَكْثَرَهُمْ لَا يَعْلَمُونَ ﴾

37. And they said: "Why is not a sign sent down to him from his Lord?" Say: "Allâh is certainly Able to send down a sign, but most of them know not."

﴿ وَمَا مِن دَآبَّةٍ فِى ٱلْأَرْضِ وَلَا طَٰٓئِرٍ يَطِيرُ بِجَنَاحَيْهِ إِلَّآ أُمَمٌ أَمْثَالُكُم ۚ مَّا فَرَّطْنَا فِى ٱلْكِتَٰبِ مِن شَىْءٍ ۚ ثُمَّ إِلَىٰ رَبِّهِمْ يُحْشَرُونَ ﴾

38. There is not a moving (living) creature on earth, nor a bird that flies with its two wings, but are communities like you. We have neglected nothing in the Book, then unto their Lord they (all) shall be gathered.

﴿ وَٱلَّذِينَ كَذَّبُواْ بِـَٔايَٰتِنَا صُمٌّ وَبُكْمٌ فِى ٱلظُّلُمَٰتِ ۗ مَن يَشَإِ ٱللَّهُ يُضْلِلْهُ وَمَن يَشَأْ يَجْعَلْهُ عَلَىٰ صِرَٰطٍ مُّسْتَقِيمٍ ﴾

39. Those who reject Our Ayât (proofs, evidences, verses, lessons, signs, revelations, etc.) are deaf and dumb in darkness. Allâh sends astray whom He wills and He guides on the Straight Path whom He wills.

Transliteration

37. Waqaloo lawla nuzzila AAalayhi ayatun min rabbihi qul inna Allaha qadirun AAala an yunazzila ayatan walakinna aktharahum la yaAAlamoona 38. Wama min dabbatin fee al-ardi wala ta-irin yateeru bijanahayhi illa omamun amthalukum ma farratna fee alkitabi min shay-in thumma ila rabbihim yuhsharoona 39. Waallatheena kaththaboo

bi-ayatina summun wabukmun fee alththulumati man yasha-i Allahu yudlilhu waman yasha/ yajAAalhu AAala siratin mustaqeemin

Tafsir Ibn Kathir

The Idolators Ask for a Miracle

Allah states that the idolators used to proclaim, "Why does not (Muhammad) bring an Ayah from his Lord," meaning, a miracle of their choice! They would sometimes say,

("We shall not believe in you, until you cause a spring to gush forth from the ground for us.") (17:90).

(Say: "Allah is certainly able to send down a sign, but most of them know not.") Certainly, Allah is able to send an Ayah (sign). But, He decided out of His wisdom to delay that, because if He sends an Ayah of their liking and they still do not believe, this will hasten their punishment as with the previous nations. Allah said in other Ayat,

(And nothing stops Us from sending the Ayat but that the people of old denied them. And We sent the she-camel to Thamud as a clear sign, but they did her wrong. And We sent not the signs except to warn, and to make them afraid (of destruction).) (17:59), and,

(If We will, We could send down to them from the heaven a sign, to which they would bend their necks in humility) (26:4).

The Meaning of Umam

Allah said,

(There is not a moving (living) creature on earth, nor a bird that flies with its two wings, but are Umam like you.) Mujahid commented, "Meaning, various species that have distinct names." Qatadah said, "Birds are an Ummah, humans are an Ummah and the Jinns are an Ummah." As-Suddi said that,

(but are Umam like you.) means, creations (or species). Allah's statement,

(We have neglected nothing in the Book,) means, the knowledge about all things is with Allah, and He never forgets any of His creatures, nor their sustenance, nor their affairs, whether these creatures live in the sea or on land. In another Ayah, Allah said;

(And no moving creature is there on earth but its provision is due from Allah. And He knows its dwelling place and its deposit (in the uterus, grave, etc.). All is in a Clear Book.) (11:6), there is a record of their names, numbers, movements, and lack of movement. In another Ayah, Allah said;

(And so many a moving creature there is, that carries not its own provision! Allah provides for it and for you. And He is the All-Hearer, the All-Knower.) (29:60) Ibn Abi Hatim reported that Ibn `Abbas said about the Ayah, (then unto their Lord they (all) shall be gathered.) "Death gathers them." It was also said that the Day of Resurrection gathers them, for in another Ayah, Allah said;

(And when the wild beasts shall be gathered together.) (81:5) `Abdur-Razzaq recorded that Abu Hurayrah said about Allah's statement,

(but are Umam like you. We have neglected nothing in the Book, then unto their Lord they (all) shall be gathered.) "All creatures will be gathered on the Day of Resurrection, the beasts, birds and all others. Allah's justice will be so perfect, that the un-horned sheep will receive retribution from the horned sheep. Allah will then command them, `Be dust!' This is when the disbeliever will say,

("Woe to me! Would that I were dust!")"(78: 40). And this was reported from the Prophet in the Hadith about the Trumpet.

The Disbelievers will be Deaf and Mute in Darkness

Allah said,

(Those who reject Our Ayat are deaf and dumb in darkness.) due to their ignorance, little knowledge and minute comprehension. Their example is that of the deaf-mute who cannot hear nor speak, as well as being blinded by darkness. Therefore, how can such a person find guidance to the path or change the condition he is in Allah said in other Ayat,

(Their parable is that of one who kindled a fire; then, when it illuminated all around him, Allah took away their light and left them in darkness. (So) they could not see. They are deaf, dumb, and blind, so they return not (to the right path)) (2:17-18), and,

(Or like the darkness in a vast deep sea, overwhelmed with a great wave topped by a great wave, topped by dark clouds, darkness, one above another, if a man stretches out his hand, he can hardly see it! And he for whom Allah has not appointed light, for him there is no light.) (24:40) This is why Allah said here,

(Allah sends astray whom He wills and He guides on the straight path whom He wills.) for He does what He wills with His creatures.

Surah: 6 Ayah: 40, Ayah: 41, Ayah: 42, Ayah: 43, Ayah: 44 & Ayah: 45

﴿ قُلْ أَرَءَيْتَكُمْ إِنْ أَتَىٰكُمْ عَذَابُ ٱللَّهِ أَوْ أَتَتْكُمُ ٱلسَّاعَةُ أَغَيْرَ ٱللَّهِ تَدْعُونَ إِن كُنتُمْ صَٰدِقِينَ ۝ ﴾

40. Say (O Muhammad (peace be upon him)) "Tell me if Allâh's Torment comes upon you, or the Hour comes upon you, would you then call upon any one other than Allâh? (Reply) if you are truthful!"

﴿ بَلْ إِيَّاهُ تَدْعُونَ فَيَكْشِفُ مَا تَدْعُونَ إِلَيْهِ إِن شَآءَ وَتَنسَوْنَ مَا تُشْرِكُونَ ۝ ﴾

41. Nay! To Him Alone you would call, and, if He wills, He would remove that (distress) for which you call upon Him, and you would forget at that time whatever partners you joined (with Him in worship)!

﴿ وَلَقَدْ أَرْسَلْنَآ إِلَىٰٓ أُمَمٍ مِّن قَبْلِكَ فَأَخَذْنَٰهُم بِٱلْبَأْسَآءِ وَٱلضَّرَّآءِ لَعَلَّهُمْ يَتَضَرَّعُونَ ۝ ﴾

42. Verily, We sent (Messengers) to many nations before you (O Muhammad (peace be upon him)) And We seized them with extreme poverty (or loss in wealth) and loss in health (with calamities) so that they might humble themselves (believe with humility).

﴿ فَلَوْلَآ إِذْ جَآءَهُم بَأْسُنَا تَضَرَّعُوا۟ وَلَٰكِن قَسَتْ قُلُوبُهُمْ وَزَيَّنَ لَهُمُ ٱلشَّيْطَٰنُ مَا كَانُوا۟ يَعْمَلُونَ ۝ ﴾

43. When Our Torment reached them, why then did they not humble themselves (believe with humility)? But their hearts became hardened, and Shaitân (Satan) made fair-seeming to them that which they used to do.

﴿ فَلَمَّا نَسُوا۟ مَا ذُكِّرُوا۟ بِهِۦ فَتَحْنَا عَلَيْهِمْ أَبْوَٰبَ كُلِّ شَىْءٍ حَتَّىٰٓ إِذَا فَرِحُوا۟ بِمَآ أُوتُوٓا۟ أَخَذْنَٰهُم بَغْتَةً فَإِذَا هُم مُّبْلِسُونَ ۝ ﴾

44. So, when they forgot (the warning) with which they had been reminded, We opened for them the gates of every (pleasant) thing, until in the midst of their enjoyment in that which they were given, all of a sudden, We took them to punishment, and lo! They were plunged into destruction with deep regrets and sorrows.

﴿ فَقُطِعَ دَابِرُ ٱلْقَوْمِ ٱلَّذِينَ ظَلَمُوا۟ وَٱلْحَمْدُ لِلَّهِ رَبِّ ٱلْعَٰلَمِينَ ۝ ﴾

45. So the roots of the people who did wrong were cut off. And all the praises and thanks are to Allâh, the Lord of the 'Alamîn (mankind, jinn, and all that exists).

Transliteration

40. Qul araaytakum in atakum AAathabu Allahi aw atatkumu alssaAAatu aghayra Allahi tadAAoona in kuntum sadiqeena   41. Bal iyyahu tadAAoona fayakshifu ma tadAAoona ilayhi in shaa watansawna ma tushrikoona   42. Walaqad arsalna ila omamin min qablika faakhathnahum bialba/sa-i waalddarra-i laAAallahum yatadarraAAoona   43. Falawla ith jaahum ba/suna tadarraAAoo walakin qasat quloobuhum wazayyana lahumu alshshaytanu ma kanoo yaAAmaloona   44. Falamma nasoo ma thukkiroo bihi fatahna AAalayhim abwaba kulli shay-in hatta itha farihoo bima ootoo akhathnahum baghtatan fa-itha hum mublisoona   45. FaqutiAAa dabiru alqawmi allatheena thalamoo waalhamdu lillahi rabbi alAAalameena

Tafsir Ibn Kathir

The Idolators Call On Allah Alone During Torment and Distress

Allah states that He does what He wills with His creatures and none can resist His decision or avert what He decrees for them. He is the One Who has no partners, Who accepts the supplication from whomever He wills. Allah said,

(Say: "Tell me if Allah's torment comes upon you, or the Hour comes upon you, would you then call upon any one other than Allah (Reply) if you are truthful!") This means, you -- disbelievers -- will not call other than Allah in this case, because you know that none except He is able to remove the affliction. Allah said,

(if you are truthful) by taking gods besides Him.

(Nay! To Him alone you call, and, if He willed, He would remove that (distress) for which you call upon Him, and you forget at that time whatever partners you joined with Him (in worship)!) for in times of necessity, you only call on Allah and forget your idols and false deities. In another Ayah, Allah said;

(And when harm touches you upon the sea, those that you call upon besides Him vanish from you except Him (Allah)) (17:67). Allah said;

(Verily, We sent (Messengers) to many nations before you. And We seized them with extreme poverty...) That is, loss of wealth and diminished provisions,

(and loss of health) various illnesses, diseases and pain,

(so that they might believe with humility) and call Allah and supplicate to Him with humbleness and humility. Allah said;

(When Our torment reached them, why then did they not believe with humility) Meaning: Why do they not believe and humble themselves before Us when We test them with disaster'

(But their hearts became hardened,) for their hearts are not soft or humble,

(and Shaytan made fair-seeming to them that which they used to do.) That is, Shirk, defiance and rebellion.

(So, when they forgot (the warning) with which they had been reminded,) by ignoring and turning away from it,

(We opened to them the gates of everything,) Meaning: `We opened the gates of provisions for them from wherever they wished, so that We deceive them.' We seek refuge with Allah from such an end. This is why Allah said,

f(until in the midst of their enjoyment in that which they were given,) such as wealth, children and provisions, (all of a sudden, We took them to punishment and lo! They were plunged into destruction with deep regrets and sorrows.) They have no hope for any type of good thing. Al-Hasan Al-Basri said, "Whomever Allah gives provision and he thinks that Allah is not testing him, has no wisdom. Whomever has little provision and thinks that Allah will not look at (provide for) him, has no wisdom." He then recited the Ayah,

(So, when they forgot (the warning) with which they had been reminded, We opened to them the gates of every (pleasant) thing, until in the midst of their enjoyment in that which they were given, all of a sudden, We took them to punishment, and lo! They were plunged into destruction with deep regrets and sorrows.) He added, "By the Lord of the Ka`bah! Allah deceived these people, when He gave them what they wished, and then they were punished." Ibn Abi Hatim recorded this statement.

Surah: 6 Ayah: 46, Ayah: 47, Ayah: 48 & Ayah: 49

﴿ قُلْ أَرَءَيْتُمْ إِنْ أَخَذَ ٱللَّهُ سَمْعَكُمْ وَأَبْصَٰرَكُمْ وَخَتَمَ عَلَىٰ قُلُوبِكُم مَّنْ إِلَٰهٌ غَيْرُ ٱللَّهِ يَأْتِيكُم بِهِۦٓ ۗ ٱنظُرْ كَيْفَ نُصَرِّفُ ٱلْءَايَٰتِ ثُمَّ هُمْ يَصْدِفُونَ ۝ ﴾

46. Say (to the disbelievers): "Tell me, if Allâh took away your hearing and your sight, and sealed up your hearts, who is there - an ilâh (a god) other than Allâh who could restore them to you?" See how variously We explain the Ayât (proofs, evidences, verses, lessons, signs, revelations, etc.), yet they turn aside.

﴿ قُلْ أَرَءَيْتَكُمْ إِنْ أَتَىٰكُمْ عَذَابُ ٱللَّهِ بَغْتَةً أَوْ جَهْرَةً هَلْ يُهْلَكُ إِلَّا ٱلْقَوْمُ ٱلظَّٰلِمُونَ ۝ ﴾

47. Say: "Tell me, if the punishment of Allâh comes to you suddenly (during the night), or openly (during the day), will any be destroyed except the Zâlimûn (polytheists and wrong-doing people)?"

﴿ وَمَا نُرْسِلُ ٱلْمُرْسَلِينَ إِلَّا مُبَشِّرِينَ وَمُنذِرِينَ ۖ فَمَنْ ءَامَنَ وَأَصْلَحَ فَلَا خَوْفٌ عَلَيْهِمْ وَلَا هُمْ يَحْزَنُونَ ۝ ﴾

48. And We send not the Messengers but as givers of glad tidings and as warners. So whosoever believes and does righteous good deeds, upon such shall come no fear, nor shall they grieve.

﴿ وَٱلَّذِينَ كَذَّبُواْ بِـَٔايَٰتِنَا يَمَسُّهُمُ ٱلْعَذَابُ بِمَا كَانُواْ يَفْسُقُونَ ۝ ﴾

49. But those who reject Our Ayât (proofs, evidences, verses, lessons, signs, revelations, etc.), the torment will touch them for their disbelief (and for their belying the Message of Muhammad (peace be upon him)) (Tafsir Al-Qurtubî).

Transliteration

46. Qul araaytum in akhatha Allahu samAAakum waabsarakum wakhatama AAala quloobikum man ilahun ghayru Allahi ya/teekum bihi onthur kayfa nusarrifu al-ayati thumma hum yasdifoona 47. Qul araaytakum in atakum AAathabu Allahi baghtatan aw jahratan hal yuhlaku illa alqawmu alththalimoona 48. Wama nursilu almursaleena illa mubashshireena wamunthireena faman amana waaslaha fala khawfun AAalayhim wala hum yahzanoona 49. Waallatheena kaththaboo bi-ayatina yamassuhumu alAAathabu bima kanoo yafsuqoona

Tafsir Ibn Kathir

Allah said to His Messenger, say, O Muhammad , to those rebellious liars,

(Tell me, if Allah took away your hearing and your sight.) just as He gave these senses to you. In another Ayah, Allah said;

(It is He Who has created you, and endowed you with hearing, seeing.) (67:23). The Ayah above might also mean that Allah will not allow the disbelievers to benefit from these senses in religious terms. This is why He said next,

(and sealed up your hearts,.) He also said in other Ayat,

(Or who owns hearing and sight) (10:31), and,

(And know that Allah comes in between a person and his heart.) Allah said;

(Is there a god other than Allah who could restore them to you) Meaning, is there anyone except Allah who is able to give you back these senses if Allah took them from you Only Allah is able to do so, and this is why He said here,

(See how variously We explain the Ayat,) and make them plain and clear, testifying to Allah's Oneness in lordship and that those worshipped besides Him are all false and unworthy.

(yet they turn aside.) After this explanation, they still turn away from the truth and hinder people from following it. Allah's statement,

(Say: "Tell me, if the punishment of Allah comes to you suddenly...") means, while you are unaware -- or during the night -- striking you all of a sudden,

(or openly) during the day, or publicly,

(will any be destroyed except the wrongdoing people) This torment only strikes those who commit injustice against themselves by associating others with Allah, while those who worship Allah alone without partners will be saved from it, and they will have no fear or sorrow. In another Ayah, Allah said;

(It is those who believe and confuse not their belief with Zulm, (wrong or Shirk).) (6:82) Allah's statement,

(And We send not the Messengers but as bearers of glad tidings and as warners.) means, the Messengers bring good news to Allah's servants, as well as, command all that is good and righteous. They also warn those who disbelieve in Allah of His anger and of all types of torment. Allah said,

(So whosoever believes and does righteous good deeds.) meaning, whoever believes in his heart with what the Messengers were sent with and makes his works righteous by imitating them;

(upon such shall come no fear,) concerning the future,

(nor shall they grieve.) about what they missed in the past and left behind them in this world. Certainly, Allah will be the Wali and Protector over what they left behind. Allah said next,

(But those who reject Our Ayat, the torment will strike them for their rebelling.) The torment will strike them because of disbelieving in the Message of the Messengers, defying Allah's commands, committing what He prohibited and transgressing His set limits.

Surah: 6 Ayah: 50, Ayah: 51, Ayah: 52, Ayah: 53 & Ayah: 54

﴿ قُل لَّآ أَقُولُ لَكُمْ عِندِى خَزَآئِنُ ٱللَّهِ وَلَآ أَعْلَمُ ٱلْغَيْبَ وَلَآ أَقُولُ لَكُمْ إِنِّى مَلَكٌ إِنْ أَتَّبِعُ إِلَّا مَا يُوحَىٰ إِلَىَّ قُلْ هَلْ يَسْتَوِى ٱلْأَعْمَىٰ وَٱلْبَصِيرُ أَفَلَا تَتَفَكَّرُونَ ﴿٥٠﴾ ﴾

50. Say (O Muhammad (peace be upon him)) "I don't tell you that with me are the treasures of Allâh, nor (that) I know the Unseen; nor I tell you that I am an angel. I but follow what is revealed to me." Say: "Are the blind and the one who sees equal? Will you not then take thought?"

﴿ وَأَنذِرْ بِهِ ٱلَّذِينَ يَخَافُونَ أَن يُحْشَرُوٓا۟ إِلَىٰ رَبِّهِمْ لَيْسَ لَهُم مِّن دُونِهِۦ وَلِىٌّ وَلَا شَفِيعٌ لَّعَلَّهُمْ يَتَّقُونَ ﴿٥١﴾ ﴾

51. And warn therewith (the Qur'ân) those who fear that they will be gathered before their Lord, when there will be neither a protector nor an intercessor for them besides Him, so that they may fear Allâh and keep their duty to Him (by abstaining from committing sins and by doing all kinds of good deeds which He has ordained).

﴿ وَلَا تَطْرُدِ ٱلَّذِينَ يَدْعُونَ رَبَّهُم بِٱلْغَدَوٰةِ وَٱلْعَشِىِّ يُرِيدُونَ وَجْهَهُۥ مَا عَلَيْكَ مِنْ حِسَابِهِم مِّن شَىْءٍ وَمَا مِنْ حِسَابِكَ عَلَيْهِم مِّن شَىْءٍ فَتَطْرُدَهُمْ فَتَكُونَ مِنَ ٱلظَّٰلِمِينَ ۝ ﴾

52. And turn not away those who invoke their Lord, morning and afternoon seeking His Face. You are accountable for them in nothing, and they are accountable for you in nothing, that you may turn them away, and thus become of the Zâlimûn (unjust).

﴿ وَكَذَٰلِكَ فَتَنَّا بَعْضَهُم بِبَعْضٍ لِّيَقُولُوٓا۟ أَهَٰٓؤُلَآءِ مَنَّ ٱللَّهُ عَلَيْهِم مِّنۢ بَيْنِنَآ أَلَيْسَ ٱللَّهُ بِأَعْلَمَ بِٱلشَّٰكِرِينَ ۝ ﴾

53. Thus We have tried some of them with others, that they might say: "Is it these (poor believers) that Allâh has favored from amongst us?" Does not Allâh know best those who are grateful?

﴿ وَإِذَا جَآءَكَ ٱلَّذِينَ يُؤْمِنُونَ بِـَٔايَٰتِنَا فَقُلْ سَلَٰمٌ عَلَيْكُمْ كَتَبَ رَبُّكُمْ عَلَىٰ نَفْسِهِ ٱلرَّحْمَةَ أَنَّهُۥ مَنْ عَمِلَ مِنكُمْ سُوٓءًۢا بِجَهَٰلَةٍ ثُمَّ تَابَ مِنۢ بَعْدِهِۦ وَأَصْلَحَ فَأَنَّهُۥ غَفُورٌ رَّحِيمٌ ۝ ﴾

54. When those who believe in Our Ayât (proofs, evidences, verses, lessons, signs, revelations, etc.) come to you, say: "Salâmun 'Alaikum" (peace be on you); your Lord has written (prescribed) Mercy for Himself, so that, if any of you does evil in ignorance, and thereafter repents and does righteous good deeds (by obeying Allâh), then surely, He is Oft-Forgiving, Most Merciful.

Transliteration

50. Qul la aqoolu lakum AAindee khaza-inu Allahi wala aAAlamu alghayba wala aqoolu lakum innee malakun in attabiAAu illa ma yooha ilayya qul hal yastawee al-aAAma waalbaseeru afala tatafakkaroona 51. Waanthir bihi allatheena yakhafoona an yuhsharoo ila rabbihim laysa lahum min doonihi waliyyun wala shafeeAAun laAAallahum yattaqoona 52. Wala tatrudi allatheena yadAAoona rabbahum bialghadati waalAAashiyyi yureedoona wajhahu ma AAalayka min hisabihim min shay-in wama min hisabika AAalayhim min shay-in fatatrudahum fatakoona mina alththalimeena 53. Wakathalika fatanna baAAdahum bibaAAdin liyaqooloo ahaola-i manna Allahu AAalayhim min baynina alaysa Allahu bi-aAAlama bialshshakireena 54. Wa-itha jaaka allatheena yu/minoona bi-ayatina faqul salamun AAalaykum kataba rabbukum AAala nafsihi alrrahmata annahu man AAamila minkum soo-an bijahalatin thumma taba min baAAdihi waaslaha faannahu ghafoorun raheemun

Tafsir Ibn Kathir

The Messenger Neither has the Key to Allah's Treasures, Nor Knows the Unseen

Allah said to His Messenger ,

(Say: "I don't tell you that with me are the treasures of Allah.") meaning, I do not own Allah's treasures or have any power over them,

(nor (that) I know the Unseen,) and I do not say that I know the Unseen, because its knowledge is with Allah and I only know what He conveys of it to me.

(nor I tell you that I am an angel.) meaning, I do not claim that I am an angel. I am only a human to whom Allah sends revelation, and He honored me with this duty and favored me with it.

(I but follow what is revealed to me.) and I never disobey the revelation in the least.

(Say: "Are the blind and the one who sees equal") meaning, `Is the one who is guided, following the truth, equal to the one misled'

(Will you not then consider) In another Ayah, Allah said;

(Shall he then who knows that what has been revealed to you from your Lord is the truth, be like him who is blind But it is only the men of understanding that pay heed.) (13:19) Allah's statement,

(And warn therewith those who fear that they will be gathered before their Lord, when there will be neither a protector nor an intercessor for them besides Him,) means, warn with this Qur'an, O Muhammad ,

(Those who live in awe for fear of their Lord) (23:57), who,

(Fear their Lord, and dread the terrible reckoning.) (13:21),

(those who fear that they will be gathered before their Lord,) on the Day of Resurrection,

(when there will be neither a protector nor an intercessor for them besides Him,) for on that Day, they will have no relative or intercessor who can prevent His torment if He decides to punish them with it,

(so that they may have Taqwa.) Therefore, warn of the Day when there will be no judge except Allah,

(so that they may have Taqwa.) and thus work good deeds in this life, so that their good deeds may save them on the Day of Resurrection from Allah's torment, and so that He will grant them multiple rewards.

Prohibiting the Messenger from Turning the Weak Away and the Order to Honor Them

Allah said,

(And turn not away those who invoke their Lord, morning and evening seeking His Face.) meaning, do not turn away those who have these qualities, instead make them your companions and associates. In another Ayah, Allah said;

(And keep yourself patiently with those who call on their Lord morning and evening, seeking His Face, and let not your eyes overlook them, desiring the pomp and glitter of the life of the world; and obey not him whose heart We have made heedless of Our remembrance, one who follows his own lusts and whose affair (deeds) has been lost.)(18:28) Allah's statement,

(invoke their Lord...) refers to those who worship Him and supplicate to Him,

(morning and evening.) referring to the obligatory prayers, according to Sa`id bin Al-Musayyib, Mujahid, Al-Hasan and Qatadah. In another Ayah, Allah said;

(And your Lord said, "Invoke Me, I will respond (to your invocation).") (40:60), I will accept your supplication. Allah said next,

(seeking His Face.) meaning, they seek Allah's Most Generous Face, by sincerity for Him in the acts of worship and obedience they perform. Allah said;

(You are accountable for them in nothing, and they are accountable for you in nothing,) This is similar to the answer Nuh gave to his people when they said,

(Shall we believe in you, when the meekest (of the people) follow you") (26:111). Nuh answered them,

(And what knowledge have I of what they used to do Their account is only with my Lord, if you could (but) know.) (26:112-113), meaning, their reckoning is for Allah not me, just as my reckoning is not up to them. Allah said here,

(that you may turn them away, and thus become of the wrongdoers.) meaning, you will be unjust if you turn them away. Allah's statement,

(Thus We have tried some of them with others) means, We tested, tried and checked them with each other,

(That they might say: "Is it these (poor believers) that Allah has favored from amongst us") This is because at first, most of those who followed the Messenger of Allah were the weak among the people, men, women, slaves, and only a few chiefs or noted men followed him. Nuh, was also addressed by his people

(Nor do we see any follow you but the meekest among us and they (too) followed you without thinking.) (11:27) KHeraclius, emperor of Rome, asked Abu Sufyan, "Do the noblemen or the weak among people follow him (Muhammad)" Abu Sufyan replied,

"Rather the weak among them." Heraclius commented, "Such is the case with followers of the Messengers." The idolators of Quraysh used to mock the weak among them who believed in the Prophet and they even tortured some of them. They used to say, "Are these the ones whom Allah favored above us," meaning, Allah would not guide these people, instead of us, to all that is good, if indeed what they embraced is good. Allah mentioned similar statements in the Qur'an from the disbelievers,

(Had it been a good thing, they (weak and poor) would not have preceded us to it!) (46:11), and,

(And when Our clear verses are recited to them, those who disbelieve say to those who believe: "Which of the two groups is best in position and station.") (19:73) Allah said in reply,

(And how many a generation (past nations) have We destroyed before them, who were better in wealth, goods and outward appearance) (19:74). Here, Allah answered the disbelievers when they said,

("Is it these (poor believers) that Allah has favored from amongst us" Does not Allah know best those who are grateful) Meaning is not Allah more knowledgeable of those who thank and appreciate Him in statement, action and heart Thus Allah directs these believers to the ways of peace, transfers them from darkness to light by His leave, and guides them to the straight path. In another Ayah, Allah said;

(As for those who strive hard for Us (Our cause), We will surely guide them to Our paths (i.e. Allah's religion). And verily, Allah is with the doers of good") (29:69). An authentic Hadith states,

«إِنَّ اللهَ لَا يَنْظُرُ إِلَى صُوَرِكُمْ وَلَا إِلَى أَلْوَانِكُمْ، وَلَكِنْ يَنْظُرُ إِلَى قُلُوبِكُمْ وَأَعْمَالِكُمْ»

(Allah does not look at your shapes or colors, but He looks at your heart and actions.) Allah's statement,

(When those who believe in Our Ayat come to you, say: "Salamun `Alaykum" (peace be on you);) means, honor them by returning the Salam and give them the good news of Allah's exclusive, encompassing mercy for them. So Allah said;

(your Lord has written Mercy for Himself,) meaning, He has obliged His Most Honored Self to grant mercy, as a favor, out of His compassion and beneficence,

(So that, if any of you does evil in ignorance...) as every person who disobeys Allah does it in ignorance,

(and thereafter repents and does righteous good deeds,) by repenting from the sins that he committed, intending not to repeat the sin in the future, but to perform righteous deeds, (then surely, He is Oft-Forgiving Most Merciful.) Imam Ahmad recorded that Abu Hurayrah said that the Messenger of Allah said,

«لَمَّا قَضَى اللهُ الْخَلْقَ كَتَبَ فِي كِتَابٍ فَهُوَ عِنْدَهُ فَوْقَ الْعَرْشِ: إِنَّ رَحْمَتِي غَلَبَتْ غَضَبِي»

(When Allah finished with the creation, He wrote in a Book that He has with Him above the Throne, `My mercy prevails over My anger'.) This Hadith was also recorded in the The Two Sahihs.

Surah: 6 Ayah: 55, Ayah: 56, Ayah: 57, Ayah: 58 & Ayah: 59

﴿ وَكَذَلِكَ نُفَصِّلُ الْآيَاتِ وَلِتَسْتَبِينَ سَبِيلُ الْمُجْرِمِينَ ۝ ﴾

55. And thus do We explain the Ayât (proofs, evidences, verses, lessons, signs, revelations, etc.) in detail, that the way of the Mujrimûn (criminals, polytheists, sinners), may become manifest.

﴿ قُلْ إِنِّي نُهِيتُ أَنْ أَعْبُدَ الَّذِينَ تَدْعُونَ مِن دُونِ اللَّهِ قُل لاَّ أَتَّبِعُ أَهْوَاءَكُمْ قَدْ ضَلَلْتُ إِذًا وَمَا أَنَا مِنَ الْمُهْتَدِينَ ۝ ﴾

56. Say (O Muhammad (peace be upon him)) "I have been forbidden to worship those whom you invoke (worship) besides Allâh." Say: "I will not follow your vain desires. If I did, I would go astray, and I would not be one of the rightly guided."

﴿ قُلْ إِنِّي عَلَى بَيِّنَةٍ مِّن رَّبِّي وَكَذَّبْتُم بِهِ مَا عِندِي مَا تَسْتَعْجِلُونَ بِهِ إِنِ الْحُكْمُ إِلاَّ لِلَّهِ يَقُصُّ الْحَقَّ وَهُوَ خَيْرُ الْفَاصِلِينَ ۝ ﴾

57. Say (O Muhammad (peace be upon him)) "I am on clear proof from my Lord (Islâmic Monotheism), but you deny it (the truth that has come to me from Allâh). I have not gotten what you are asking for impatiently (the torment). The decision is only for Allâh, He declares the truth, and He is the Best of judges."

﴿ قُل لَّوْ أَنَّ عِندِي مَا تَسْتَعْجِلُونَ بِهِ لَقُضِيَ الأَمْرُ بَيْنِي وَبَيْنَكُمْ وَاللَّهُ أَعْلَمُ بِالظَّالِمِينَ ۝ ﴾

58. Say: "If I had that which you are asking for impatiently (the torment), the matter would have been settled at once between me and you, but Allâh knows best the Zâlimûn (polytheists and wrong-doers)."

Chapter 6: Al-An'am (Cattle, Livestock), Verses 001-110

$$\text{وَعِندَهُۥ مَفَاتِحُ ٱلْغَيْبِ لَا يَعْلَمُهَآ إِلَّا هُوَۚ وَيَعْلَمُ مَا فِى ٱلْبَرِّ وَٱلْبَحْرِۚ وَمَا تَسْقُطُ مِن وَرَقَةٍ إِلَّا يَعْلَمُهَا وَلَا حَبَّةٍ فِى ظُلُمَٰتِ ٱلْأَرْضِ وَلَا رَطْبٍ وَلَا يَابِسٍ إِلَّا فِى كِتَٰبٍ مُّبِينٍ}$$

59. And with Him are the keys of the Ghaib (all that is hidden), none knows them but He. And He knows whatever there is in the land and in the sea; not a leaf falls, but he knows it. There is not a grain in the darkness of the earth nor anything fresh or dry, but is written in a Clear Record.

Transliteration

55. Wakathalika nufassilu al-ayati walitastabeena sabeelu almujrimeena 56. Qul innee nuheetu an aAAbuda allatheena tadAAoona min dooni Allahi qul la attabiAAu ahwaakum qad dalaltu ithan wama ana mina almuhtadeena 57. Qul innee AAala bayyinatin min rabbee wakaththabtum bihi ma AAindee ma tastaAAjiloona bihi ini alhukmu illa lillahi yaqussu alhaqqa wahuwa khayru alfasileena 58. Qul law anna AAindee ma tastaAAjiloona bihi laqudiya al-amru baynee wabaynakum waAllahu aAAlamu bialththalimeena 59. WaAAindahu mafatihu alghaybi la yaAAlamuha illa huwa wayaAAlamu ma fee albarri waalbahri wama tasqutu min waraqatin illa yaAAlamuha wala habbatin fee thulumati al-ardi wala ratbin wala yabisin illa fee kitabin mubeenin

Tafsir Ibn Kathir

The Prophet Understands What He Conveys; Torment is in Allah's Hands Not the Prophet's

Allah says, just as We mentioned the clear signs that testify and direct to the path of guidance, all the while chastising useless arguments and defiance,

(And thus do We explain the Ayat in detail,) that is, whatever responsible adults need explained to them, in the affairs of life and religion,

(That the way of the criminals may become manifest.) so that the path of the criminals who defy the Prophets is apparent and clear. This Ayah was also said to mean, so that you, O Muhammad , are aware of the path of the criminals. Allah's statement,

(Say: "I am on clear proof from my Lord...") means: I have a clear understanding of the Law of Allah that He has revealed to me,

(but you deny it.) meaning, but you disbelieve in the truth that came to me from Allah.

(I do not have what you are hastily seeking) meaning, the torment,

(The decision is only for Allah,) for the ruling of this is with Allah. If He wills, He will punish you soon in response to your wish! If He wills, He will give you respite, out of His great wisdom. This is why Allah said,

(He declares the truth, and He is the best of judges.) and the best in reckoning between His servants. Allah's statement,

(Say: "If I had that which you are asking for impatiently (the torment), the matter would have been settled at once between you and I,") means, if I have what you ask for, I will surely send down what you deserve of it,

(but Allah knows best the wrongdoers) Someone might ask about the meaning of this Ayah compared to the Hadith in the Two Sahihs, from `A'ishah, may Allah be pleased with her, that she said to the Messenger, "O Allah's Messenger ! Have you encountered a day harder than the day (of the battle) of Uhud" The Prophet replied,

«لَقَدْ لَقِيتُ مِنْ قَوْمِكِ، وَكَانَ أَشَدَّ مَا لَقِيتُ مِنْهُمْ يَوْمَ الْعَقَبَةِ، إِذْ عَرَضْتُ نَفْسِي عَلَى ابْنِ عَبْدِيَالِيلَ بْنِ عَبْدِكُلَالٍ، فَلَمْ يُجِبْنِي إِلَى مَا أَرَدْتُ، فَانْطَلَقْتُ وَأَنَا مَهْمُومٌ عَلَى وَجْهِي، فَلَمْ أَسْتَفِقْ إِلَّا بِقَرْنِ الثَّعَالِبِ، فَرَفَعْتُ رَأْسِي، فَإِذَا أَنَا بِسَحَابَةٍ قَدْ ظَلَّلَتْنِي، فَنَظَرْتُ فَإِذَا فِيهَا جِبْرِيلُ عَلَيْهِ السَّلَامُ، فَنَادَانِي فَقَالَ: إِنَّ اللهَ قَدْ سَمِعَ قَوْلَ قَوْمِكَ لَكَ، وَمَا رَدُّوا عَلَيْكَ، وَقَدْ بَعَثَ إِلَيْكَ مَلَكَ الْجِبَالِ، لِتَأْمُرَهُ بِمَا شِئْتَ فِيهِمْ، قَالَ: فَنَادَانِي مَلَكُ الْجِبَالِ وَسَلَّمَ عَلَيَّ، ثُمَّ قَالَ: يَا مُحَمَّدُ إِنَّ اللهَ قَدْ سَمِعَ قَوْلَ قَوْمِكَ لَكَ، وَقَدْ بَعَثَنِي رَبُّكَ إِلَيْكَ، لِتَأْمُرَنِي بِأَمْرِكَ فِيمَا شِئْتَ، إِنْ شِئْتَ أَطْبَقْتُ عَلَيْهِمُ الْأَخْشَبَيْنِ»

(Your people have troubled me alot and the worst trouble was on the day of `Aqabah when I presented myself to Ibn `Abd Yalil bin `Abd Kulal, who did not respond to my call. So I departed, overwhelmed with severe sorrow, proceeded on and could not relax until I found myself at Qarn Ath-Tha`alib where I raised my head towards the sky to see a cloud unexpectedly shading me. I looked up and saw Jibril in it and he called me saying, `Indeed Allah has heard what you said to the people and what they have responded to you. Therefore, Allah has sent the Angel of the Mountains to you so that you may order him to do whatever you wish to these people.' The Angel of the Mountains called and greeted me, and then said, `O Muhammad! verily, Allah has heard how your people responded to you and He has sent me to you so that you could order me to do what you wish. If you like, I will let Al-Akhshabayn (two mountains to the north and south of Makkah) fall on them.' The Prophet said,

«بَلْ أَرْجُو أَنْ يُخْرِجَ اللهُ مِنْ أَصْلَابِهِمْ، مَنْ يَعْبُدُ اللهَ لَا يُشْرِكُ بِهِ شَيْئًا»

No, but I hope that Allah will let them generate offspring who will worship Allah Alone, and will worship none besides Him.) This is the wording of Muslim. Tormenting the disbelievers of Quraysh was offered to the Prophet, but he chose patience and asked Allah for respite for them, so that Allah might let them generate offspring who will not associate anything with Him in worship. Therefore, how can we combine the meaning of this Hadith and the honorable Ayah,

(Say: "If I had that which you are asking for impatiently (the torment), the matter would have been settled at once between you and I, but Allah knows best the wrongdoers.") The answer to this question is, Allah knows the best, that the Ayah states that if the punishment that they asked for was in the Prophet's hand at the time, he would have sent it on them as they asked. As for the Hadith, the disbelievers did not ask the Prophet to send the torment down on them. Rather, the angel responsible for the mountains offered him the choice to let the two mountains to the north and south of Makkah close in on the disbelievers and crush them. The Prophet did not wish that and asked for respite out of compassion for them.

Only Allah Knows the Unseen

Allah said next,

(And with Him are the keys of the Ghayb (all that is hidden), none knows them but He.) Al-Bukhari recorded that Salim bin `Abdullah said that his father said that the Messenger of Allah said,

«مَفَاتِيحُ الْغَيْبِ خَمْسٌ لَا يَعْلَمُهُنَّ إِلَّا اللهُ»

(The keys of the Unseen are five and none except Allah knows them:

(Verily, Allah! With Him (Alone) is the knowledge of the Hour, He sends down the rain, and knows that which is in the wombs. No person knows what he will earn tomorrow, and no person knows in what land he will die. Verily, Allah is All-Knower, All-Aware)") (31:34). Allah's statement,

(And He knows whatever there is on the land and in the sea;) means, Allah's honored knowledge encompasses everything, including the creatures living in the sea and on land, and none of it, not even the weight of an atom on earth or in heaven, ever escapes His knowledge. Allah's statement,

(not a leaf falls, but He knows it.) means, He knows the movements of everything including inanimate things. Therefore, what about His knowledge of the living creatures, especially, those whom the Divine laws have been imposed upon such as mankind and the Jinns In another Ayah, Allah said;

(Allah knows the fraud of the eyes, and all that the breasts conceal.) (40:19)

Surah: 6 Ayah: 60, Ayah: 61 & Ayah: 62

﴿ وَهُوَ ٱلَّذِى يَتَوَفَّىٰكُم بِٱلَّيْلِ وَيَعْلَمُ مَا جَرَحْتُم بِٱلنَّهَارِ ثُمَّ يَبْعَثُكُمْ فِيهِ لِيُقْضَىٰٓ أَجَلٌ مُّسَمًّى ۖ ثُمَّ إِلَيْهِ مَرْجِعُكُمْ ثُمَّ يُنَبِّئُكُم بِمَا كُنتُمْ تَعْمَلُونَ ۝ ﴾

60. It is He, Who takes your souls by night (when you are asleep), and has knowledge of all that you have done by day, then he raises (wakes) you up again that a term appointed (your life period) be fulfilled, then (in the end) unto Him will be your return. Then He will inform you of that which you used to do.

﴿ وَهُوَ ٱلْقَاهِرُ فَوْقَ عِبَادِهِۦ ۖ وَيُرْسِلُ عَلَيْكُمْ حَفَظَةً حَتَّىٰٓ إِذَا جَآءَ أَحَدَكُمُ ٱلْمَوْتُ تَوَفَّتْهُ رُسُلُنَا وَهُمْ لَا يُفَرِّطُونَ ۝ ﴾

61. He is the Irresistible, (Supreme) over His slaves, and He sends guardians (angels guarding and writing all of one's good and bad deeds) over you, until when death approaches one of you, Our Messengers (angel of death and his assistants) take his soul, and they never neglect their duty.

﴿ ثُمَّ رُدُّوٓا۟ إِلَى ٱللَّهِ مَوْلَىٰهُمُ ٱلْحَقِّ ۚ أَلَا لَهُ ٱلْحُكْمُ وَهُوَ أَسْرَعُ ٱلْحَـٰسِبِينَ ۝ ﴾

62. Then they are returned to Allâh, their True Maulâ (True Master (God), the Just Lord (to reward them)) Surely, for Him is the judgement and He is the Swiftest in taking account.

Transliteration

60. Wahuwa allathee yatawaffakum biallayli wayaAAlamu ma jarahtum bialnnahari thumma yabAAathukum feehi liyuqda ajalun musamman thumma ilayhi marjiAAukum thumma yunabbi-okum bima kuntum taAAmaloona 61. Wahuwa alqahiru fawqa AAibadihi wayursilu AAalaykum hafathatan hatta itha jaa ahadakumu almawtu tawaffat-hu rusuluna wahum la yufarritoona 62. Thumma ruddoo ila Allahi mawlahumu alhaqqi ala lahu alhukmu wahuwa asraAAu alhasibeena

Tafsir Ibn Kathir

The Servants are in Allah's Hands Before and After Death

Allah states that He brings death to His servants in their sleep at night, for sleep is minor death. Allah said in other Ayat,

(And (remember) when Allah said: "O `Isa! I will take you and raise you to Myself...") (3:55), and,

(It is Allah Who takes away the souls at the time of their death, and those that die not during their sleep. He keeps those (souls) for which He has ordained death and sends the rest for a term appointed.)(39:42), ,thus mentioning both minor and major death. Allah says,

(It is He, Who takes your souls by night (when you are asleep), and has knowledge of all that you have done by day,) meaning, He knows the deeds and actions that you perform during the day. This Ayah demonstrates Allah's perfect knowledge of His creation, by day and night, and in their movements and idleness. Allah said in other Ayat,

(It is the same (to Him) whether any of you conceal his speech or declare it openly, whether he be hid by night or go forth freely by day.) (13:10), and

(It is out of His mercy that He made night and day, so that you may rest therein), by night,

(and that you may seek of His bounty) by day. Allah said,

(And (We) have made the night as a covering. And (We) have made the day for livelihood.) (78:10-11). Allah said here,

(It is He, Who takes your souls by night (when you are asleep), and has knowledge of all that you have done by day,) (6:60), Then said,

(then he raises (wakes) you up again,) by day, according to Mujahid, Qatadah and As-Suddi. Allah's statement,

(that a term appointed be fulfilled) refers to the life span of every person,

(then (in the end), unto Him will be your return.) on the Day of Resurrection,

(Then He will inform you of what you used to do.) He will reward you, good for good, and evil for evil. Allah's statement,

(He is the Qahir over His servants.) The Qahir means, the one who controls everything, all are subservient to His supreme grace, greatness and majesty,

(and He sends guardians over you,) angels who guard mankind. In another Ayah, Allah said;

(For each (person), there are angels in succession, before and behind him. They guard him by the command of Allah.) (13:11), watching his deeds and recording them. Allah said,

(But verily, over you (are appointed angels in charge of mankind) to watch you.) (82:10), and,

((Remember!) that the two receivers (recording angels) receive, one sitting on the right and one on the left. Not a word does he utter, but there is a watcher by him, ready.) (50:17-18). Allah's statement,

(until when death approaches one of you...) refers to, when one's life span comes to an end and he is dying,

(Our messengers take his soul...) meaning, there are angels who are responsible for this job. Ibn `Abbas and several others said that the Angel of Death has angels who pull the soul from its body and when it reaches the throat, the Angel of Death captures it. Allah said;

(and they never neglect their duty.) They guard the soul of the dead person and take it to wherever Allah wills, to `Illiyyin if he was among the righteous, and to Sijjin if he was among the wicked (disbelievers, sinners, etc.), we seek refuge with Allah from this end. Allah said next,

(Then they are returned to Allah, their Master, the Just Lord.) Imam Ahmad recorded that Abu Hurayrah said that the Prophet said,

«إِنَّ الْمَيِّتَ تَحْضُرُهُ الْمَلَائِكَةُ فَإِذَا كَانَ الرَّجُلُ الصَّالِحُ، قَالُوا: اخْرُجِي أَيَّتُهَا النَّفْسُ الطَّيِّبَةُ كَانَتْ فِي الْجَسَدِ الطَّيِّبِ، اخْرُجِي حَمِيدَةً، وَأَبْشِرِي بِرَوْحٍ وَرَيْحَانٍ وَرَبٍّ غَيْرِ غَضْبَانَ، فَلَا تَزَالُ يُقَالُ لَهَا ذَلِكَ حَتَّى تَخْرُجَ، ثُمَّ يُعْرَجُ بِهَا إِلَى السَّمَاءِ، فَيُسْتَفْتَحُ لَهَا فَيُقَالُ: مَنْ هَذَا؟ فَيُقَالُ: فُلَانٌ، فَيُقَالُ: مَرْحَبًا بِالنَّفْسِ الطَّيِّبَةِ، كَانَتْ فِي الْجَسَدِ الطَّيِّبِ، ادْخُلِي حَمِيدَةً وَأَبْشِرِي بِرَوْحٍ وَرَيْحَانٍ وَرَبٍّ غَيْرِ غَضْبَانَ، فَلَا تَزَالُ يُقَالُ لَهَا ذَلِكَ حَتَّى يُنْتَهَى بِهَا إِلَى السَّمَاءِ الَّتِي فِيهَا اللهُ عَزَّ وَجَلَّ، وَإِذَا كَانَ الرَّجُلُ السَّوْءُ، قَالُوا: اخْرُجِي أَيَّتُهَا النَّفْسُ الْخَبِيثَةُ كَانَتْ فِي الْجَسَدِ الْخَبِيثِ، اخْرُجِي ذَمِيمَةً وَأَبْشِرِي بِحَمِيمٍ وَغَسَّاقٍ، وَآخَرَ مِنْ شَكْلِهِ أَزْوَاجٍ، فَلَا تَزَالُ يُقَالُ لَهَا ذَلِكَ حَتَّى تَخْرُجَ، ثُمَّ يُعْرَجُ بِهَا إِلَى السَّمَاءِ، فَيُسْتَفْتَحُ لَهَا فَيُقَالُ: مَنْ هَذَا؟ فَيُقَالُ: فُلَانٌ، فَيُقَالُ: لَا مَرْحَبًا بِالنَّفْسِ الْخَبِيثَةِ كَانَتْ فِي الْجَسَدِ الْخَبِيثِ، ارْجِعِي ذَمِيمَةً، فَإِنَّهُ لَا يُفْتَحُ لَكَ أَبْوَابُ السَّمَاءِ، فَتُرْسَلُ مِنَ السَّمَاءِ ثُمَّ تَصِيرُ إِلَى الْقَبْرِ، فَيُجْلَسُ الرَّجُلُ الصَّالِحُ، فَيُقَالُ لَهُ مِثْلُ مَا قِيلَ فِي الْحَدِيثِ الْأَوَّلِ، وَيُجْلَسُ الرَّجُلُ السَّوْءُ فَيُقَالُ لَهُ مِثْلُ مَا قِيلَ فِي الْحَدِيثِ الثَّانِي»

Chapter 6: Al-An'am (Cattle, Livestock), Verses 001-110

(The angels attend the dying person. If he is a righteous person, the angels will say, `O pure soul from a pure body! Come out with honor and receive the good news of rest, satisfaction and a Lord Who is not angry.' The angels will keep saying this until the soul leaves its body, and they will then raise it up to heaven and will ask that the door be opened for the soul and it will be asked, `Who is this' It will be said, `(The soul of) so-and-so.' It will be said, `Welcome, to the pure soul that inhabited the pure body. Enter with honor and receive the good news of rest, satisfaction and a Lord Who is not angry.' This statement will be repeated until the soul reaches the heaven above which there is Allah. If the dying person is evil, the angels will say,`Get out (of your body), O wicked soul from a wicked body! Get out in disgrace and receive the news of boiling fluid, a fluid dark, murky, intensely cold and other (torments) of similar kind - all together - to match them.' This statement will be said repeatedly until the evil soul leaves its body. The soul will be raised up to heaven and a request will be made that the door be opened for it. It will be asked, `Who is this' It will be said, `(The soul of) so and so.' It will be said, `No welcome to the wicked soul from the wicked body. Return with disgrace, for the doors of heaven will not be opened for you.' So it will be thrown from heaven until it returns to the grave. So the righteous person sits and similar is said to him as before. And the evil person sits and similar is said to him as before.) It is also possible that the meaning of,

(Then they are returned...) refers to the return of all creation to Allah on the Day of Resurrection, when He will subject them to His just decision. Allah said in other Ayat,

(Say: "(Yes) verily, those of old, and those of later times. All will surely be gathered together for an appointed meeting of a known Day.") (56:49-50) and,

(And We shall gather them all together so as to leave not one of them behind...) (18:47) until,

(And your Lord treats no one with injustice.) (18:49) Allah said here,

(their Master, the Just Lord. Surely, His is the judgement and He is the swiftest in taking account.) (6:62)

Surah: 6 Ayah: 63, Ayah: 64 & Ayah: 65

﴿ قُلْ مَن يُنَجِّيكُم مِّن ظُلُمَـٰتِ ٱلْبَرِّ وَٱلْبَحْرِ تَدْعُونَهُۥ تَضَرُّعًا وَخُفْيَةً لَّئِنْ أَنجَىٰنَا مِنْ هَـٰذِهِۦ لَنَكُونَنَّ مِنَ ٱلشَّـٰكِرِينَ ۝ ﴾

63. Say (O Muhammad (peace be upon him)) "Who rescues you from the darkness of the land and the sea (dangers like storms), (when) you call upon Him in humility and in secret (saying): If He (Allâh) only saves us from this (danger), we shall truly be grateful."

﴿ قُلِ ٱللَّهُ يُنَجِّيكُم مِّنْهَا وَمِن كُلِّ كَرْبٍ ثُمَّ أَنتُمْ تُشْرِكُونَ ۝ ﴾

64. Say (O Muhammad (peace be upon him)) "Allâh rescues you from this and from all (other) distresses, and yet you worship others besides Allâh."

﴿ قُلْ هُوَ ٱلْقَادِرُ عَلَىٰٓ أَن يَبْعَثَ عَلَيْكُمْ عَذَابًا مِّن فَوْقِكُمْ أَوْ مِن تَحْتِ أَرْجُلِكُمْ أَوْ يَلْبِسَكُمْ شِيَعًا وَيُذِيقَ بَعْضَكُم بَأْسَ بَعْضٍ ۗ ٱنظُرْ كَيْفَ نُصَرِّفُ ٱلْـَٔايَـٰتِ لَعَلَّهُمْ يَفْقَهُونَ ﴿٦٥﴾ ﴾

65. Say: "He has power to send torment on you from above or from under your feet, or to cover you with confusion in party strife, and make you to taste the violence of one another." See how variously We explain the Ayât (proofs, evidences, lessons, signs, revelations, etc.), so that they may understand.

Transliteration

63. Qul man yunajjeekum min thulumati albarri waalbahri tadAAoonahu tadarruAAan wakhufyatan la-in anjana min hathihi lanakoonanna mina alshshakireena   64. Quli Allahu yunajjeekum minha wamin kulli karbin thumma antum tushrikoona   65. Qul huwa alqadiru AAala an yabAAatha AAalaykum AAathaban min fawqikum aw min tahti arjulikum aw yalbisakum shiyAAan wayutheeqa baAAdakum ba/sa baAAdin onthur kayfa nusarrifu al-ayati laAAallahum yafqahoona

Tafsir Ibn Kathir

Allah's Compassion and Generosity, and His Power and Torment

Allah mentions how He favors His servants, saving them during times of need, in the darkness of land and at sea, such as when storms strike. In such cases, they call on Allah alone, without partners, in supplication. In other Ayat, Allah said,

(And when harm strikes you at sea, those that you call upon besides Him vanish from you except Him.) (17:67),

(He it is Who enables you to travel through the land and the sea, till when you are in the ships and they sail with them with a favorable wind, and they rejoice, then comes a stormy wind and the waves come to them from all sides, and they think that they are encircled therein, they invoke Allah, making their faith pure for Him alone, saying: "If You deliver us from this, we shall truly be of the grateful".) (10:22), and,

(Is not He (better than your gods) Who guides you in the darkness of the land and the sea, and Who sends the winds as heralds of glad tidings, going before His mercy Is there any god with Allah High Exalted be Allah above all that they associate as partners (with Him)!) (27:63). Allah said in this honorable Ayah,

(Say: "Who rescues you from the dark recesses of the land and the sea, when you call upon Him begging and in secret.") i.e., in public and secret,

((Saying): `If He (Allah) only saves us...) from this distress,

(we shall truly be grateful.) thereafter. Allah said,

Chapter 6: Al-An'am (Cattle, Livestock), Verses 001-110

(Say: "Allah rescues you from these (dangers) and from all distress, and yet you commit Shirk.") meaning, yet you call other gods besides Him in times of comfort. Allah said;

(Say: "He has the power to send torment on you from above or from under your feet,") He said this after His statement,

(And yet you commit Shirk.) Allah said next,

(Say: "He has the power to send torment on you..."), after He saves you. Allah said in Surah Subhan (chapter 17),

(Your Lord is He Who drives the ship for you through the sea, in order that you may seek of His bounty. Truly! He is Ever Merciful towards you. And when harm strikes you upon the sea, those that you call upon besides Him vanish from you except Him. But when He brings you safely to land, you turn away (from Him). And man is ever ungrateful. Do you then feel secure that He will not cause a side of the land to swallow you up, or that He will not send against you a storm of stones Then, you shall find no guardian. Or do you feel secure that He will not send you back a second time to sea, and send against you a hurricane of wind and drown you because of your disbelief, then you will not find any avenger therein against Us) (17:66-69). Al-Bukhari, may Allah grant him His mercy, commented on Allah's statement,

(Say: "He has the power to send torment on you from above or from under your feet, or to Yalbisakum in party strife, and make you taste the violence of one another." See how variously We explain the Ayat, so that they may understand.) "Yalbisakum means, `cover you with confusion', So it means to, `divide into parties and sects'. Jabir bin `Abdullah said, `When this Ayah was revealed,

(Say: "He has power to send torment on you from above") Allah's Messenger said,

«أَعُوذُ بِوَجْهِكَ»

(I seek refuge with Your Face.) (or from under your feet,) he again said,

«أَعُوذُ بِوَجْهِكَ»

(I seek refuge with Your Face.)

(or to cover you with confusion in party strife, and make you to taste the violence of one another.) he said,

«هَذِهِ أَهْوَنُ أَوْ أَيْسَرُ»

(This is less burdensome or easier.)"' Al-Bukhari recorded this Hadith again in the book of Tawhid (in his Sahih), and An-Nasa'i also recorded it in the book of Tafsir.

Another Hadith

Imam Ahmad recorded that Sa`d bin Abi Waqqas said, We accompanied the Messenger of Allah and passed by the Masjid of Bani Mu`awiyah. The Prophet went in and offered a two Rak`ah prayer, and we prayed behind him. He supplicated to his Lord for a long time and then said,

«سَأَلْتُ رَبِّي ثَلَاثًا: سَأَلْتُهُ أَنْ لَا يُهْلِكَ أُمَّتِي بِالْغَرَقِ فَأَعْطَانِيهَا، وَسَأَلْتُهُ أَنْ لَا يُهْلِكَ أُمَّتِي بِالسَّنَةِ فَأَعْطَانِيهَا، وَسَأَلْتُهُ أَنْ لَا يَجْعَلَ بَأْسَهُمْ بَيْنَهُمْ فَمَنَعَنِيهَا»

(I asked my Lord for three: I asked Him not to destroy my Ummah (Muslims) by drowning and He gave that to me. I asked Him not to destroy my Ummah by famine and He gave that to me. And I asked Him not to make them taste the violence of one another, but He did not give that to me.) Muslim, but not Al-Bukhari, recorded this Hadith in the book on Fitan (trials) (of his Sahih).

Another Hadith

Imam Ahmad recorded that Khabbab bin Al-Aratt, who attended the battle of Badr with the Messenger of Allah, said, "I met Allah's Messenger during a night in which he prayed throughout it, until dawn. When the Messenger of Allah ended his prayer, I said, `O Allah's Messenger! This night, you have performed a prayer that I never saw you perform before.' Allah's Messenger said,

«أَجَلْ إِنَّهَا صَلَاةُ رَغَبٍ وَرَهَبٍ، سَأَلْتُ رَبِّي عَزَّ وَجَلَّ فِيهَا ثَلَاثَ خِصَالٍ، فَأَعْطَانِي اثْنَتَيْنِ وَمَنَعَنِي وَاحِدَةً، سَأَلْتُ رَبِّي عَزَّ وَجَلَّ أَنْ لَا يُهْلِكَنَا بِمَا أَهْلَكَ بِهِ الْأُمَمَ قَبْلَنَا فَأَعْطَانِيهَا، وَسَأَلْتُ رَبِّي عَزَّ وَجَلَّ أَنْ لَا يُظْهِرَ عَلَيْنَا عَدُوًّا مِنْ غَيْرِنَا فَأَعْطَانِيهَا، وَسَأَلْتُ رَبِّي عَزَّ وَجَلَّ أَنْ لَا يُلْبِسَنَا شِيَعًا فَمَنَعَنِيهَا»

(Yes, it was a prayer of eagerness and fear. During this prayer, I asked my Lord for three things and He gave me two and refused to give me the third. I asked my Lord not to destroy us with what He destroyed the nations before us and He gave me that. I asked my Lord not to make our enemies prevail above us and He gave me that. I asked my Lord not to cover us with confusion in party strife, but He refused.) An-Nasa'i, Ibn Hibban in his Sahih, and At-Tirmidhi also recorded it. In the book on Fitan, in Al-Jami`, At-Tirmidhi said, "Hasan Sahih". Allah's statement,

(or to cover you with confusion in party strife,) means, He causes you to be in disarray and separate into opposing parties and groups. Al-Walibi (`Ali bin Abi Talhah) reported that Ibn `Abbas said that this Ayah refers to desires. Mujahid and several others said similarly. A Hadith from the Prophet, collected from various chains of narration, states,

«وَسَتَفْتَرِقُ هَذِهِ الأُمَّةُ عَلَى ثَلَاثٍ وَسَبْعِينَ فِرْقَةً، كُلُّهَا فِي النَّارِ إِلَّا وَاحِدَةٌ»

(And this Ummah (Muslims) will divide into seventy-three groups, all of them in the Fire except one.) Allah said;

(and make you taste the violence of one another.) meaning, some of you will esperience torture and murder from one another, according to Ibn `Abbas and others. Allah said next,

(See how variously We explain the Ayat,) by making them clear, plain and duly explained,

(So that they may understand.) and comprehend Allah's Ayat, proofs and evidences.

Surah: 6 Ayah: 66, Ayah: 67, Ayah: 68 & Ayah: 69

﴿ وَكَذَّبَ بِهِ قَوْمُكَ وَهُوَ ٱلْحَقُّ قُل لَّسْتُ عَلَيْكُم بِوَكِيلٍ ۝ ﴾

66. But your people (O Muhammad (peace be upon him)) have denied it (the Qur'ân) though it is the truth. Say: "I am not a Wakîl (guardian) over you."

﴿ لِّكُلِّ نَبَإٍ مُّسْتَقَرٌّ وَسَوْفَ تَعْلَمُونَ ۝ ﴾

67. For every news there is a reality and you will come to know.

﴿ وَإِذَا رَأَيْتَ ٱلَّذِينَ يَخُوضُونَ فِي ءَايَـٰتِنَا فَأَعْرِضْ عَنْهُمْ حَتَّىٰ يَخُوضُواْ فِي حَدِيثٍ غَيْرِهِ ۚ وَإِمَّا يُنسِيَنَّكَ ٱلشَّيْطَـٰنُ فَلَا تَقْعُدْ بَعْدَ ٱلذِّكْرَىٰ مَعَ ٱلْقَوْمِ ٱلظَّـٰلِمِينَ ۝ ﴾

68. And when you (Muhammad (peace be upon him)) see those who engage in a false conversation about Our Verses (of the Qur'ân) by mocking at them, stay away from them till they turn to another topic. And if Shaitân (Satan) causes you to forget, then after the remembrance sit not you in the company of those people who are the Zâlimûn (polytheists and wrong-doers).

﴿ وَمَا عَلَى ٱلَّذِينَ يَتَّقُونَ مِنْ حِسَابِهِم مِّن شَىْءٍ وَلَـٰكِن ذِكْرَىٰ لَعَلَّهُمْ يَتَّقُونَ ۝ ﴾

69. Those who fear Allâh, keep their duty to Him and avoid evil are not responsible for them (the disbelievers) in any case, but (their duty) is to remind them, that

they may fear Allah (and refrain from mocking at the Qur'ân). (The provision of this Verse was abrogated by the Verse 4:140).

Transliteration

66. Wakaththaba bihi qawmuka wahuwa alhaqqu qul lastu AAalaykum biwakeelin 67. Likulli naba-in mustaqarrun wasawfa taAAlamoona 68. Wa-itha raayta allatheena yakhoodoona fee ayatina faaAArid AAanhum hatta yakhoodoo fee hadeethin ghayrihi wa-imma yunsiyannaka alshshaytanu fala taqAAud baAAda alththikra maAAa alqawmi alththalimeena 69. Wama AAala allatheena yattaqoona min hisabihim min shay-in walakin thikra laAAallahum yattaqoona

Tafsir Ibn Kathir

The Invitation to the Truth is Guidance Without Coercion

Allah said,

(But have denied it) denied the Qur'an, guidance and clear explanation that you (O Muhammad) have brought them,

(your people) meaning, Quraysh,

(though it is the truth.) beyond which there is no other truth.

(Say: "I am not responsible for your affairs.") meaning, I have not been appointed a guardian or watcher over you. Allah also said;

(And say: "The truth is from your Lord." Then whosoever wills, let him believe, and whosoever wills, let him disbelieve.) (18:29), This means, my duty is to convey the Message and your duty is to hear and obey. Those who follow me, will acquire happiness in this life and the Hereafter. Those who defy me will become miserable in this life and the Hereafter. So Allah said;

(For every news there is a reality...) meaning, for every news, there is a reality, in that, this news will occur, perhaps after a while, according to Ibn `Abbas and others. Allah said in other Ayat,

(And you shall certainly know the truth of it after a while.) (38:88) and,

((For) each and every matter there is a decree (from Allah).) (13:38). This, indeed, is a warning and a promise that will surely occur,

(and you will come to know.) Allah's statement,

(And when you see those who engage in false conversation about Our verses (of the Qur'an)), by denying and mocking them.

The Prohibition of Sitting with Those Who Deny and Mock Allah's Ayat

(stay away from them till they turn to another topic.) until they talk about a subject other than the denial they were engaged in.

(And if Shaytan causes you to forget...) This command includes every member of this Ummah. No one is to sit with those who deny and distort Allah's Ayat and explain them incorrectly. If one forgets and sits with such people,

(then after the remembrance sit not you) after you remember,

(in the company of those people who are the wrongdoers.). A Hadith states,

《رُفِعَ عَنْ أُمَّتِي الْخَطَأُ وَالنِّسْيَانُ وَمَا اسْتُكْرِهُوا عَلَيْهِ》

(My Ummah was forgiven unintentional errors, forgetfulness and what they are coerced to do.) The Ayah above (6:68) is the Ayah mentioned in Allah's statement,

(And it has already been revealed to you in the Book that when you hear the Verses of Allah being denied and mocked at, then sit not with them, until they engage in a talk other than that; (but if you stayed with them) certainly in that case you would be like them.) (4:140), for, if you still sit with them, agreeing to what they say, you will be just like them. Allah's statement,

(There is no responsibility for them upon those who have Taqwa,) means, when the believers avoid sitting with wrongdoers in this case, they will be innocent of them and they will have saved themselves from their sin. Allah's statement,

(but (their duty) is to remind them, that they may avoid that.), means, We commanded you to ignore and avoid them, so that they become aware of the error they are indulging in, that they may avoid this behavior and never repeat it again.

Surah: 6 Ayah: 70

﴿ وَذَرِ ٱلَّذِينَ ٱتَّخَذُوا۟ دِينَهُمْ لَعِبًا وَلَهْوًا وَغَرَّتْهُمُ ٱلْحَيَوٰةُ ٱلدُّنْيَا وَذَكِّرْ بِهِۦٓ أَن تُبْسَلَ نَفْسٌۢ بِمَا كَسَبَتْ لَيْسَ لَهَا مِن دُونِ ٱللَّهِ وَلِىٌّ وَلَا شَفِيعٌ وَإِن تَعْدِلْ كُلَّ عَدْلٍ لَّا يُؤْخَذْ مِنْهَآ أُو۟لَٰٓئِكَ ٱلَّذِينَ أُبْسِلُوا۟ بِمَا كَسَبُوا۟ لَهُمْ شَرَابٌ مِّنْ حَمِيمٍ وَعَذَابٌ أَلِيمٌۢ بِمَا كَانُوا۟ يَكْفُرُونَ ﴾

70. And leave alone those who take their religion as play and amusement, and whom the life of this world has deceived. But remind (them) with it (the Qur'ân) lest a person be given up to destruction for that which he has earned, when he will find for himself no protector or intercessor besides Allâh, and even if he offers every ransom, it will not be accepted from him. Such are they who are given up to destruction because of that which they have earned. For them will be a drink of boiling water and a painful torment because they used to disbelieve.

Transliteration

70. Wathari allatheena ittakhathoo deenahum laAAiban walahwan wagharrat-humu alhayatu alddunya wathakkir bihi an tubsala nafsun bima kasabat laysa laha min dooni Allahi waliyyun wala shafeeAAun wa-in taAAdil kulla AAadlin la yu/khath minha ola-ika allatheena obsiloo bima kasaboo lahum sharabun min hameemin waAAathabun aleemun bima kanoo yakfuroona

Tafsir Ibn Kathir

Allah said,

(And leave alone those who take their religion as play and amusement, and are deceived by the life of this world.) The Ayah commands to leave such people, ignore them and give them respite, for soon, they will taste a tremendous torment. This is why Allah said,

(But remind with it) meaning, remind the people with this Qur'an and warn them against Allah's revenge and painful torment on the Day of Resurrection. Allah said;

(lest a soul Tubsal for that which one has earned,) meaning, so that it is not Tubsal. Ad-Dahhak from Ibn `Abbas, Mujahid, `Ikrimah, Al-Hasan and As-Suddi said that Tubsal means, be submissive. Al-Walibi said that Ibn `Abbas said that Tubsal means, `be exposed'. Qatadah said that Tubsal means, `be prevented', Murrah and Ibn Zayd said that it means, `be recompensed', Al-Kalbi said, `be reckoned'. All these statements and expressions are similar, for they all mean exposure to destruction, being kept away from all that is good, and being restrained from attaining what is desired. Allah also said;

(Every person is restrained by what he has earned. Except those on the Right.) (74:38-39), and

(when he will find for himself no protector or intercessor besides Allah,) and,

(and even if he offers every ransom, it will not be accepted from him.) meaning, whatever the ransom such people offer, it will not be accepted from them. Allah said in a similar statement,

(Verily, those who disbelieved, and died while they were disbelievers, the (whole) earth full of gold will not be accepted from anyone of them.) (3:91) Allah said here,

(Such are they who are given up to destruction because of that which they have earned. For them will be a drink of boiling water and a painful torment because they used to disbelieve.)

Surah: 6 Ayah: 71, Ayah: 72 & Ayah: 73

﴿ قُلْ أَنَدْعُواْ مِن دُونِ ٱللَّهِ مَا لَا يَنفَعُنَا وَلَا يَضُرُّنَا وَنُرَدُّ عَلَىٰٓ أَعْقَابِنَا بَعْدَ إِذْ هَدَىٰنَا ٱللَّهُ كَٱلَّذِى ٱسْتَهْوَتْهُ ٱلشَّيَٰطِينُ فِى ٱلْأَرْضِ حَيْرَانَ لَهُۥٓ أَصْحَٰبٌ يَدْعُونَهُۥٓ إِلَى ٱلْهُدَى ٱئْتِنَا ۗ قُلْ إِنَّ هُدَى ٱللَّهِ هُوَ ٱلْهُدَىٰ ۖ وَأُمِرْنَا لِنُسْلِمَ لِرَبِّ ٱلْعَٰلَمِينَ ﴿٧١﴾ ﴾

71. Say (O Muhammad (peace be upon him)) "Shall we invoke others besides Allâh (false deities), that can do us neither good nor harm, and shall we turn back on our heels after Allâh has guided us (to true Monotheism)? - like one whom the Shayâtin (devils) have made to go astray in the land in confusion, his companions calling him to guidance (saying): 'Come to us.' " Say: "Verily, Allâh's Guidance is the only guidance, and we have been commanded to submit (ourselves) to the Lord of the 'Alamîn (mankind, jinn and all that exists);

﴿ وَأَنْ أَقِيمُواْ ٱلصَّلَوٰةَ وَٱتَّقُوهُ ۚ وَهُوَ ٱلَّذِىٓ إِلَيْهِ تُحْشَرُونَ ﴿٧٢﴾ ﴾

72. And to perform As-Salât (Iqâmat-as-Salât)", and to be obedient to Allâh and fear Him, and it is He to Whom you shall be gathered.

﴿ وَهُوَ ٱلَّذِى خَلَقَ ٱلسَّمَٰوَٰتِ وَٱلْأَرْضَ بِٱلْحَقِّ ۖ وَيَوْمَ يَقُولُ كُن فَيَكُونُ ۚ قَوْلُهُ ٱلْحَقُّ ۚ وَلَهُ ٱلْمُلْكُ يَوْمَ يُنفَخُ فِى ٱلصُّورِ ۚ عَٰلِمُ ٱلْغَيْبِ وَٱلشَّهَٰدَةِ ۚ وَهُوَ ٱلْحَكِيمُ ٱلْخَبِيرُ ﴿٧٣﴾ ﴾

73. It is He Who has created the heavens and the earth in truth, and on the Day (i.e. the Day of Resurrection) He will say: "Be!", - and it is! His Word is the truth. His will be the dominion on the Day when the Trumpet will be blown. All-Knower of the unseen and the seen. He is the All-Wise, Well-Aware (of all things).

Transliteration

71. Qul anadAAoo min dooni Allahi ma la yanfaAAuna wala yadurruna wanuraddu AAala aAAqabina baAAda ith hadana Allahu kaallathee istahwat-hu alshshayateenu fee al-ardi hayrana lahu as-habun yadAAoonahu ila alhuda i/tina qul inna huda Allahi huwa alhuda waomirna linuslima lirabbi alAAalameena 72. Waan aqeemoo alssalata waittaqoohu wahuwa allathee ilayhi tuhsharoona 73. Wahuwa allathee khalaqa alssamawati waal-arda bialhaqqi wayawma yaqoolu kun fayakoonu qawluhu alhaqqu walahu almulku yawma yunfakhu fee alssoori AAalimu alghaybi waalshshahadati wahuwa alhakeemu alkhabeeru

Tafsir Ibn Kathir

The Parable of Those Who Revert to Disbelief After Faith and Good Deeds

As-Suddi said, "Some idolators said to some Muslims, `Follow us and abandon the religion of Muhammad.' Allah sent down the revelation,

(Say: "Shall we invoke others besides Allah, that can do us neither good nor harm, and shall we turn on our heels...") by reverting to disbelief,

("...after Allah has guided us.") for if we do this, our example will be like he whom the devils have caused to wander in confusion throughout the land. Allah says here, your example, if you revert to disbelief after you believed, is that of a man who went with some people on a road, but he lost his way and the devils led him to wander in confusion over the land. Meanwhile, his companions on the road were calling him to come to them saying, `Come back to us, for we are on the path.' But, he refused to go back to them. This is the example of he who follows the devil after recognizing Muhammad, and Muhammad is the person who is calling the people to the path, and the path is Islam." Ibn Jarir recorded this statement. Allah's statement, j

(Like one whom the Shayatin (devils) have made to go astray (wandering) through the land,) refers to ghouls,

(calling him) by his name, his father's and his grandfather's names. So he follows the devils' call thinking that it is a path of guidance, but by the morning he will find himself destroyed and perhaps they eat him. The Jinns will then let him wander in a wasteland where he will die of thirst. This is the example of those who follow the false gods that are being worshipped instead of Allah, Most Honored. Ibn Jarir also recorded this. Allah said,

(Say: "Verily, Allah's guidance is the only guidance,") Allah said in other instances,

(And whomsoever Allah guides, for him there will be none to misguide him.) (39:37), and,

(If you covet for their guidance, then verily Allah guides not those whom He makes to go astray. And they will have no helpers.) (17:37) Allah's statement,

(and we have been commanded to submit to the Lord of all that exists.) means, we were commanded to worship Allah in sincerity to Him alone, without partners.

(And to perform the Salah, and have Taqwa of Him.) meaning, we were commanded to perform the prayer and to fear Allah in all circumstances,

(and it is He to Whom you shall be gathered.) on the Day of Resurrection.

(It is He Who has created the heavens and the earth in truth.) meaning, in justice, and He is their Originator and Owner Who governs their affairs and the affairs of their inhabitants. Allah said, (and on the Day He will say: "Be!" it shall become.) Referring to the Day of Resurrection, which will come faster than the blink of an eye, when Allah says to it, `Be.'

As-Sur; The Trumpet

Allah's statement,

(on the Day when the Sur will be blown...) refers to His statement,

(and on the Day He will say: "Be!" it shall become.) as we stated above. Or, it means,

(His will be the dominion on the Day when the Sur will be blown.) Allah said in other Ayat,

(Whose is the kingdom this Day It is Allah's, the One, the Irresistible!) (40:16), and,

(The sovereignty on that Day will be the true (sovereignty), belonging to the Most Beneficent (Allah), and it will be a hard Day for the disbelievers.) (25:26) The Sur is the Trumpet into which the angel Israfil, peace be upon him, will blow. The Messenger of Allah said,

(Israfil has held the Sur in his mouth and lowered his forehead, awaiting the command to blow in it.) Muslim recorded this Hadith in his Sahih. Imam Ahmad recorded that `Abdullah bin `Amr said, "A bedouin man said, `O Allah's Messenger! What is the Sur' He said,

》قَرْنٌ يُنْفَخُ فِيهِ《

(A Trumpet which will be blown.)"

Surah: 6 Ayah: 74, Ayah: 75, Ayah: 76, Ayah: 77, Ayah: 78 & Ayah: 79

﴿ ۞ وَإِذْ قَالَ إِبْرَاهِيمُ لِأَبِيهِ ءَازَرَ أَتَتَّخِذُ أَصْنَامًا ءَالِهَةً إِنِّي أَرَاكَ وَقَوْمَكَ فِي ضَلَالٍ مُّبِينٍ ۝ ﴾

74. And (remember) when Ibrâhîm (Abraham) said to his father Azar: "Do you take idols as âlihâ (gods)? Verily, I see you and your people in manifest error."

﴿ وَكَذَلِكَ نُرِى إِبْرَاهِيمَ مَلَكُوتَ ٱلسَّمَـٰوَٰتِ وَٱلْأَرْضِ وَلِيَكُونَ مِنَ ٱلْمُوقِنِينَ ۝ ﴾

75. Thus did we show Ibrâhîm (Abraham) the kingdom of the heavens and the earth that he be one of those who have Faith with certainty.

$$\left\{\text{فَلَمَّا جَنَّ عَلَيْهِ ٱلَّيْلُ رَءَا كَوْكَبًا ۖ قَالَ هَـٰذَا رَبِّى ۖ فَلَمَّا أَفَلَ قَالَ لَآ أُحِبُّ ٱلْـَٔافِلِينَ ۝}\right\}$$

76. When the night covered him over with darkness he (peace be upon him) a star. He said: "This is my lord." But when it set, he said: "I like not those that set."

$$\left\{\text{فَلَمَّا رَءَا ٱلْقَمَرَ بَازِغًا قَالَ هَـٰذَا رَبِّى ۖ فَلَمَّا أَفَلَ قَالَ لَئِن لَّمْ يَهْدِنِى رَبِّى لَأَكُونَنَّ مِنَ ٱلْقَوْمِ ٱلضَّآلِّينَ ۝}\right\}$$

77. When he saw the moon rising up, he said: "This is my lord." But when it set, he said: "Unless my Lord guides me, I shall surely be among the people who went astray."

$$\left\{\text{فَلَمَّا رَءَا ٱلشَّمْسَ بَازِغَةً قَالَ هَـٰذَا رَبِّى هَـٰذَآ أَكْبَرُ ۖ فَلَمَّآ أَفَلَتْ قَالَ يَـٰقَوْمِ إِنِّى بَرِىٓءٌ مِّمَّا تُشْرِكُونَ ۝}\right\}$$

78. When he saw the sun rising up, he said: "This is my lord. This is greater." But when it set, he said: "O my people! I am indeed free from all that you join as partners (in worship with Allâh).

$$\left\{\text{إِنِّى وَجَّهْتُ وَجْهِىَ لِلَّذِى فَطَرَ ٱلسَّمَـٰوَٰتِ وَٱلْأَرْضَ حَنِيفًا ۖ وَمَآ أَنَا۠ مِنَ ٱلْمُشْرِكِينَ ۝}\right\}$$

79. Verily, I have turned my face towards Him Who has created the heavens and the earth Hanîfa, (Islâmic Monotheism, i.e. worshipping none but Allâh Alone), and I am not of Al-Mushrikûn (see V.2:105)".

Transliteration

74. Wa-ith qala ibraheemu li-abeehi azara atattakhithu asnaman alihatan innee araka waqawmaka fee dalalin mubeenin 75. Wakathalika nuree ibraheema malakoota alssamawati waal-ardi waliyakoona mina almooqineena 76. Falamma janna AAalayhi allaylu raa kawkaban qala hatha rabbee falamma afala qala la ohibbu al-afileena 77. Falamma raa alqamara bazighan qala hatha rabbee falamma afala qala la-in lam yahdinee rabbee laakoonanna mina alqawmi alddalleena 78. Falamma raa alshshamsa bazighatan qala hatha rabbee hatha akbaru falamma afalat qala ya qawmi innee baree-on mimma tushrikoona 79. Innee wajjahtu wajhiya lillathee fatara alssamawati waal-arda haneefan wama ana mina almushrikeena

Tafsir Ibn Kathir

Ibrahim Advises his Father

Ibrahim advised, discouraged and forbade his father from worshipping idols, just as Allah stated,

(And (remember) when Ibrahim said to his father Azar: "Do you take idols as gods") meaning, do you worship an idol instead of Allah

(Verily, I see you and your people...) who follow your path,

(in manifest error) wandering in confusion unaware of where to go. Therefore, you are in disarray and ignorance, and this fact is clear to all those who have sound reason. Allah also said,

(And mention in the Book (the Qur'an, the story of) Ibrahim. Verily! He was a man of truth, a Prophet. When he said to his father: "O my father! Why do you worship that which hears not, sees not and cannot avail you in anything O my father! Verily! There has come to me of knowledge that which came not unto you. So follow me. I will guide you to a straight path. O my father! Worship not Shaytan. Verily! Shaytan has been a rebel against the Most Beneficent (Allah). O my father! Verily! I fear lest a torment from the Most Beneficent (Allah) overtakes you, so that you become a companion of Shaytan (in the Hell-fire)." He (the father) said: "Do you reject my gods, O Ibrahim If you stop not (this), I will indeed stone you. So get away from me safely before I punish you." Ibrahim said: "Peace be on you! I will ask forgiveness of my Lord for you. Verily! He is unto me, Ever Most Gracious. And I shall turn away from you and from those whom you invoke besides Allah. And I shall call on my Lord; and I hope that I shall not be unanswered in my invocation to my Lord.") (19:41-48) Ibrahim continued asking for forgiveness for his father for the rest of his father's life. When his father died an idolator and Ibrahim realized this fact, he stopped asking Allah for forgiveness for him and disassociated himself from him. Allah said,

(And invoking for his father's forgiveness was only because of a promise he had made to him. But when it became clear to him that he was an enemy to Allah, he dissociated himself from him. Verily Ibrahim was patient in supplication and forbearing.) (9:114). It was recorded in the Sahih that Ibrahim will meet his father Azar on the Day of Resurrection and Azar will say to him, "My son! This Day, I will not disobey you." Ibrahim will say, "O Lord! You promised me not to disgrace me on the Day they are resurrected; and what will be more disgraceful to me than cursing and dishonoring my father" Then Allah will say, "O Ibrahim! Look behind you!" He will look and there he will see (that his father was changed into) a male hyena covered in dung, which will be caught by the legs and thrown in the (Hell) Fire."

Tawhid Becomes Apparent to Ibrahim

Allah's statement,

(Thus did We show Ibrahim the kingdom of the heavens and the earth...) (6:75), means, when he contemplated about the creation of the heaven and earth, We showed Ibrahim the proofs of Allah's Oneness over His dominion and His creation, which indicate that there is no god or Lord except Allah. Allah said in other Ayat;

(Say: "Behold all that is in the heavens and the earth.") (10:101), and,

(See they not what is before them and what is behind them, of the heaven and the earth If We will, We sink the earth with them, or cause a piece of the sky to fall upon them. Verily, in this is a sign for every servant who turns to Allah.) (34:9) Allah said next,

(When the night overcame him) covered him with darkness,

(He saw a Kawkab) a star.

(He said: "This is my lord." But when it Afala,) meaning, set, he said,

(I like not those that set.) Qatadah commented, "Ibrahim knew that his Lord is Eternal and never ceases."

(When he saw the moon rising up, he said: "This is my lord." But when it set, he said: "Unless my Lord guides me, I shall surely be among the misguided people." When he saw the sun rising up, he said: "This is my lord.") this radiating, rising star is my lord,

(This is greater) bigger than the star and the moon, and more radiant.

(But when it Afalat) set,

(he said: "O my people! I am indeed free from all that you join as partners in worship with Allah. Verily, I have turned my face..."), meaning, I have purified my religion and made my worship sincere,

("towards Him Who has created the heavens and the earth,") Who originated them and shaped them without precedence,

(Hanifan) avoiding Shirk and embracing Tawhid. This is why he said next,

("and I am not of the idolators.")

Prophet Ibrahim Debates with his People

We should note here that, in these Ayat, Ibrahim, peace be upon him, was debating with his people, explaining to them the error of their way in worshipping idols and images. In the first case with his father, Ibrahim explained to his people their error in worshipping the idols of earth, which they made in the shape of heavenly angels, so that they intercede on their behalf with the Glorious Creator. His people thought that they are too insignificant to worship Allah directly, and this is why they turned to the worship of angels as intercessors with Allah for their provisions, gaining victory and attaining their various needs. He then explained to them the error and deviation of worshipping the seven planets, which they said were the Moon, Mercury, Venus, the Sun, Mars, Jupiter and Saturn. The brightest of these objects and the most honored to them was the Sun, the Moon then Venus. Ibrahim, may Allah's peace and blessings be on him, first proved that Venus is not worthy of being worshipped, for it is subservient to a term and course appointed that it does not defy, nor swerving right or left. Venus does not have any say in its affairs, for it is only a heavenly object that Allah created and made bright out of His wisdom. Venus rises from the east and sets in the west where it disappears from sight. This rotation is repeated the next night, and so forth. Such an object is not worthy of being a god. Ibrahim then went on to mention the Moon in the same manner in which he mentioned Venus, and then the Sun. When he proved that these three objects were not gods, although they are the brightest objects the eyes can see,

(he said: "O my people! I am indeed free from all that you join as partners in worship with Allah.") meaning, I am free from worshipping these objects and from taking them as protectors. Therefore, if they are indeed gods as you claim, then all of you bring your plot against me and do not give me respite.

(Verily, I have turned my face towards Him Who has created the heavens and the earth, Hanifan, and I am not one of the idolators.) meaning, I worship the Creator of these things, Who originated and decreed them, and Who governs their affairs and made them subservient. It is He in Whose Hand is the dominion of all things, and He is the Creator, Lord, King and God of all things in existence. In another Ayah, Allah said:

(Indeed your Lord is Allah, Who created the heavens and the earth in six Days, and then He Istawa (rose over) the Throne. He brings the night as a cover over the day, seeking it rapidly, and (He created) the sun, the moon, the stars, subjecting them to His command. Surely, His is the creation and commandment. Blessed be Allah, the Lord of all that exists!) (7:54). Allah described Prophet Ibrahim,

(And indeed We bestowed aforetime on Ibrahim his (portion of) guidance, and We were well-acquainted with him. When he said to his father and his people: "What are these images, to which you are devoted") (21:51-52). These Ayat indicate that Ibrahim was debating with his people about the Shirk they practiced.

Surah: 6 Ayah: 80, Ayah: 81, Ayah: 82 & Ayah: 83

﴿ وَحَاجَّهُ قَوْمُهُ ۚ قَالَ أَتُحَٰجُّوٓنِّى فِى ٱللَّهِ وَقَدْ هَدَىٰنِ ۚ وَلَآ أَخَافُ مَا تُشْرِكُونَ بِهِۦٓ إِلَّآ أَن يَشَآءَ رَبِّى شَيْـًٔا ۗ وَسِعَ رَبِّى كُلَّ شَىْءٍ عِلْمًا ۗ أَفَلَا تَتَذَكَّرُونَ ۝ ﴾

80. His people disputed with him. He said: "Do you dispute with me concerning Allâh while He has guided me, and I fear not those whom you associate with Him (Allâh) in worship. (Nothing can happen to me) except when my Lord (Allâh) wills something. My Lord comprehends in His Knowledge all things. Will you not then remember?

﴿ وَكَيْفَ أَخَافُ مَا أَشْرَكْتُمْ وَلَا تَخَافُونَ أَنَّكُمْ أَشْرَكْتُم بِاللَّهِ مَا لَمْ يُنَزِّلْ بِهِ عَلَيْكُمْ سُلْطَانًا فَأَيُّ الْفَرِيقَيْنِ أَحَقُّ بِالْأَمْنِ إِن كُنتُمْ تَعْلَمُونَ ۝ ﴾

81. And how should I fear those whom you associate in worship with Allâh (though they can neither benefit nor harm), while you fear not that you have joined in worship with Allâh things for which He has not sent down to you any authority. (So) which of the two parties has more right to be in security? If you but know."

﴿ الَّذِينَ ءَامَنُوا وَلَمْ يَلْبِسُوا إِيمَانَهُم بِظُلْمٍ أُوْلَئِكَ لَهُمُ الْأَمْنُ وَهُم مُّهْتَدُونَ ۝ ﴾

82. It is those who believe (in the Oneness of Allâh and worship none but Him Alone) and confuse not their belief with Zulm (wrong i.e. by worshipping others besides Allâh), for them (only) there is security and they are the guided.

﴿ وَتِلْكَ حُجَّتُنَا ءَاتَيْنَاهَا إِبْرَاهِيمَ عَلَىٰ قَوْمِهِ نَرْفَعُ دَرَجَاتٍ مَّن نَّشَاءُ إِنَّ رَبَّكَ حَكِيمٌ عَلِيمٌ ۝ ﴾

83. And that was Our Proof which We gave Ibrâhîm (Abraham) against his people. We raise whom We will in degrees. Certainly your Lord is All-Wise, All-Knowing.

Transliteration

80. Wahajjahu qawmuhu qala atuhajjoonnee fee Allahi waqad hadani wala akhafu ma tushrikoona bihi illa an yashaa rabbee shay-an wasiAAa rabbee kulla shay-in AAilman afala tatathakkaroona 81. Wakayfa akhafu ma ashraktum wala takhafoona annakum ashraktum biAllahi ma lam yunazzil bihi AAalaykum sultanan faayyu alfareeqayni ahaqqu bial-amni in kuntum taAAlamoona 82. Allatheena amanoo walam yalbisoo eemanahum bithulmin ola-ika lahumu al-amnu wahum muhtadoona 83. Watilka hujjatuna ataynaha ibraheema AAala qawmihi narfaAAu darajatin man nashao inna rabbaka hakeemun AAaleemun

Tafsir Ibn Kathir

Allah states that His Khalil, Prophet Ibrahim, said when his people mentioned various doubts and disputed with him about the Tawhid that he called to:

(Do you dispute with me about Allah while He has guided me). The Ayah means, do you argue with me about Allah, other than Whom there is no god worthy of worship, while He has guided me to the Truth and made me aware of it Therefore, how can I ever consider your misguided statements and false doubts Ibrahim said next,

(and I fear not those whom you associate with Allah in worship. (Nothing can happen to me) except when my Lord wills something.) Ibrahim said, among the proofs to the falsehood of your creed, is that these false gods that you worship do not bring about any effect, and I do not fear them or care about them. Therefore, if these gods are able to cause harm, then use them against me and do not give me respite. Ibrahim's statement,

(except when my Lord wills something.) means, only Allah causes benefit or harm.

(My Lord comprehends in His knowledge all things.) meaning, Allah's knowledge encompasses all things and nothing escapes His complete observation,

(Will you not then remember) what I explained to you, considering your idols as false gods and refraining from worshipping them This reasoning from Prophet Ibrahim is similar to the argument that Prophet Hud used against his people, `Ad. Allah mentioned this incident in His Book, when He said,

(They said: "O Hud! No evidence have you brought us, and we shall not leave our gods for your (mere) saying! And we are not believers in you. All that we say is that some of our gods have seized you with evil." He said: "I call Allah to witness - and bear you witness - that I am free from that which you ascribe as partners in worship with Him (Allah). So plot against me, all of you, and give me no respite. I put my trust in Allah, my Lord and your Lord! There is not a moving creature but He has grasp of its forelock. Verily, my Lord is on the straight path (the truth).") (11:53-56) Ibrahim's statement,

(And how should I fear those whom you associate. ..) means, how should I fear the idols that you worship instead of Allah,

(while you fear not that you have joined in worship with Allah things for which He has not sent down to you any Sultan.) meaning, proof, according to Ibn `Abbas and others among the Salaf. Allah said in similar Ayat;

(Or have they partners who have instituted for them a religion which Allah has not allowed) (42:21), and,

(They are but names which you have named, you and your fathers, for which Allah has sent down no authority.) (53:21) His statement,

((So) which of the two parties has more right to be in security If you but know.) means, which of the two parties is on the truth, those who worship Him in Whose Hand is harm and benefit, or those who worship what cannot bring harm or benefit, without authority to justify worshipping them Who among these two parties has more right to be saved from Allah's torment on the Day of Resurrection Allah said,

(It is those who believe and confuse not their belief with Zulm (wrong), for them (only) there is security and they are the guided.) Therefore, those who worship Allah alone without partners, will acquire safety on the Day of Resurrection, and they are the guided ones in this life and the Hereafter.

Shirk is the Greatest Zulm (Wrong)

Al-Bukhari recorded that `Abdullah said, "When the Ayah,

(and confuse not their belief with Zulm (wrong).) was revealed, the Companions of the Prophet said, `And who among us did not commit Zulm against himself' The Ayah,

(Verily! Joining others in worship with Allah is a great Zulm (wrong) indeed.) (31:13), was later revealed." Imam Ahmad recorded that `Abdullah said, "When this Ayah was revealed,

(It is those who believe and confuse not their belief with Zulm (wrong),) it was hard on the people. They said, `O Allah's Messenger! Who among us did not commit Zulm against himself' He said,

«إِنَّهُ لَيْسَ الَّذِي تَعْنُونَ، أَلَمْ تَسْمَعُوا مَا قَالَ الْعَبْدُ الصَّالِحُ»

(It is not what you understood from it. Did you not hear what the righteous servant (Luqman) said,

(O my son! Join not in worship others with Allah. Verily! Shirk is a great Zulm (wrong) indeed.)) (31:13). Therefore, it is about Shirk. Allah's statement,

(And that was Our proof which We gave Ibrahim against his people.) means, We directed him to proclaim Our proof against them. Mujahid and others said that `Our proof' refers to,

(And how should I fear those whom you associate in worship with Allah (though they can neither benefit nor harm), while you fear not that you have joined in worship with Allah things for which He has not sent down to you any Sultan. (So) which of the two parties has more right to be in security) Allah has testified Ibrahim's statement and affirmed security and guidance, saying;

(It is those who believe and confuse not their belief with Zulm, for them there is security and they are the guided.) Allah said,

(And that was Our proof which We gave Ibrahim against his people. We raise in degrees whom We will.) And;

(Certainly your Lord is All-Wise, All-Knowing.) He is All-Wise in His statements and actions, All-Knower of those whom He guides or misguides, and whether the proof was established against them or not. Allah also said,

(Truly! Those, against whom the Word (wrath) of your Lord has been justified, will not believe. Even if every sign should come to them -- until they see the painful torment.) (10:96-97) This is why Allah said here,

(Certainly your Lord is All-Wise, All-Knowing.)

Surah: 6 Ayah: 84, Ayah: 85, Ayah: 86, Ayah: 87, Ayah: 88, Ayah: 89 & Ayah: 90

﴿ وَوَهَبْنَا لَهُۥ إِسْحَٰقَ وَيَعْقُوبَ ۚ كُلًّا هَدَيْنَا ۚ وَنُوحًا هَدَيْنَا مِن قَبْلُ ۖ وَمِن ذُرِّيَّتِهِۦ دَاوُۥدَ وَسُلَيْمَٰنَ وَأَيُّوبَ وَيُوسُفَ وَمُوسَىٰ وَهَٰرُونَ ۚ وَكَذَٰلِكَ نَجْزِى ٱلْمُحْسِنِينَ ۝ ﴾

84. And We bestowed upon him Ishâq (Isaac) and Ya'qûb (Jacob), each of them We guided, and before him, We guided Nûh (Noah), and among his progeny Dâwûd (David), Sulaimân (Solomon), Ayyûb (Job), Yûsuf (Joseph), Mûsâ (Moses), and Hârûn (Aaron). Thus do We reward Al-Muhsinûn (the good-doers).

﴿ وَزَكَرِيَّا وَيَحْيَىٰ وَعِيسَىٰ وَإِلْيَاسَ ۖ كُلٌّ مِّنَ ٱلصَّٰلِحِينَ ۝ ﴾

85. And Zakariyâ (Zachariya), and Yahya (John) and 'Isâ (Jesus) and Iliyâs (Elias), each one of them was of the righteous.

﴿ وَإِسْمَٰعِيلَ وَٱلْيَسَعَ وَيُونُسَ وَلُوطًا ۚ وَكُلًّا فَضَّلْنَا عَلَى ٱلْعَٰلَمِينَ ۝ ﴾

86. And Ismâ'îl (Ishmael) and Al-Yas'â (Elisha), and Yûnus (Jonah) and Lût (Lot), and each one of them We preferred above the 'Alamîn (mankind and jinn (of their times))

﴿ وَمِنْ ءَابَآئِهِمْ وَذُرِّيَّٰتِهِمْ وَإِخْوَٰنِهِمْ ۖ وَٱجْتَبَيْنَٰهُمْ وَهَدَيْنَٰهُمْ إِلَىٰ صِرَٰطٍ مُّسْتَقِيمٍ ۝ ﴾

87. And also some of their fathers and their progeny and their brethren, We chose them, and We guided them to the Straight Path.

﴿ ذَٰلِكَ هُدَى ٱللَّهِ يَهْدِى بِهِۦ مَن يَشَآءُ مِنْ عِبَادِهِۦ ۚ وَلَوْ أَشْرَكُوا۟ لَحَبِطَ عَنْهُم مَّا كَانُوا۟ يَعْمَلُونَ ۝ ﴾

88. This is the Guidance of Allâh with which He guides whomsoever He wills of His slaves. But if they had joined in worship others with Allâh, all that they used to do would have been of no benefit to them.

﴿ أُو۟لَٰٓئِكَ ٱلَّذِينَ ءَاتَيْنَٰهُمُ ٱلْكِتَٰبَ وَٱلْحُكْمَ وَٱلنُّبُوَّةَ ۚ فَإِن يَكْفُرْ بِهَا هَٰٓؤُلَآءِ فَقَدْ وَكَّلْنَا بِهَا قَوْمًا لَّيْسُوا۟ بِهَا بِكَٰفِرِينَ ۝ ﴾

89. They are those whom We gave the Book, Al-Hukm (understanding of the religious laws), and Prophethood. But if these disbelieve therein (the Book, Al-

Hukm and Prophethood), then, indeed We have entrusted it to a people (such as the Companions of Prophet Muhammad (peace be upon him)) who are not disbelievers therein.

﴿أُوْلَـٰٓئِكَ ٱلَّذِينَ هَدَى ٱللَّهُ ۖ فَبِهُدَىٰهُمُ ٱقْتَدِهْ ۗ قُل لَّآ أَسْـَٔلُكُمْ عَلَيْهِ أَجْرًا ۖ إِنْ هُوَ إِلَّا ذِكْرَىٰ لِلْعَـٰلَمِينَ ۞﴾

90. They are those whom Allâh had guided. So follow their guidance. Say: "No reward I ask of you for this (the Qur'ân). It is only a reminder for the 'Alamîn (mankind and jinn)."

Transliteration

84. Wawahabna lahu ishaqa wayaAAqooba kullan hadayna wanoohan hadayna min qablu wamin thurriyyatihi dawooda wasulaymana waayyooba wayoosufa wamoosa waharoona wakathalika najzee almuhsineena 85. Wazakariyya wayahya waAAeesa wailyasa kullun mina alssaliheena 86. Wa-ismaAAeela wailyasaAAa wayoonusa walootan wakullan faddalna AAala alAAalameena 87. Wamin aba-ihim wathurriyyatihim wa-ikhwanihim waijtabaynahum wahadaynahum ila siratin mustaqeemin 88. Thalika huda Allahi yahdee bihi man yashao min AAibadihi walaw ashrakoo lahabita AAanhum ma kanoo yaAAmaloona 89. Ola-ika allatheena ataynahumu alkitaba waalhukma waalnnubuwwata fa-in yakfur biha haola-i faqad wakkalna biha qawman laysoo biha bikafireena 90. Ola-ika allatheena hada Allahu fabihudahumu iqtadih qul la as-alukum AAalayhi ajran in huwa illa thikra lilAAalameena

Tafsir Ibn Kathir

Ibrahim Receives the News of Ishaq and Ya`qub During His Old Age

Allah states that after Ibrahim became old and he, and his wife, Sarah, lost hope of having children, He gave them Ishaq. The angels came to Ibrahim on their way to the people of Prophet Lut (to destroy them) and they delivered the good news of a child to Ibrahim and his wife. Ibrahim's wife was amazed at the news,

(She said (in astonishment): "Woe unto me! Shall I bear a child while I am an old woman, and here is my husband, an old man Verily! This is a strange thing!" They said: "Do you wonder at the decree of Allah The mercy of Allah and His blessings be on you, O the family (of Ibrahim). Surely, He (Allah) is All-Praiseworthy, All-Glorious.") (11:72-73) The angels also gave them the good news that Ishaq will be a Prophet and that he will have offspring of his own. In another Ayah, Allah said;

(And We gave him the good news of Ishaq a Prophet from the righteous.)(37:112), which perfects this good news and completes the favor. Allah said,

(of Ishaq, and after him, of Ya`qub...) (11:71), meaning, this child will have another child in your lifetime, so that your eyes are comforted by him, just as your eyes will be comforted by his father. Certainly, one becomes jubilant and joyous when he becomes a grandfather, because this means that his offspring will continue to exist. It was also expected that if an elderly couple had children, due to the child's weakness, he would have no offspring. This is why Allah delivered the good news of Ishaq and of his son Ya`qub, whose name literally means `multiplying and having offspring'. This was a reward for Ibrahim who left his people and migrated from their land so that he could worship Allah alone. Allah compensated Ibrahim with better than his people and tribe when He gave him righteous children of his own, who would follow his religion, so that his eyes would be comforted by them. In another Ayah, Allah said; a

(So when he turned away from them and from those whom they worshipped besides Allah, We gave him Ishaq and Ya`qub, and each one of them We made a Prophet.) (19:49) Allah said here,

(And We bestowed upon him Ishaq and Ya`qub, each of them We guided,) Allah said;

(and before him, We guided Nuh...) meaning, We guided Nuh before and gave him righteous offspring, just as We guided Ibrahim and gave him righteous children.

Qualities of Nuh and Ibrahim

Each of these two Prophets had special qualities. When Allah caused the people of the earth to drown, except those who believed in Nuh and accompanied him in the ark, Allah made the offspring of Nuh the dwellers of the earth thereafter. Ever since that occurred, the people of the earth were and still are the descendants of Nuh. As for Ibrahim, Allah did not send a Prophet after him but from his descendants. Allah said in other Ayat,

(And We ordained among his (Ibrahim's) offspring prophethood and the Book.) (29:27),

(And indeed, We sent Nuh and Ibrahim, and placed in their offspring Prophethood and the Book.) (57:26), and,

(Those were they unto whom Allah bestowed His grace from among the Prophets, of the offspring of Adam, and of those whom We carried (in the ship) with Nuh, and of the offspring of Ibrahim and Isra'il and from among those whom We guided and chose. When the verses of the Most Beneficent (Allah) were recited unto them, they fell down prostrating and weeping.) (19:58) Allah said in this honorable Ayah here,

(and among his progeny...) meaning, We guided from among his offspring,

(Dawud, Sulayman...) from the offspring of Nuh, according to Ibn Jarir. It is also possible that the Ayah refers to Ibrahim since it is about him that the blessings were originally mentioned here, although Lut is not from his offspring, for he was Ibrahim's nephew, the son of his brother Maran, the son of Azar. It is possible to say that Lut was mentioned in Ibrahim's offspring as a generalization. As Allah said,

(Or were you witnesses when death approached Ya`qub When he said unto his sons, "What will you worship after me" They said, "We shall worship your God, and the God of your fathers, Ibrahim, Isma`il, Ishaq, One God, and to Him we submit.") (2:133).

Here, Isma`il was mentioned among the ascendants of Ya`qub, although he was Ya`qub's uncle. Similarly Allah said,

(So the angels prostrated themselves, all of them together. Except Iblis -- he refused to be among those to prostrate.) (15:30-31). Allah included Iblis in His order to the angels to prostrate, and chastised him for his opposition, all because he was similar to them in that (order), so he was considered among them in general, although he was a Jinn. Iblis was created from fire while the angels were created from light. Mentioning `Isa in the offspring of Ibrahim, or Nuh as we stated above, is proof that the grandchildren from a man's daughter's side are included among his offspring. `Isa is included among Ibrahim's progeny through his mother, although `Isa did not have a father. Ibn Abi Hatim recorded that Abu Harb bin Abi Al-Aswad said, "Al-Hajjaj sent to Yahya bin Ya`mar, saying, `I was told that you claim that Al-Hasan and Al-Husayn are from the offspring of the Prophet , did you find it in the Book of Allah I read the Qur'an from beginning to end and did not find it.' Yahya said, `Do you not read in Surat Al-An`am,

(and among his progeny Dawud, Sulayman...) until,

(and Yahya and `Isa...) Al-Hajjaj said, `Yes.' Yahya said, `Is not `Isa from the offspring of Ibrahim, although he did not have a father' Al-Hajjaj said, `You have said the truth.'" For example, when a man leaves behind a legacy, a trust, or gift to his "offspring" then the children of his daughters are included. But if a man gives something to his "sons", or he leaves a trust behind for them, then that would be particular to his male children and their male children. Allah's statement,

(And also some of their fathers and their progeny and their brethren,) (6:87), mentions that some of these Prophets' ascendants and descendants were also guided and chosen. So Allah said,

(We chose them, and We guided them to a straight path.)

Shirk Eradicates the Deeds, Even the Deeds of the Messengers

Allah said next,

(This is the guidance of Allah with which He guides whomsoever He wills of His servants.) meaning, this occurred to them by Allah's leave and because He directed them to guidance. Allah said;

(But if they had joined in worship others with Allah, all that they used to do would have been of no benefit to them.) This magnifies the serious danger of Shirk and the gravity of committing it. In another Ayah, Allah said;

(And indeed it has been revealed to you, as it was to those (Allah's Messengers) before you: "If you join others in worship with Allah, surely your deeds will be in vain.") (39:65) `If' here does not mean that this would ever occur, as is similar in Allah's statement;

(Say: "If the Most Beneficent had a son, then I am the first of Allah's worshippers.") (43:81), and

(If We intended to take a pastime (a wife or a son, etc.) We could surely have taken it from Us, if We were going to do (that)) (21:17), and,

(If Allah willed to take a son, He could have chosen whom He pleased out of those whom He created. But glory be to Him! He is Allah, the One, the Compelling.) (39:4) Allah said,

(They are those whom We gave the Book, Al-Hukm, and prophethood.) We bestowed these bounties on them, as a mercy for the servants, and out of our kindness for creation.

(But if they disbelieve therein...) in the prophethood, or the three things; the Book, the Hukm and the prophethood,

(They...) refers to the people of Makkah, according to Ibn `Abbas, Sa`id bin Al-Musayyib, Ad-Dahhak, Qatadah, As-Suddi, and others.

(then, indeed We have entrusted it to a people who are not disbelievers therein.) This Ayah means, if the Quraysh and the rest of the people of the earth - Arabs and non-Arabs, illiterate and the People of the Scripture - disbelieve in these bounties, then We have entrusted them to another people, the Muhajirun and Ansar, and those who follow their lead until the Day of Resurrection,

(who are not disbelievers therein.) They will not deny any of these favors, not even one letter. Rather, they will believe in them totally, even the parts that are not so clear to some of them. We ask Allah to make us among them by His favor, generosity and kindness. Addressing His servant and Messenger, Muhammad , Allah said;

(They are...) the Prophets mentioned here, along with their righteous fathers, offspring and bretheren,

(those whom Allah had guided.) meaning, they alone are the people of guidance,

(So follow their guidance.) Imitate them. This command to the Messenger certainly applies to his Ummah, according to what he legislates and commands them. While mentioning this Ayah, Al-Bukhari recorded that Mujahid asked Ibn `Abbas, "Is there an instance where prostration is warranted in (Surah) Sad" Ibn `Abbas said, "Yes." He then recited,

(...And We bestowed upon him Ishaq and Ya`qub...) until,

(...So follow their guidance.) He commented, "He (our Prophet, Muhammad) was among them." In another narration, Mujahid added that Ibn `Abbas said, "Your Prophet was among those whose guidance we were commanded to follow." Allah's statement,

(Say: "No reward I ask of you for this.") means, I do not ask you for any reward for delivering the Qur'an to you, nor anything else,

("It is only a reminder for the `Alamin (mankind and Jinns).") so they are reminded by it and guided from blindness to clarity, from misguidance to guidance, and from disbelief to faith.

Surah: 6 Ayah: 91 & Ayah: 92

﴿ وَمَا قَدَرُواْ ٱللَّهَ حَقَّ قَدْرِهِۦٓ إِذْ قَالُواْ مَآ أَنزَلَ ٱللَّهُ عَلَىٰ بَشَرٍ مِّن شَىْءٍۗ قُلْ مَنْ أَنزَلَ ٱلْكِتَٰبَ ٱلَّذِى جَآءَ بِهِۦ مُوسَىٰ نُورًا وَهُدًى لِّلنَّاسِۖ تَجْعَلُونَهُۥ قَرَاطِيسَ تُبْدُونَهَا وَتُخْفُونَ كَثِيرًاۖ وَعُلِّمْتُم مَّا لَمْ تَعْلَمُوٓاْ أَنتُمْ وَلَآ ءَابَآؤُكُمْۖ قُلِ ٱللَّهُۖ ثُمَّ ذَرْهُمْ فِى خَوْضِهِمْ يَلْعَبُونَ ۝ ﴾

91. They (the Jews, Quraish pagans, idolaters) did not estimate Allâh with an estimation due to Him when they said: "Nothing did Allâh send down to any human being (by revelation)." Say (O Muhammad (peace be upon him)) "Who then sent down the Book which Mûsâ (Moses) brought, a light and a guidance to mankind which you (the Jews) have made into (separate) papersheets, disclosing (some of it) and concealing much. And you (believers in Allâh and His Messenger Muhammad (peace be upon him)) were taught (through the Qur'ân) that which neither you nor your fathers knew." Say: "Allâh (sent it down)." Then leave them to play in their vain discussions. (Tafsir Al-Qurtubî).

﴿ وَهَٰذَا كِتَٰبٌ أَنزَلْنَٰهُ مُبَارَكٌ مُّصَدِّقُ ٱلَّذِى بَيْنَ يَدَيْهِ وَلِتُنذِرَ أُمَّ ٱلْقُرَىٰ وَمَنْ حَوْلَهَاۚ وَٱلَّذِينَ يُؤْمِنُونَ بِٱلْءَاخِرَةِ يُؤْمِنُونَ بِهِۦۖ وَهُمْ عَلَىٰ صَلَاتِهِمْ يُحَافِظُونَ ۝ ﴾

92. And this (the Qur'ân) is a blessed Book which We have sent down, confirming (the revelations) which came before it, so that you may warn the Mother of Towns (i.e. Makkah) and all those around it. Those who believe in the Hereafter believe in it (the Qur'ân), and they are constant in guarding their Salât (prayers).

Transliteration

91. Wama qadaroo Allaha haqqa qadrihi ith qaloo ma anzala Allahu AAala basharin min shay-in qul man anzala alkitaba allathee jaa bihi moosa nooran wahudan lilnnasi tajAAaloonahu qarateesa tubdoonaha watukhfoona katheeran waAAullimtum ma lam taAAlamoo antum wala abaokum quli Allahu thumma tharhum fee khawdihim yalAAaboona 92. Wahatha kitabun anzalnahu mubarakun musaddiqu allathee bayna yadayhi walitunthira omma alqura waman hawlaha waallatheena yu/minoona bial-akhirati yu/minoona bihi wahum AAala salatihim yuhafithoona

Tafsir Ibn Kathir

The Messenger is but a Human to Whom the Book was Revealed by Inspiration

Allah says that those who rejected His Messengers did not give Allah due consideration. Ibn `Abbas, Mujahid and `Abdullah bin Kathir said that this Ayah was revealed about the Quraysh. It was also said that it was revealed about some Jews.

(They said: "Nothing did Allah send down to any human being (by inspiration).") Allah also, said,

(Is it a wonder for mankind that We have inspired to a man from among themselves (saying): "Warn mankind.") (10:2), and,

(And nothing prevented men from believing when the guidance came to them, except that they said: "Has Allah sent a man as Messenger" Say: "If there were on the earth, angels walking about in peace and security, We should certainly have sent down for them from the heaven an angel as a Messenger.") (17:94-95). Allah said here,

(They did not estimate Allah with an estimation due to Him when they said: "Nothing did Allah send down to any human being (by inspiration).") Allah answered them,

(Say : "Who then sent down the Book which Musa brought, a light and a guidance to mankind") meaning, say, O Muhammad , to those who deny the concept that Allah sent down Books by revelation, answering them specifically,

(Who then sent down the Book which Musa brought) in reference to the Tawrah that you and all others know that Allah sent down to Musa, son of `Imran. Allah sent the Tawrah as a light and a guidance for people, so that it could shed light on the answers to various disputes, and to guide away from the darkness of doubts. Allah's statement, .

(which you have made into (separate) papersheets, disclosing (some of it) and concealing (much).) means, you made the Tawrah into separate sheets which you copied from the original and altered, changed and distorted as you wished. You then said, "this is from Allah," meaning it is in the revealed Book of Allah, when in fact, it is not from Allah. This is why Allah said here,

(which you have made into (separate) papersheets, disclosing (some of it) and concealing (much).) Allah said;

(And you were taught that which neither you nor your fathers knew.) meaning, Who sent down the Qur'an in which Allah taught you the news of those who were before you and the news of what will come after, that neither you nor your fathers had knowledge of. Allah's statement,

(Say: "Allah.") `Ali bin Abi Talhah reported that Ibn `Abbas said, "Meaning, `Say, Allah sent it down.'" Allah said,

(Then leave them to play in their vain discussions.) leave them to play in ignorance and misguidance until the true news comes to them from Allah. Then, they will know whether the good end is theirs or for the fearful servants of Allah. Allah said,

(And this is a Book,) the Qur'an,

(Blessed, which We have sent down, confirming which came before it, so that you may warn the Mother of Towns) that is, Makkah,

(and all those around it...) refering to the Arabs and the rest of the children of Adam, Arabs and non-Arabs alike. Allah said in other Ayat,

(Say: "O mankind! Verily, I am sent to you all as the Messenger of Allah.") (7:158), and

("that I may therewith warn you and whomsoever it may reach.") (6:19), and

(but those of the sects who reject it, the Fire will be their promised meeting place) (11:17) and,

(Blessed be He Who sent down the criterion to His servant that he may be a warner to the `Alamin (mankind and Jinn).) (25:1), and,

(And say to those who were given the Scripture and to those who are illiterates: "Do you submit yourselves" If they do, they are rightly guided; but if they turn away, your duty is only to convey the Message; and Allah is All-Seer of (His) servants.) (3:20). It is recorded in the Two Sahihs, that the Messenger of Allah said,

》أُعْطِيتُ خَمْسًا لَمْ يُعْطَهُنَّ أَحَدٌ مِنَ الْأَنْبِيَاءِ قَبْلِي《

(I have been given five things which were not given to any one else before me.) The Prophet mentioned among these five things,

》وَكَانَ النَّبِيُّ يُبْعَثُ إِلَى قَوْمِهِ خَاصَّةً، وَبُعِثْتُ إِلَى النَّاسِ عَامَّةً《

(Every Prophet was sent only to his nation, but I have been sent to all people.) This is why Allah said,

(Those who believe in the Hereafter believe in it,) meaning, those who believe in Allah and the Last Day, believe in this blessed Book, the Qur'an, which We revealed to you, O Muhammad ,

(and they are constant in guarding their Salah.) for they perform what Allah ordered them, offering the prayers perfectly and on time.

Surah: 6 Ayah: 93 & Ayah: 94

﴿ وَمَنْ أَظْلَمُ مِمَّنِ ٱفْتَرَىٰ عَلَى ٱللَّهِ كَذِبًا أَوْ قَالَ أُوحِىَ إِلَىَّ وَلَمْ يُوحَ إِلَيْهِ شَىْءٌ وَمَن قَالَ سَأُنزِلُ مِثْلَ مَآ أَنزَلَ ٱللَّهُ وَلَوْ تَرَىٰٓ إِذِ ٱلظَّٰلِمُونَ فِى غَمَرَٰتِ ٱلْمَوْتِ وَٱلْمَلَٰٓئِكَةُ بَاسِطُوٓا۟ أَيْدِيهِمْ أَخْرِجُوٓا۟ أَنفُسَكُمُ ٱلْيَوْمَ تُجْزَوْنَ عَذَابَ ٱلْهُونِ بِمَا كُنتُمْ تَقُولُونَ عَلَى ٱللَّهِ غَيْرَ ٱلْحَقِّ وَكُنتُمْ عَنْ ءَايَٰتِهِۦ تَسْتَكْبِرُونَ ۝ ﴾

93. And who can be more unjust than he who invents a lie against Allâh, or says: "a revelation has come to me" whereas no revelation has come to him in anything ; and who says, "I will reveal the like of what Allâh has revealed." And if you could but see when the Zâlimûn (polytheists and wrong-doers) are in the agonies of death, while the angels are stretching forth their hands (saying): "Deliver your souls! This day you shall be recompensed with the torment of degradation because of what you used to utter against Allâh other than the truth. And you used to reject His Ayât (proofs, evidences, verses, lessons, signs, revelations, etc.) with disrespect!"

﴿ وَلَقَدْ جِئْتُمُونَا فُرَٰدَىٰ كَمَا خَلَقْنَٰكُمْ أَوَّلَ مَرَّةٍ وَتَرَكْتُم مَّا خَوَّلْنَٰكُمْ وَرَآءَ ظُهُورِكُمْ وَمَا نَرَىٰ مَعَكُمْ شُفَعَآءَكُمُ ٱلَّذِينَ زَعَمْتُمْ أَنَّهُمْ فِيكُمْ شُرَكَٰٓؤُا۟ لَقَد تَّقَطَّعَ بَيْنَكُمْ وَضَلَّ عَنكُم مَّا كُنتُمْ تَزْعُمُونَ ۝ ﴾

94. And truly you have come unto Us alone (without wealth, companions or anything else) as We created you the first time. You have left behind you all that which We had bestowed on you. We see not with you your intercessors whom you claimed to be partners with Allâh. Now all relations between you and them have been cut off, and all that you used to claim has vanished from you.

Transliteration

93. Waman athlamu mimmani iftara AAala Allahi kathiban aw qala oohiya ilayya walam yooha ilayhi shay-on waman qala saonzilu mithla ma anzala Allahu walaw tara ithi aththalimoona fee ghamarati almawti waalmala-ikatu basitoo aydeehim akhrijoo anfusakumu alyawma tujzawna AAathaba alhooni bima kuntum taqooloona AAala Allahi ghayra alhaqqi wakuntum AAan ayatihi tastakbiroona   94. Walaqad ji/tumoona furada kama khalaqnakum awwala marratin wataraktum ma khawwalnakum waraa thuhoorikum wama nara maAAakum shufaAAaakumu allatheena zaAAamtum annahum feekum shurakao laqad taqattaAAa baynakum wadalla AAankum ma kuntum tazAAumoona

Tafsir Ibn Kathir

None is Worse Than One who Invents a Lie Against Allah and Claims that Revelation Came to Him

Allah said,

(And who can be more unjust than he who invents a lie against Allah,) Therefore, none is more unjust than one who lies about Allah claiming that He has partners or a son, or falsely claiming that Allah sent him as a Prophet;

(or says: "I have received inspiration," whereas he is not inspired with anything;) `Ikrimah and Qatadah said that this Ayah was revealed about Musaylimah Al-Kadhdhab.

(and who says, "I will reveal the like of what Allah has revealed.") This refers to he, who claims that the lies he invents rival the revelation that came from Allah. In another Ayah, Allah said,

(And when Our verses (of the Qur'an) are recited to them, they say: "We have heard this (the Qur'an); if we wish we can say the like of this.")

The Condition of These Unjust People Upon Death and on the Day of Resurrection

Allah, the Most Honored, said,

(And if you could but see when the wrongdoers are in the agonies of death...) suffering from the hardhips, agonies and afflictions of death,

(while the angels are stretching forth their hands...) beating them. Allah said in other Ayat:

(If you do stretch your hand against me to kill me..) (5:28)and,

(And stretch forth their hands and their tongues against you with evil.)(60:2) Ad-Dahhak and Abu Salih said that, `stretch forth their hands,' means, `with torment'. In another Ayah, Allah said,

(And if you could see when the angels take away the souls of those who disbelieve they smite their faces and their backs.)(8:50) Allah said,

(while the angels are stretching forth their hands) beating them, until their souls leave their bodies, saying,

("Deliver your souls!") When the disbeliever is near death, the angels will convey the `good news' to him of torment, vengeance, chains, restraints, Hell, boiling water and the anger of the Most Beneficent, Most Merciful. The soul will then scatter in the body of the disbeliever and refuse to get out of it. The angels will keep beating the disbeliever until his soul exits from his body,

((Saying): "Deliver your souls! This day you shall be recompensed with the torment of degradation because of what you used to say about Allah other than the truth.") This Ayah means, today, you will be utterly humiliated because you used to invent lies against Allah and arrogantly refused to follow His Ayat and obey His Mesengers. There are many Hadiths, of Mutawatir grade, that explain what occurs when the believers and disbelievers die, and we will mention these Hadiths when explaining Allah's statement,

(Allah will keep firm those who believe, with the word that stands firm in this world, and in the Hereafter.) (14:27) Allah said next,

(And truly you have come unto Us alone as We created you the first time.) (6:94), and this statement will be said on the Day of Return. In another Ayah, Allah said,

(And they will be set before your Lord in rows, (and Allah will say): "Now indeed, you have come to Us as We created you the first time.') (18:48), meaning, just as We started your creation, We brought you back, although you used to deny Resurrection and reject its possibility. Therefore, this is the Day of Resurrection! Allah said,

(You have left behind you all that which We had bestowed on you.) (6:94), The wealth and the money that you collected in the life of the world, you left all this behind you. It is recorded in the Sahih that Allah's Messenger said,

«يَقُولُ ابْنُ آدَمَ مَالِي مَالِي وَهَلْ لَكَ مِنْ مَالِكَ إِلَّا مَا أَكَلْتَ فَأَفْنَيْتَ، أَوْ لَبِسْتَ فَأَبْلَيْتَ، أَوْ تَصَدَّقْتَ فَأَمْضَيْتَ، وَمَا سِوَى ذَلِكَ فَذَاهِبٌ وَتَارِكُهُ لِلنَّاسِ»

(The Son of Adam says, `My money, my money!' But, what part of your money do you have, other than what you eat of it and is thus spent, what you wear and tear and what you gave in chairty and thus remains (in the record of good deeds) Other than that, you will depart and leave it to the people.) Al-Hasan Al-Basri said, "On the Day of Resurrection, the Son of Adam will be brought, as if he were a golden chariot and Allah, the Most Honored, will ask, `Where is what you collected' He will reply, `O Lord! I collected it and left it as intact as ever.' Allah will say to him, `O Son of Adam! Where is what you sent forth for yourself (of righteous, good deeds),' and he will realize that he did not send forth anything for himself." Al-Hasan then recited the Ayah,

(And truly you have come unto Us alone as We created you the first time. You have left behind you all that which We had bestowed on you.) Ibn Abi Hatim recorded this statement. Allah said;

(We see not with you your intercessors whom you claimed to be your partners.) This chastises and criticizes the disbelievers for the rivals, idols and images that they worshipped in this life, thinking they will avail them in this life and upon Resurrection, if there is Resurrection, as they thought. On the Day of Resurrection, all relationships will be cut off, misguidance will be exposed, and those whom they used to call upon as gods will disappear from them. Allah will then call them, while the rest of creation is listening,

(Where are My (so-called) partners whom you used to assert) (28:62) And,

(And it will be said to them: "Where are those that you used to worship. Instead of Allah Can they help you or help themselves") (26:92-93) Allah said here,

(We see not with you your intercessors whom you claimed were partners.) meaning partners in worship. That is, partners in a share of your worship.

(Now you and they have been cut off) or, the Ayah is recited with the meaning: all connections, means, and ties between you and them have been severed.

(and vanished from you) you have lost,

(all that you used to claim) of hope in the benefit of the idols and rivals (you worshipped with Allah). Allah said in other Ayat,

(When those who were followed, declare themselves innocent of those who followed (them), and they see the torment, then all their relations will be cut off from them. And those who followed will say: "If only we had one more chance to return, we would disown them as they have disowned us." Thus Allah will show them their deeds as regret for them. And they will never get out of the Fire.) (2:166-167), and

(Then, when the Trumpet is blown, there will be no kinship among them that Day, nor will they ask of one another.) (23:101), and

(You have taken (for worship) idols instead of Allah, and the love between you is only in the life of this world, but on the Day of Resurrection, you shall disown each other, and curse each other, and your abode will be the Fire, and you shall have no helper.) (29:25), and

(And it will be said (to them): "Call upon your partners", and they will call upon them, but they will give no answer to them.) (28:64), and

(And the Day whereon We shall gather them all together, then We shall say to those who committed Shirk...) (10:28) until,

(And their invented false deities will vanish from them.) (10:30)

Surah: 6 Ayah: 95, Ayah: 96 & Ayah: 97

﴿ ۞ إِنَّ ٱللَّهَ فَالِقُ ٱلْحَبِّ وَٱلنَّوَىٰ ۖ يُخْرِجُ ٱلْحَىَّ مِنَ ٱلْمَيِّتِ وَمُخْرِجُ ٱلْمَيِّتِ مِنَ ٱلْحَىِّ ۚ ذَٰلِكُمُ ٱللَّهُ ۖ فَأَنَّىٰ تُؤْفَكُونَ ﴾

95. Verily! It is Allâh Who causes the seed-grain and the fruit-stone (like date-stone) to split and sprout. He brings forth the living from the dead, and it is He Who brings forth the dead from the living. Such is Allâh, then how are you deluded away from the truth?

﴿ فَالِقُ ٱلْإِصْبَاحِ وَجَعَلَ ٱلَّيْلَ سَكَنًا وَٱلشَّمْسَ وَٱلْقَمَرَ حُسْبَانًا ۚ ذَٰلِكَ تَقْدِيرُ ٱلْعَزِيزِ ٱلْعَلِيمِ ۝ ﴾

96. (He is the) Cleaver of the daybreak. He has appointed the night for resting, and the sun and the moon for reckoning. Such is the measuring of the All-Mighty, the All-Knowing.

﴿ وَهُوَ ٱلَّذِى جَعَلَ لَكُمُ ٱلنُّجُومَ لِتَهْتَدُواْ بِهَا فِى ظُلُمَٰتِ ٱلْبَرِّ وَٱلْبَحْرِ ۗ قَدْ فَصَّلْنَا ٱلْءَايَٰتِ لِقَوْمٍ يَعْلَمُونَ ۝ ﴾

97. It is He Who has set the stars for you, so that you may guide your course with their help through the darkness of the land and the sea. We have (indeed) explained in detail Our Ayât (proofs, evidences, verses, lessons, signs, Revelations, etc.) for people who know.

Transliteration

95. Inna Allaha faliqu alhabbi waalnnawa yukhriju alhayya mina almayyiti wamukhriju almayyiti mina alhayyi thalikumu Allahu faanna tu/fakoona   96. Faliqu al-isbahi wajaAAala allayla sakanan waalshshamsa waalqamara husbanan thalika taqdeeru alAAazeezi alAAaleemi   97. Wahuwa allathee jaAAala lakumu alnnujooma litahtadoo biha fee thulumati albarri waalbahri qad fassalna al-ayati liqawmin yaAAlamoona

Tafsir Ibn Kathir

Recognizing Allah Through Some of His Ayat

Allah states that He causes the seed grain and the fruit stone to split and sprout in the ground, producing various types, colors, shapes, and tastes of grains and produce. The Ayah,

(Who causes the seed grain and the fruit stone to split and sprout.) is explained by the next statement,

(He brings forth the living from the dead, and it is He Who brings forth the deed from the living.) meaning, He brings the living plant from the seed grain and the fruit stone, which is a lifless and inanimate object. Allah said,

(And a sign for them is the dead land. We gave it life, and We brought forth from it grains, so that they eat thereof.) (36:33) until,

(as well as of their own (human) kind (male and female), and of that which they know not.) (36:36) Allah's statement, (and it is He Who brings forth the dead from the living.) There are similar expressions in meaning such as, He brings the egg from the chicken, and the opposite. Others said that it means, He brings the wicked offspring from the righteous parent and the opposite, and there are other possible meanings for the Ayah. Allah said,

(Such is Allah,) meaning, He Who does all this, is Allah, the One and Only without partners,

(then how are you deluded away from the truth) meaning, look how you are deluded from Truth to the falsehood of worshipping others besides Allah. Allah's statement,

((He is the) Cleaver of the daybreak. He has appointed the night for resting,) means, He is the Creator of light and darkness. Allah said in the beginning of the Surah,

(And originated the darkness and the light.) Indeed, Allah causes the darkness of the night to disappear and brings forth the day, thus bringing brighteness to the world and light to the horizon, while dissipating darkness and ending the night with its depth of darkness and starting the day with its brightness and light. Allah said,

(He brings the night as a cover over the day, seeking it rapidly.) (7:54) In this Ayah, Allah reminds of His ability to create diversified things in opposites, testifying to His perfect greatness and supreme power. Allah states that He is the Cleaver of the daybreak and mentioned its opposite, when He said,

(He has appointed the night for resting,) meaning, created darkness, in order for the creation to become halt and rest during it. Allah said in other Ayat,

(By the forenoon. And by the night when it is still.) (93:1-2),

(By the night as it envelops. And by the day as it appears in brightness.) (92:1,2) and,

(And by the day as it shows up (the sun's) brightness. And by the night as it conceals it.) (91:3-4) Allah's statement,

(...And the sun and the moon for reckoning.) means, the sun and the moon have specific orbits, according to a term appointed with magnificent precision that never changes or alters. Both the sun and the moon have distinct positions that they assume in summer and winter, effecting changes in the length of night and day. Allah said in other Ayat,

(It is He Who made the sun a shining thing and the Moon as a light and measured out stages for it.) (10:5),

(It is not for the sun to overtake the moon, nor does the night outstrip the day. They all float, each in an orbit.) (36:40), And,

(The sun and the moon; and the stars are subjected by His command.) (16:12) Allah's statement,

(Such is the measuring of the Almighty, the All-Knowing.) means, all of this occurs according to the decree and due measurement of the Almighty Who is never resisted or contradicted. He is the Knower of all things and nothing ever escapes His knowledge, not even the weight of an atom on earth or in heavens. Allah often mentions the creation of the night, the day, the sun and the moon and then ends His Speech by mentioning His attributes of power and knowledge, as in this Ayah above (6:96), and in His statement,

(And a sign for them is the night, We withdraw therefrom the day, and behold, they are in darkness. And the sun runs on its fixed course for a term. That is the decree of the Almighty, the All-Knowing.) (36:37-38) In the beginning of Surat Ha-Mim As-Sajdah, after mentioning the creation of the heavens and earth and all that is in them, Allah said:

(And We adorned the nearest (lowest) heaven with lamps (stars) to be an adornment as well as to guard. Such is the decree of Him, the Almighty, the All-Knower.) (41:12) Allah said next,

(It is He Who has set the stars for you, so that you may guide your course with their help through the darkness of the land and the sea.) Some of the Salaf said; Whoever believes in other than three things about these stars, then he has made a mistake, and lied against Allah. Indeed Allah made them as decorations for the heavens, and to shoot at the Shayatin, and for directions in the dark recesses of the land and sea. Then, Allah said,

(We have explained in detail Our Ayat.) meaning, We made them clear and plain,

(for people who know.) who have sound minds and are able to recognize the truth and avoid falsehood.

Surah: 6 Ayah: 98 & Ayah: 99

﴿ وَهُوَ ٱلَّذِىٓ أَنشَأَكُم مِّن نَّفْسٍ وَٰحِدَةٍ فَمُسْتَقَرٌّ وَمُسْتَوْدَعٌ قَدْ فَصَّلْنَا ٱلْءَايَٰتِ لِقَوْمٍ يَفْقَهُونَ ۝ ﴾

98. It is He Who has created you from a single person (Adam), and has given you a place of residing (on the earth or in your mother's wombs) and a place of storage (in the earth (in your graves) or in your father's loins). Indeed, We have explained in detail Our revelations (this Qur'ân) for people who understand.

﴿ وَهُوَ ٱلَّذِىٓ أَنزَلَ مِنَ ٱلسَّمَآءِ مَآءً فَأَخْرَجْنَا بِهِۦ نَبَاتَ كُلِّ شَىْءٍ فَأَخْرَجْنَا مِنْهُ خَضِرًا نُّخْرِجُ مِنْهُ حَبًّا مُّتَرَاكِبًا وَمِنَ ٱلنَّخْلِ مِن طَلْعِهَا قِنْوَانٌ دَانِيَةٌ وَجَنَّٰتٍ مِّنْ

أَعْنَابٍ وَٱلزَّيْتُونَ وَٱلرُّمَّانَ مُشْتَبِهًا وَغَيْرَ مُتَشَـٰبِهٍ ٱنظُرُوٓا۟ إِلَىٰ ثَمَرِهِۦٓ إِذَآ أَثْمَرَ وَيَنْعِهِۦٓ إِنَّ فِى ذَٰلِكُمْ لَءَايَـٰتٍ لِّقَوْمٍ يُؤْمِنُونَ ۞

99. It is He Who sends down water (rain) from the sky, and with it We bring forth vegetation of all kinds, and out of it We bring forth green stalks, from which We bring forth thick clustered grain. And out of the date-palm and its spathe come forth clusters of dates hanging low and near, and gardens of grapes, olives and pomegranates, each similar (in kind) yet different (in variety and taste). Look at their fruits when they begin to bear, and the ripeness thereof. Verily! In these things there are signs for people who believe.

Transliteration

98. Wahuwa allathee anshaakum min nafsin wahidatin famustaqarrun wamustawdaAAun qad fassalna al-ayati liqawmin yafqahoona 99. Wahuwa allathee anzala mina alssama-i maan faakhrajna bihi nabata kulli shay-in faakhrajna minhu khadiran nukhriju minhu habban mutarakiban wamina alnnakhli min talAAiha qinwanun daniyatun wajannatin min aAAnabin waalzzaytoona waalrrummana mushtabihan waghayra mutashabihin onthuroo ila thamarihi itha athmara wayanAAihi inna fee thalikum laayatin liqawmin yu/minoona

Tafsir Ibn Kathir

Allah said,

(It is He Who has created you from a single person,) (6:98) in reference to Adam, peace be upon him. In another Ayah, Allah said;

(O mankind! Have Taqwa of your Lord, Who created you from a single person, and from him He created his mate, and from them both He created many men and women.)(4:1) Allah said,

(Mustaqar and Mustawda`) Ibn Mas`ud, Ibn `Abbas, Abu `Abdur-Rahman As-Sulami, Qays bin Abu Hazim, Mujahid, `Ata', Ibrahim An-Nakha`i, Ad-Dahhak, Qatadah, As-Suddi and `Ata' Al-Khurasani and others said that,

(Mustaqar), `in the wombs'. They, or most of them, also said that,

(And Mustawda`,) means, `in your father's loins'. Ibn Mas`ud and several others said that, Mustaqar, means residence in this life, while, Mustawda`, means the place of storage after death (the grave). Allah's statement,

(Indeed, We have explained in detail Our revelations for people who understand.) refers to those who comprehend and understand Allah's Words and its meanings. Allah said next,

(It is He Who sends down water (rain) from the sky) in due measure, as a blessing and provision for the servants, relief and means of survival for the creatures and mercy from Allah for His creation. Allah's statement,

(And with it We bring forth vegetation of all kinds,) is similar to,

(And We have made from water every living thing.) (21:30)

(and out of it We bring forth green stalks,) green produce and trees, on which We grow seeds and fruits.

(from which We bring forth thick clustered grain.) lined on top of each other in clusters, like an ear or spike of grain.

(And out of the date-palm and its sprouts come forth clusters) of dates

(hanging low) Within reach and easy to pick. `Ali bin Abi Talhah Al-Walibi said that Ibn `Abbas said that,

(clusters hanging low) refers to short date trees whose branches hang low, close to the ground. This was recorded by Ibn Jarir. Allah's statement

(and gardens of grapes,) means, We bring forth gardens of grapes. Grapes and dates are the most precious fruits to the people of Al-Hijaz (Western Arabia), and perhaps both are the best fruits in this world. Allah has reminded His servants of His favor in making these two fruits for them, when He said,

(And from the fruits of date-palms and grapes, you derive strong drink and a goodly provision.) (16:67) before intoxicating drinks were prohibited, and;

(And We have made therein gardens of date-palms and grapes.) (36:34). Allah said,

(olives and pomegranates, each similar yet different.) The leaves are similar in shape and appearence, yet different in the shape, and taste. And the kind of fruit each plant produces is different, according to the explanation of Qatadah and several others. Allah's statement,

(Look at their fruits when they begin to bear, and Yan`ih.) means, when the fruits become ripe, according to Al-Bara' bin `Azib, Ibn `Abbas, Ad-Dahhak, `Ata' Al-Khurasani, As-Suddi, Qatadah and others. This Ayah means, contemplate the ability of the Creator of these fruits, Who brought them into existence after they were dry wood, and they later became grapes and dates; and similar is the case with the various colors, shapes, tastes and fragrance of whatever Allah created. Allah said,

(And in the earth are neighbouring tracts, and gardens of vines, and green crops, and date-palms, growing out, two or three from a single stem root, or otherwise, watered with the same water, yet some of them We make better than others to eat.) (13:4) This is why Allah said here,

(In these things there are...) O people,

(signs...) and proofs that testify to the perfect ability, wisdom and mercy of He Who created these things, (for people who believe.) in Allah and obey His Messengers.

Surah: 6 Ayah: 100

﴿وَجَعَلُواْ لِلَّهِ شُرَكَآءَ ٱلْجِنَّ وَخَلَقَهُمْ وَخَرَقُواْ لَهُ بَنِينَ وَبَنَـٰتٍۭ بِغَيْرِ عِلْمٍ سُبْحَـٰنَهُۥ وَتَعَـٰلَىٰ عَمَّا يَصِفُونَ ۝﴾

100. Yet, they join the jinn as partners in worship with Allâh, though He has created them (the jinn); and they attribute falsely without knowledge sons and daughters to Him. Be He Glorified and Exalted above all that (evil) they attribute to Him.

Transliteration

100. WajaAAaloo lillahi shurakaa aljinna wakhalaqahum wakharaqoo lahu baneena wabanatin bighayri AAilmin subhanahu wataAAala AAamma yasifoona

Tafsir Ibn Kathir

Rebuking the Idolators

This Ayah refutes the idolators who worshipped others besides Allah and associated the Jinns with Him in worship. Glory be to Allah above this Shirk and Kufr. If someone asks, how did the idolators worship the Jinns, although they only were idol worshippers The answer is that in fact, they worshipped the idols by obeying the Jinns who commanded them to do so. Allah said in other Ayat,

(They invoke nothing but female deities besides Him, and they invoke nothing but Shaytan, a persistent rebel! Allah cursed him. And he (Shaytan) said: "I will take an appointed portion of your servants. Verily, I will mislead them, and surely, I will arouse in them false desires; and certainly, I will order them to slit the ears of cattle, and indeed I will order them to change the nature created by Allah." And whoever takes Shaytan as a protector instead of Allah, has surely suffered a manifest loss. He (Shaytan) makes promises to them, and arouses in them false desires; and Shaytan's promises are nothing but deceptions.) (4:117-120) and,

(Will you then take him (Iblis) and his offspring as protectors and helpers rather than Me) (18:50) Ibrahim said to his father,

("O my father! Worship not Shaytan. Verily! Shaytan has been a rebel against the Most Beneficent (Allah).") (19:44) Allah said,

(Did I not ordain for you, O Children of Adam, that you should not worship Shaytan. Verily, he is a plain enemy to you. And that you should worship Me. That is a straight path.) (36:60-61) On the Day of Resurrection, the angels will proclaim,

(Glorified be You! You are our Protector instead of them. Nay, but they used to worship the Jinn; most of them were believers in them.) (34:41) This is why Allah said here,

(Yet, they join the Jinns as partners in worship with Allah, though He has created them.) (6:100), Alone without partners. Consequently, how is it that another deity is being worshipped along with Him As Ibrahim said,

("Worship you that which you (yourselves) carve While Allah has created you and what you make!") (37:95-96) Allah alone is the Creator without partners. Therefore, He Alone deserves to be worshipped without partners. Allah said next,

(And they Kharaqu (attribute falsely) without knowledge, sons and daughters to Him.) Allah mentions the misguidance of those who were led astray and claimed a son or offspring for Him, as the Jews did with `Uzayr, the Christians with `Isa and the Arab pagans with the angels whom they claimed were Allah's daughters. Allah is far holier than what the unjust, polytheist people associate with Him. The word, Kharaqu, means `falsely attributed, invented, claimed and lied', according to the scholars of the Salaf. Allah's statement next,

(Be He Glorified and Exalted above (all) that they attribute to Him.) means, He is holier than, hallowed, and Exalted above the sons, rivals, equals and partners that these ignorant, misled people attribute to Him.

Surah: 6 Ayah: 101

﴿ بَدِيعُ ٱلسَّمَٰوَٰتِ وَٱلْأَرْضِ أَنَّىٰ يَكُونُ لَهُۥ وَلَدٌ وَلَمْ تَكُن لَّهُۥ صَٰحِبَةٌ وَخَلَقَ كُلَّ شَىْءٍ وَهُوَ بِكُلِّ شَىْءٍ عَلِيمٌ ﴾

101. He is the Originator of the heavens and the earth. How can He have children when He has no wife? He created all things and He is the All-Knower of everything.

Transliteration

101. BadeeAAu alssamawati waal-ardi anna yakoonu lahu waladun walam takun lahu sahibatun wakhalaqa kulla shay-in wahuwa bikulli shay-in AAaleemun

Tafsir Ibn Kathir

Meaning of Badi'

(He is the Badi` of the heavens and the earth) Meaning He originated, created, invented and brought them into existence without precedence, as Mujahid and As-Suddi said. This is why the word for innovation - Bid`ah - comes from it, because it is something that did not have a precedence.

(How can He have children when He has no wife) for the child is the offspring of two compatible spouses. Allah does not have an equal, none of His creatures are similar to Him, for He alone created the entire creation. Allah said;

(And they say: "The Most Beneficent (Allah) has begotten a son." Indeed you have brought forth (said) a terrible evil thing.) (19:88-89), until,

(And everyone of them will come to Him alone on the Day of Resurrection.)(19:95).

(He created all things and He is the All-Knower of everything.) He has created everything and He is All-Knower of all things. How can He have a wife from His creation who is suitable for His majesty, when there is none like Him How can He have a child then Verily, Allah is Glorified above having a son.

Surah: 6 Ayah: 102 & Ayah: 103

﴿ ذَٰلِكُمُ ٱللَّهُ رَبُّكُمْ لَآ إِلَٰهَ إِلَّا هُوَ خَٰلِقُ كُلِّ شَىْءٍ فَٱعْبُدُوهُ وَهُوَ عَلَىٰ كُلِّ شَىْءٍ وَكِيلٌ ﴾

102. Such is Allâh, your Lord! Lâ ilâha illa Huwa (none has the right to be worshipped but He), the Creator of all things. So worship Him (Alone), and He is the Wakîl (Trustee, Disposer of affairs, Guardian) over all things.

﴿ لَّا تُدْرِكُهُ ٱلْأَبْصَٰرُ وَهُوَ يُدْرِكُ ٱلْأَبْصَٰرَ وَهُوَ ٱللَّطِيفُ ٱلْخَبِيرُ ﴾

103. No vision can grasp Him, but He Grasps all vision. He is Al-Latîf (the Most Subtle and Courteous), Well-Acquainted with all things.

Transliteration

102. Thalikumu Allahu rabbukum la ilaha illa huwa khaliqu kulli shay-in faoAAbudoohu wahuwa AAala kulli shay-in wakeelun   103. La tudrikuhu al-absaru wahuwa yudriku al-absara wahuwa allateefu alkhabeeru

Tafsir Ibn Kathir

Allah is Your Lord

Allah said,

(Such is Allah, your Lord!) Who created everything and has neither a son nor a wife,

(None has the right to be worshipped but He, the Creator of all things. So worship Him,) Alone without partners, and attest to His Oneness, affirming that there is no deity worthy of worship except Him. Allah has neither descendants, nor acsendants, wife, equal or rival,

(And He is the Guardian over all things.) meaning, Trustee, Watcher and Disposer of affairs for all things in existence, giving them provisions and protection by day and night. Seeing Allah in the Hereafter Allah said,

(No vision can grasp Him) in this life. The vision will be able to look at Allah in the Hereafter, as affirmed and attested to by the numerous Hadiths from the Prophet through authentic chains of narration in the collections of the Sahihs, Musnad and Sunan collections. As for this life, Masruq narrated that `A'ishah said, "Whoever claims that Muhammad has seen his Lord, will have uttered a lie against Allah, for Allah the Most Honored, says,

(No vision can grasp Him, but His grasp is over all vision.)" In the Sahih (Muslim) it is recorded that Abu Musa Al-Ash`ari narrated from the Prophet,

»إِنَّ اللهَ لَا يَنَامُ وَلَا يَنْبَغِي لَهُ أَنْ يَنَامَ، يَخْفِضُ الْقِسْطَ وَيَرْفَعُهُ، يُرْفَعُ إِلَيْهِ عَمَلُ النَّهَارِ قَبْلَ اللَّيْلِ، وَعَمَلُ اللَّيْلِ قَبْلَ النَّهَارِ، حِجَابُهُ النُّورُ أَوِ النَّارُ لَوْ كَشَفَهُ لَأَحْرَقَتْ سُبُحَاتُ وَجْهِهِ مَا انْتَهَى إِلَيْهِ بَصَرُهُ مِنْ خَلْقِهِ«

(Verily, Allah does not sleep and it does not befit His majesty that He should sleep. He lowers the scale (of everything) and raises it. The deeds of the day are ascended to Him before the night, and the deeds of the night before the day. His Veil is the Light -- or Fire -- and if He removes it (the veil), the Light of His Face will burn every created thing that His sight reaches.) In the previous (revealed) Books there is this statement, "When Musa requested to see Him, Allah said to Musa: `O Musa! Verily, no living thing sees Me, but it dies and no dried things sees me, but it rolls up.' " Allah said,

(So when his Lord appeared to the mountain, He made it collapse to dust, and Musa fell down unconscious. Then when he recovered his senses he said: "Glory be to You, I turn to You in repentance and I am the first of the believers.") (7:143). These Ayat, Hadiths and statements do not negate the fact that Allah will be seen on the Day of Resurrection by His believing servants, in the manner that He decides, all the while preserving His might and grace as they are. The Mother of the Faithful, `A'ishah, used to affirm that Allah will be seen in the Hereafter, but denied that it could occur in this life, mentioning this Ayah as evidence,

(No vision can grasp Him, but His grasp is over all vision.) Her denial was a denial of the ability to encompass Him, meaning to perfectly see His grace and magnificence as He is, for that is not possible for any human, angel or anything created. Allah's statement,

(but His grasp is over all vision.) means, He encompasses all vision and He has full knowledge of them, for He created them all. In another Ayah, Allah said;

(Should not He Who has created know And He is the Most Subtle, Well Acquainted (with all things).) (67:14) It is also possible that `all vision' refers to those who have the vision. As-Suddi said that Allah's statement,

(No vision can grasp Him, but His grasp is over all vision.) means, "Nothing sees Him (in this life), but He sees all creation." Abu Al-`Aliyah said that Allah's statement,

(He is the Most Subtle, Well-Acquainted (with all things).) means, "He is the Most Subtle, bringing forth all things, Well-Acquainted with their position and place." Allah knows best. In another Ayah, Allah mentions Luqman's advice to his son,

(O my son! If it be (anything) equal to the weight of grain of mustard seed, and though it be in a rock, or in the heavens or in the earth, Allah will bring it forth. Verily, Allah is Most Subtle, Well Acquainted) (31:16)

Surah: 6 Ayah: 104 & Ayah: 105

﴿ قَدْ جَآءَكُم بَصَآئِرُ مِن رَّبِّكُمْ ۖ فَمَنْ أَبْصَرَ فَلِنَفْسِهِ ۖ وَمَنْ عَمِيَ فَعَلَيْهَا ۚ وَمَآ أَنَا۟ عَلَيْكُم بِحَفِيظٍ ۝ ﴾

104. Verily, proofs have come to you from your Lord, so whosoever sees, will do so for (the good of) his own self, and whosoever blinds himself, will do so to his own harm, and I (Muhammad (peace be upon him)) am not a watcher over you.

﴿ وَكَذَٰلِكَ نُصَرِّفُ ٱلْءَايَٰتِ وَلِيَقُولُوا۟ دَرَسْتَ وَلِنُبَيِّنَهُۥ لِقَوْمٍ يَعْلَمُونَ ۝ ﴾

105. Thus We explain variously the Verses so that they (the disbelievers) may say: "You have studied (the Books of the people of the Scripture and brought this Qur'ân from that)" and that We may make the matter clear for the people who have knowledge.

Transliteration

104. Qad jaakum basa-iru min rabbikum faman absara falinafsihi waman AAamiya faAAalayha wama ana AAalaykum bihafeethin   105. Wakathalika nusarrifu al-ayati waliyaqooloo darasta walinubayyinahu liqawmin yaAAlamoona

Tafsir Ibn Kathir

The Meaning of Basa'ir

Basa'ir are the proofs and evidences in the Qur'an and the Message of Allah's Messenger . The Ayah,

(so whosoever sees, will do so for (the good of) himself.) is similar to,

(So whosoever receives guidance, he does so for the good of himself, and whosoever goes astray, he does so at his own loss.) (10:108) After Allah mentioned the Basa'ir, He said,

(And whosoever blinds himself, will do so against himself,) meaning, he will only harm himself. Allah said,

(Verily, it is not the eyes that grow blind, but it is the hearts which are in the breasts that grow blind.) (22:46)

(And I (Muhammad) am not a Hafiz over you.) neither responsible, nor a watcher over you. Rather, I only convey, Allah guides whom He wills and misguides whom He wills. Allah said,

Chapter 6: Al-An'am (Cattle, Livestock), Verses 001-110

(Thus We explain variously the verses...)(6:105), meaning, just as We explained the Ayat in this Surah, such as explaining Tawhid and that there is no deity worthy of worship except Allah. This is how We explain the Ayat and make them plain and clear in all circumstances, to suffice the ignorance of the ignorant; and so that the idolators and disbelievers who deny you say, `O Muhammad! You have Darasta with those who were before you from among the People of the Book and learned with them'. Ibn `Abbas, Mujahid, Sa`id bin Jubayr and Ad-Dahhak said similarly. At-Tabarani narrated that `Amr bin Kaysan said that he heard Ibn `Abbas saying, "Darasta, means, `recited, argued and debated.'" This is similar to Allah's statement about the denial and rebellion of the disbelievers, e

(Those who disbelieve say, "This (the Qur'an) is nothing but a lie that he has invented, and others have helped him at it, so that they have produced an unjust wrong (thing) and a lie." And they say, "Tales of the ancients, which he has written down, and they are dictated to him morning and afternoon.") (25:4-5) Allah described the chief liar of the disbelievers (Al-Walid bin Al-Mughirah Al-Makhzumi),

(Verily, he thought and plotted. So let him be cursed! How he plotted! And once more let him be cursed, how he plotted! Then he thought. Then he frowned and he looked in a bad tempered way. Then he turned back and was proud. Then he said, "This is nothing but magic from that of old. This is nothing but the word of a human being!") (74:18-25) Allah said next,

(And that We may make the matter clear for the people who have knowledge.) The Ayah means, so that We explain the matter to a people who know truth, and thus follow it, and know falsehood, and thus avoid it. Allah's wisdom is perfect, He allows the disbelievers to stray, and He guides the people who have knowledge. Allah said in other Ayat,

(By it He misleads many, and many He guides thereby.) (2:26), and;

(That He (Allah) may make what is thrown in by Shaytan a trial for those in whose hearts is a disease and whose hearts are hardened.) (22:53) and,

(And verily, Allah is the Guide of those who believe, to the straight path.) (22:54),

(And We have set none but angels as guardians of the Fire, and We have fixed their number only as a trial for the disbelievers, in order that the People of the Scripture may arrive at a certainty and the believers may increase in faith, and that no doubts may be left for the People of the Scripture and the believers, and that those in whose hearts is a disease (of hypocrisy) and the disbelievers may say, "What does Allah intend by this example" Thus Allah leads astray whom He wills and guides whom He wills. And none can know the hosts of your Lord but He.) (74:31), and;

(And We send down in the Qur'an that which is a healing and a mercy to the believers, and it increases the wrongdoers in nothing but loss.) (17:82), and,

(Say, "It is for those who believe, a guide and a healing. And as for those who disbelieve, there is heaviness in their ears, and it is blindness for them. They are those who are called from a place far away.") (41:44) There are similar Ayat that testify that Allah sent down the Qur'an as guidance to those who fear Him and that He guides or misguides whom He wills by the Qur'an.

Surah: 6 Ayah: 106 & Ayah: 107

﴿ ٱتَّبِعْ مَآ أُوحِىَ إِلَيْكَ مِن رَّبِّكَ لَآ إِلَـٰهَ إِلَّا هُوَ وَأَعْرِضْ عَنِ ٱلْمُشْرِكِينَ ۝ ﴾

106. Follow what has been revealed to you (O Muhammad (peace be upon him)) from your Lord, Lâ ilâha illa Huwa (none has the right to be worshipped but He) and turn aside from Al-Mushrikûn.

﴿ وَلَوْ شَآءَ ٱللَّهُ مَآ أَشْرَكُوا۟ وَمَا جَعَلْنَـٰكَ عَلَيْهِمْ حَفِيظًا وَمَآ أَنتَ عَلَيْهِم بِوَكِيلٍ ۝ ﴾

107. Had Allâh willed, they would not have taken others besides Him in worship. And We have not made you a watcher over them nor are you a Wakîl (disposer of affairs, guardian, trustee) over them.

Transliteration

106. IttabiAA ma oohiya ilayka min rabbika la ilaha illa huwa waaAArid AAani almushrikeena   107. Walaw shaa Allahu ma ashrakoo wama jaAAalnaka AAalayhim hafeethan wama anta AAalayhim biwakeelin

Tafsir Ibn Kathir

The Command to Follow the Revelation

Allah commands His Messenger and those who followed his path,

(Follow what has been inspired to you from your Lord,) meaning, follow it, obey it and act according to it. What has been revealed to you from your Lord is the Truth, no doubt, and there is no deity worthy of worship except Him,

(and turn aside from the idolators) meaning, forgive them, be forbearing and endure their harm until Allah brings relief to you, supports you and makes you triumphant over them. Know -- O Muhammad -- that there is a wisdom behind misleading the idolators, and that had Allah willed, He would have directed all people to guidance,

(Had Allah willed, they would not have taken others besides Him in worship.) Allah's is the perfect will and wisdom in all decrees and decisions, and He is never questioned about what He does, while they all will be questioned. Allah's statement,

(And We have not made you Hafiz over them.) means, a watcher who observes their statements and deeds,

(Nor are you set over them to dispose of their affairs.) or to control their provision. Rather, your only job is to convey, just as Allah said,

(So remind them, you are only one who reminds. You are not a dictator over them.) (88:21-22) and,

(Your duty is only to convey and on Us is the reckoning.) (13:40)

Surah: 6 Ayah: 108

﴿ وَلَا تَسُبُّواْ ٱلَّذِينَ يَدْعُونَ مِن دُونِ ٱللَّهِ فَيَسُبُّواْ ٱللَّهَ عَدْوًۢا بِغَيْرِ عِلْمٍ ۗ كَذَٰلِكَ زَيَّنَّا لِكُلِّ أُمَّةٍ عَمَلَهُمْ ثُمَّ إِلَىٰ رَبِّهِم مَّرْجِعُهُمْ فَيُنَبِّئُهُم بِمَا كَانُواْ يَعْمَلُونَ ۝ ﴾

108. And insult not those whom they (disbelievers) worship besides Allâh, lest they insult Allâh wrongfully without knowledge. Thus We have made fair-seeming to each people its own doings; then to their Lord is their return and He shall then inform them of all that they used to do.

Transliteration

108. Wala tasubboo allatheena yadAAoona min dooni Allahi fayasubboo Allaha AAadwan bighayri AAilmin kathalika zayyanna likulli ommatin AAamalahum thumma ila rabbihim marjiAAuhum fayunabbi-ohum bima kanoo yaAAmaloona

Tafsir Ibn Kathir

The Prohibition of Insulting the False gods of the Disbelievers, So that they Do not Insult Allah

Allah prohibits His Messenger and the believers from insulting the false deities of the idolators, although there is a clear benefit in doing so. Insulting their deities will lead to a bigger evil than its benefit, for the idolators might retaliate by insulting the God of the believers, Allah, none has the right to be worshipped but He. `Ali bin Abi Talhah said that Ibn `Abbas commented on this Ayah (6:108); "They (disbelievers) said, `O Muhammad! You will stop insulting our gods, or we will insult your Lord.' Thereafter, Allah prohibited the believers from insulting the disbelievers' idols,

(lest they insult Allah wrongfully without knowledge.)" `Abdur-Razzaq narrated that Ma`mar said that Qatadah said, "Muslims used to insult the idols of the disbelievers and the disbelievers would retaliate by insulting Allah wrongfully without knowledge. Allah revealed,

(And insult not those whom they worship besides Allah.)" On this same subject -- abandoning what carries benefit to avert a greater evil - it is recorded in the Sahih that the Messenger of Allah said,

«مَلْعُونٌ مَنْ سَبَّ وَالِدَيْه»

(Cursed is he who insults his own parents!) They said, "O Allah's Messenger! And how would a man insult his own parents" He said,

$$\text{«يَسُبُّ أَبَا الرَّجُلِ فَيَسُبُّ أَبَاهُ وَيَسُبُّ أُمَّهُ فَيَسُبُّ أُمَّهُ»}$$

(He insults a man's father, and that man insults his father, and insults his mother and that man insults his mother.) Allah's statement,

(Thus We have made fair seeming to each people its own doings;) means, as We made fair seeming to the idolators loving their idols and defending them, likewise We made fair seeming to every previous nation the misguidance they indulged in. Allah's is the most perfect proof, and the most complete wisdom in all that He wills and chooses.

(then to their Lord is their return,) gathering and final destination,

(and He shall then inform them of all that they used to do.) He will compensate them for their deeds, good for good and evil for evil.

Surah: 6 Ayah: 109 & Ayah: 110

$$\text{﴿ وَأَقْسَمُواْ بِٱللَّهِ جَهْدَ أَيْمَـٰنِهِمْ لَئِن جَآءَتْهُمْ ءَايَةٌ لَّيُؤْمِنُنَّ بِهَا ۚ قُلْ إِنَّمَا ٱلْآيَـٰتُ عِندَ ٱللَّهِ ۖ وَمَا يُشْعِرُكُمْ أَنَّهَآ إِذَا جَآءَتْ لَا يُؤْمِنُونَ ﴾}$$

109. And they swear their strongest oaths by Allâh, that if there came to them a sign, they would surely believe therein. Say: "Signs are but with Allâh and what will make you (Muslims) perceive that (even) if it (the sign) came, they will not believe?"

$$\text{﴿ وَنُقَلِّبُ أَفْـِٔدَتَهُمْ وَأَبْصَـٰرَهُمْ كَمَا لَمْ يُؤْمِنُواْ بِهِۦٓ أَوَّلَ مَرَّةٍ وَنَذَرُهُمْ فِى طُغْيَـٰنِهِمْ يَعْمَهُونَ ﴾}$$

110. And We shall turn their hearts and their eyes away (from guidance), as they refused to believe therein for the first time, and We shall leave them in their trespass to wander blindly.

Transliteration

109. Waaqsamoo biAllahi jahda aymanihim la-in jaat-hum ayatun layu/minunna biha qul innama al-ayatu AAinda Allahi wama yushAAirukum annaha itha jaat la yu/minoona 110. Wanuqallibu af-idatahum waabsarahum kama lam yu/minoo bihi awwala marratin wanatharuhum fee tughyanihim yaAAmahoona

Tafsir Ibn Kathir

Asking for Miracles and Swearing to Believe if They Come

Allah states that the idolators swore their strongest oaths by Allah,

(that if there came to them a sign...) a miracle or phenomenon, (they would surely believe therein.) affirming its truth,

(Say: "Signs are but with Allah.") (6:109) meaning: Say, O Muhammad - to those who ask you for signs out of defiance, disbelief and rebellion, not out of the desire for guidance and knowledge - "The matter of sending signs is for Allah. If He wills, He sends them to you, and if He wills, He ignores your request." Allah said next,

(And what will make you perceive that (even) if it came, they will not believe) It was said that `you' in `make you preceive' refers to the idolators, according to Mujahid. In this case, the Ayah would mean, what makes you -- you idolators -- preceive that you are truthful in the vows that you swore Therefore, in this recitation, the Ayah means, the idolators will still not believe if the sign that they asked for came. It was also said that `you' in, `what will make you preceive', refers to the believers, meaning, what will make you preceive, O believers, that the idolators will still not believe if the signs come. Allah also said,

("What prevented you (O Iblis) that you did not prostrate, when I commanded you") (7:12) and,

(And a ban is laid on every town (population) which We have destroyed that they shall not return (to this world again).) (21:95) These Ayat mean: `What made you, O Iblis, refrain from prostrating, although I commanded you to do so, and, in the second Ayah, that village shall not return to this world again. In the Ayah above (6:109), the meaning thus becomes: What makes you perceive, O believers, who wish eagerly for the disbelievers to believe, that if the Ayat came to them they would believe Allah said next, (And We shall turn their hearts and their eyes away, as they refused to believe therein for the first time,) Al-`Awfi said that Ibn `Abbas said about this Ayah, "When the idolators rejected what Allah sent down, their hearts did not settle on any one thing and they turned away from every matter (of benefit)." Mujahid said that Allah's statement,

(and We shall turn their hearts and their eyes away,) means, We prevent them from the faith, and even if every sign came to them, they will not believe, just as We prevented them from faith the first time. Similar was said by `Ikrimah and `Abdur-Rahman bin Zayd bin Aslam. `Ali bin Abi Talhah said that Ibn `Abbas said, "Allah mentions what the servants will say before they say it and what they will do before they do it. Allah said; (And none can inform you like Him Who is the All-Knower.) (35:14) and, (Lest a person should say, "Alas, my grief that I was undutiful to Allah.") (39:56) until, ("If only I had another chance, then I should indeed be among the doers of good.") (39:58). So Allah, glory be to Him, states that if they were sent back to life, they would not accept the guidance,

(But if they were returned, they would certainly revert to that which they were forbidden. And indeed they are liars.) (6:28) Allah said, (And We shall turn their hearts and their eyes away (from guidance), as they refused to believe therein for the first time,) meaning: `If they were sent back to this life, they would be prevented from embracing the guidance, just as We prevented them from it the first time, when they were in the life of this world." Allah said, (and We shall leave them...) and abandon them,

(in their trespass...) meaning, disbelief, according to Ibn `Abbas and As-Suddi. Abu Al-`Aliyah, Ar-Rabi` bin Anas and Qatadah said that `their trespass' means, `their misguidance'. m

(to wander blindly) or playfully, according to Al-A`mash. Ibn `Abbas, Mujahid, Abu Al-`Aliyah, Ar-Rabi`, Abu Malik and others commented, "to wander in their disbelief."

www.ingramcontent.com/pod-product-compliance
Lightning Source LLC
Chambersburg PA
CBHW081113080526
44587CB00021B/3568